주한미군지위협정(SOFA)

한 · 미
합동위원회 3

주한미군지위협정(SOFA)

한·미
합동위원회 3

| 머리말

미국은 오래전부터 우리나라 외교에 있어서 가장 긴밀하고 실질적인 우호·협력관계를 맺어 온 나라다. 6·25전쟁 정전 협정이 체결된 후 북한의 재침을 막기 위한 대책으로서 1953년 11월 한미 상호방위조약이 체결되었다. 이는 미군이 한국에 주둔하는 법적 근거였고, 그렇게 주둔하게 된 미군의 시설, 구역, 사업, 용역, 출입국, 통관과 관세, 재판권 등 포괄적인 법적 지위를 규정하는 것이 바로 주한미군지위협정(SOFA)이다. 그러나 이와 관련한 협상은 계속된 난항을 겪으며 한미 상호방위조약이 체결로부터 10년이 훌쩍 넘은 1967년이 돼서야 정식 발효에 이를 수 있었다. 그럼에도 당시 미군 범죄에 대한 한국의 재판권은 심한 제약을 받았으며, 1980년대 후반 민주화 운동과 함께 미군 범죄 문제가 사회적 이슈로 떠오르자 협정을 개정해야 한다는 목소리가 커지게 되었다. 이에 1991년 2월 주한미군지위협정 1차 개정이 진행되었고, 이후에도 여러 사건이 발생하며 2001년 4월 2차 개정이 진행되어 현재에 이르고 있다.

본 총서는 외교부에서 작성하여 최근 공개한 주한미군지위협정(SOFA) 관련 자료를 담고 있다. 1953년 한미 상호방위조약 체결 이후부터 1967년 발효가 이뤄지기까지의 자료와 더불어, 이후 한미 합동위원회을 비롯해 민·형사재판권, 시설, 노무, 교통 등 각 분과위원회의 회의록과 운영 자료, 한국인 고용인 문제와 관련한 자료, 기타 관련 분쟁 자료 등을 포함해 총 42권으로 구성되었다. 전체 분량은 약 2만 2천여 쪽에 이른다.

2024년 3월

한국학술정보(주)

| 일러두기

· 본 총서에 실린 자료는 2022년 4월과 2023년 4월에 각각 공개한 외교문서 4,827권, 76만 여 쪽 가운데 일부를 발췌한 것이다.

· 각 권의 제목과 순서는 공개된 원본을 최대한 반영하였으나, 주제에 따라 일부는 적절히 변경하였다.

· 원본 자료는 A4 판형에 맞게 축소하거나 원본 비율을 유지한 채 A4 페이지 안에 삽입 하였다. 또한 현재 시점에선 공개되지 않아 '공란'이란 표기만 있는 페이지 역시 그대로 실었다.

· 외교부가 공개한 문서 각 권의 첫 페이지에는 '정리 보존 문서 목록'이란 이름으로 기록물 종류, 일자, 명칭, 간단한 내용 등의 정보가 수록되어 있으며, 이를 기준으로 0001번부터 번호가 매겨져 있다. 이는 삭제하지 않고 총서에 그대로 수록하였다.

· 보고서 내용에 관한 더 자세한 정보가 필요하다면, 외교부가 온라인상에 제공하는 『대한 민국 외교사료요약집』 1991년과 1992년 자료를 참조할 수 있다.

| 차례

머리말 4

일러두기 5

SOFA 한.미국 합동위원회 회의록, 제70-72차. 1972 7

분류번호	729.41 1972 70-72차	등록번호	127	보존기간	영구
기능명칭	SOFA 한미 합동위원회 회의록, 제70-72차. 1972				
생 산 과	안보담당관실		생산년도		1972

주 :
1. 제70차   1972. 1. 28
2. 제71차   1972. 2. 24
3. 제72차   1972. 3. 28

	M/F No.	

결 번

넘버링 오류

결 번

넘버링 오류

1. 제70차, 1972.1.28

기 안 용 지

분류기호 문서번호	미이 723 -	(전화번호)	전결규정 조 항 **국장** 전결사항

처 리 기 간		
시 행 일 자		
보 존 년 한		국 ～～～ 장

보 조 기 관	북미 2과장		협 조

기 안 책 임 자	정태익 북미 2과 (72. 1. 24.)

경 유		발 신	(도장: No.2283 1972. 1. 25 외무부)
수 신	수신처 참조		
참 조			
제 목	한.미 합동위원회 회의개최 통지		

오는 1972년 1월 28일 (금요일) 15:30 외무부 회의실 (420호실)

에서 한.미 합동위원회 제 70차 회의가 개최될 예정이오니 각 위원께서는

회의에 필히 참석하여 주시기 바랍니다. 끝.

이에 따른 처리과장는 북미2부위께 있음. 끝.

수신처 : 법무부장관 (법무실장, 검찰국장, 출입국관미국장),

국방부장관 (기획국장, 시설국장), 재무부장관 (관세국장),

상공부장관 (상역국장), 교통부장관 (종합수송담당관),

노동청장 (노정국장).

	정서
	관인
	발송

공동서식 1—2 (갑)
1967. 4. 4 승인

190mm×268mm 중량 7g/m²
조 달 청 1,000,000매 인쇄)

(1. FOR YOUR INFORMATION: The new ROK Representative,
Mr. KIM Dong Whie, will hand to you for the record a copy of the
official notification from the ROK Ministry of Foreign Affairs to the
US Embassy in Seoul, dated 4 January 1972, informing the US Govern-
ment of his appointment as the new ROK Representative to the Joint
Committee, succeeding his predecessor, Mr. KOO Choong Whay.
It is proposed that the US Representative, after accepting a copy of
the ROK Representative's credentials, respond as follows.)

2. Mr. Kim, I am very happy to accept a copy of your credentials
informing my Government of your appointment as the Republic of
Korea Representative to the Republic of Korea-United States Joint
Committee. On behalf of my Government and of the United States component of the Joint Committee, I wish to extend to you a warm and
hearty welcome in your important new position. I have been informed
that you had an important part in the negotiation of the Republic of
Korea-United States Status of Forces Agreement while you were serving
as the Chief of the Treaty Section in the Ministry of Foreign Affairs
during the years 1965-1966. It is indeed a pleasure to have you return
as your Government's representative to work on the implementation of
this important agreement which you helped negotiate. The Status of
Forces Agreement will have been in effect for five years on 9 February

6

AGENDA ITEM I continued

1972. Through the friendly cooperation and diligent work of officials of our two Governments, this important Agreement has been implemented effectively, thereby promoting our mutual defense interests and enhancing the traditional friendship between our two peoples. As you assume the position of the Republic of Korea Representative to the Joint Committee, Mr. Kim, I wish to assure you of our desire to continue to work together with you and your colleagues on our common tasks in the Joint Committee in a spirit of close and friendly cooperation and mutual understanding of our defense objectives.

(3. FOR YOUR INFORMATION: The ROK Representative will make an appropriate response to the US Representative's welcome. After concluding his response, he will give the US Representative an opportunity to introduce a new member of the US component of the Joint Committee prior to turning to the next item on the agenda.)

4. Before we take up the next agenda item, I would like to take this opportunity to introduce a new member of the United States component of the Joint Committee, Colonel Carl G. Schneider, Vice Commander, United States Air Forces Korea, who is replacing Colonel Robert G. Eklund who has departed Korea. Colonel Schneider served a tour with the United States Air Force in Korea during the Korean

2

AGENDA ITEM I continued

War, and in his most recent assignment, he served as Wing Commander, Moody Air Force Base, Georgia. On behalf of the United States component of the Joint Committee, I wish to extend a warm welcome to Colonel Schneider to the Joint Committee.

(4. FOR YOUR INFORMATION: The ROK Representative will also extend his welcome to Colonel Schneider.)

3

AGENDA ITEM II

US Presentation

(1. FOR YOUR INFORMATION: The ROK Representative will invite the US Representative to present ten new tasks for assignment to the Facilities and Areas Subcommittee.)

2. The United States Representative would like to present ten new tasks for assignment to the Facilities and Areas Subcommittee. These new tasks consist of two requests for the acquisition of real estate on a permanent use basis, one request for the acquisition of an easement and seven requests for the release of parcels of real estate. All details concerning these new tasks are contained in memoranda which have been distributed to both sides.

3. It is proposed that these ten new tasks be assigned to the Facilities and Areas Subcommittee.

(4. FOR YOUR INFORMATION: The ROK SOFA Secretary has indicated that the ROK Representative will concur in this proposal. Since the ROK Representative has no new Facilities and Areas tasks to present at this meeting, he will propose proceeding to the next agenda item.)

AGENDA ITEM IV   US Presentation

    (1. FOR YOUR INFORMATION: The ROK Representative will request his US counterpart to present eight recommendations received from the Facilities and Areas Subcommittee.)

    2. The United States Representative has eight recommendations of the Facilities and Areas Subcommittee to present. These comprise two recommendations for the acquisition of land for permanent use, two recommendations concerning the extension of Temporary Use Permits, three recommendations for release of parcels of real estate, and one recommendation for the withdrawal of a previously made request for the conversion of land under acquisition from a temporary use to a permanent use basis.

    3. It is proposed that the Joint Committee approve these eight recommendations of the Facilities and Areas Subcommittee.

    (4. FOR YOUR INFORMATION: The ROK SOFA Secretary has indicated that the ROK Representative will concur in this proposal. Since the ROK Representative has no Facilities and Areas recommendations to present at this meeting, he will propose proceeding to the next agenda item.)

10

AGENDA ITEM V   US Presentation

(1. FOR YOUR INFORMATION: The ROK Representative will ask the US Representative to present this item.)

2. The Transportation Subcommittee reached agreement on a distinctive new license plate for privately-owned vehicles of United States Forces Korea personnel and invited contractors on 20 December 1971. In order to expedite the re-registration process and the issuing of the new license plates, the Joint Committee approved the recommendation of the Transportation Subcommittee by exigent action on 30 December 1971.

3. I am pleased to announce that the United States Forces Korea began to re-register privately-owned vehicles and to issue the new license plates in the Seoul area on 25 January. We hope to complete this process throughout Korea as quickly as possible.

4. The United States Representative proposes to include in the minutes of this meeting the recommendation of the Transportation Subcommittee approved by exigent action of the Joint Committee on 30 December 1971.

(5. FOR YOUR INFORMATION: The ROK Secretary has indicated that the ROK Representative will concur in this action.)

(1. FOR YOUR INFORMATION: The ROK Representative will

present the fifth report of the Ad Hoc Subcommittee on Civil-Military

Relations and request Joint Committee approval for the report and the

five recommendations included therein. These recommendations

include two from the Panel on Health and Sanitation, two from the Panel

on Narcotics and Drug Control, and one from the Panel on Race Rela-

tions and Equality of Treatment. The ROK Representative will also

probably mention the formation of the new ROK Government cabinet-

level "Base Community Clean-Up Committee, " which was presented

by the ROK Ad Hoc Subcommittee Chairman at the last Subcommittee

meeting and is included in the minutes of the sixth meeting of the Ad

Hoc Subcommittee.)

2. The United States Representative is pleased to concur in ap-

proval of the fifth report of the Ad Hoc Subcommittee on Civil-Military

Relations, including the five recommendations of three of its panels.

This will bring to 19 the number of approved recommendations of the

Ad Hoc Subcommittee, and the seven Ad Hoc Subcommittee panels continue

to work on many other recommendations. The continued progress of

the Ad Hoc Subcommittee, coupled with the vigorous efforts of the

ROK Government to deal with the problems of the camp communities

AGENDA ITEM VI continued

through its own "Base Community Clean-Up Committee, " greatly

enhances the prospects for significant improvement in the situation

in the Korean communities adjacent to US military installations. These

developments should facilitate continuation of the traditional friendly

relations between the United States serviceman and the Korean people

and should assist in maximizing the contribution of these servicemen

in the mutual defense of the Republic of Korea. On behalf of my

Government, I would like to take note of and to commend my colleagues

in the Government of the Republic of Korea for their increasingly

vigorous efforts to improve civil-military relations and thereby

strengthen our mutual defense position.

2

(1. FOR YOUR INFORMATION: The Foreign Organization Employees Union and USFK reached agreement on two labor disputes in a Memorandum of Understanding signed 24 December 1971. The Memorandum was signed by the President of the FOEU as well as the Director of Civilian Personnel, and countersigned by the Director of the ROK Labor Affairs Bureau of the Office of Labor Affairs. The disputes which were resolved in accordance with this memorandum involved an increase in wage schedules for USFK's Korean employees, effective 1 January 1972, as well as an adjustment in the USFK severance pay plan for short tenure employees.)

2. The United States Representative proposes that the Memorandum of Understanding of 24 December 1971, which terminated two recent labor disputes between the United States Forces Korea and the Foreign Organization Employees Union be recorded in the minutes of this Joint Committee meeting. One of the disputes involved the wage schedules for United States Forces Korea Korean employees and the new schedules became effective 1 January 1972. The other dispute involved severance pay for a small number of short tenure United States Forces Korea Korean employees and also became effective 1 January 1972. These two disputes have been referred for conciliation to the Office of Labor Affairs of the Government of the Republic of Korea in accordance

14

AGENDA ITEM VII continued

with paragraph 4 of Article XVII of the Status of Forces Agreement.
The Memorandum of Understanding was signed by officials of the
Foreign Organization Employees Union and United States Forces Korea,
and was countersigned by Mr. HAN Chin Hui, Director, Labor Affairs
Bureau of the Office of Labor Affairs. The United States Representative would like to express his sincere appreciation for the assistance
of the officials of the Government of the Republic of Korea in the
amicable settlement of these labor disputes, in accordance with the
provisions of the Labor Article of the Status of Forces Agreement.
Settlement of these two disputes under the provisions of the Status of
Forces Agreement again demonstrates the effectiveness of the Labor
Article of that Agreement in the maintenance of fair and friendly
relations between the United States Forces Korea and its Korean
employees.

(3. FOR YOUR INFORMATION: The ROK SOFA Secretary has
indicated that the ROK Representative will concur in the inclusion of
the Memorandum of Understanding of 24 December 1971 in the minutes
of this meeting.)

2

(1. FOR YOUR INFORMATION: The ROK Representative will invite the US Representative to present this agenda item.)

2. The United States Representative wishes to present memoranda to the Joint Committee informing the Government of the Republic of Korea of the designation of six United States invited contractors under Article XV of the Status of Forces Agreement. These designations were made after consultations between Republic of Korea and United States Commerce Subcommittee personnel in accordance with Joint Committee procedures. The invited contractors so designated are Lyon Associates, Incorporated; Daniel, Mann, Johnson, and Mendenhall; Trans Asia Engineering Company; Associated American Engineers Overseas, Incorporated; Collins Radio Company; and National Cash Register Company. All companies have one contract except National Cash Register which has two. The contract of American Engineers Overseas, Incorporated is in joint venture with a Korean firm.

3. Pertinent data concerning employees of these invited contractors will be provided to the Government of the Republic of Korea in accordance with mutually agreed procedures.

(4. FOR YOUR INFORMATION: The ROK SOFA Secretary has indicated that the ROK Representative will acknowledge the designation of these invited contractors.)

16

AGENDA ITEM IX   US Presentation

    (1. FOR YOUR INFORMATION: The ROK Representative will invite the US Representative to present this agenda item.)

    2. Since the Status of Forces Agreement went into effect on 9 February 1967, the University of Maryland has been listed as a United States Invited Contractor on all invited contractor lists. This listing was a continuation of the pre-Status of Forces Agreement status of the University of Maryland and was not subject to the consultation and designation procedures of the Commerce Subcommittee and the Joint Committee.

    3. The Commerce Subcommittee has consulted and reviewed this matter. In accordance with this review, the United States is withdrawing the designation of the University of Maryland as a United States invited contractor and henceforth will consider personnel of this organization as members of the civilian component as defined in Article I b of the Status of Forces Agreement.

    (4. FOR YOUR INFORMATION: The ROK SOFA Secretary has indicated the ROK Representative will acknowledge this change in status.)

17

(1. FOR YOUR INFORMATION: The ROK Representative will invite the US Representative to present this agenda item.)

2. The United States Representative wishes to note for the record that the United States Status of Forces Agreement Secretariat has furnished the following information to the Republic of Korea Status of Forces Agreement Secretariat in accordance with the provisions of the Status of Forces Agreement and Joint committee decisions.

a. Five copies of reports on the United States armed forces disposition of cases for the month of November 1971.

b) One copy of pertinent information on cargo consigned to United States armed forces non-appropriated fund organizations in the Republic of Korea, for the months of November and December 1971.

c. Twenty copies of the report of United States armed forces personnel, the civilian component, invited contractors, and the dependents of each, entering or departing the Republic of Korea during the months of November and December.

d. Twenty copies of the quarterly listing of all United States invited contractors and their contracts as of 31 December 1971.

18

(1. FOR YOUR INFORMATION: The ROK Representative will
propose that a special press release commemorating the fifth anniversary of the entry into force of the SOFA on 9 February 1972 be issued
by the Joint Committee on or about 8 February 1972. The press release would be developed by the ROK and US SOFA Secretariats in
collaboration with the ROK and US public information and other appropriate offices and would be approved by both the ROK and US Representatives prior to its release. The question of a ROK Government -
sponsored press conference or a joint ROK-US press conference involving the two Representatives on 8 or 9 February has been considered
by ROK officials and they feel it is better to have just the formal press
release as far as ROK media are concerned. The ROK Representative
has indicated that he would be glad to participate with the US Representative on an AFKN TV program on 9 February 1972 in which the
focus would be upon the SOFA and the five years of Joint Committee
operations including reference to the recent joint activities in the Ad
Hoc Subcommittee on Civil-Military Relations which should be of
special interest to the US military personnel.)

2. The United States Representative is glad to concur with the
ROK Representative's proposal that a joint ROK-US press release
be issued in connection with the fifth anniversary of the entry into

119

force of the Republic of Korea-United States Status of Forces Agreement on 9 February 1972. I also agree that our respective Secretariats in cooperation with other appropriate Korean and American officials should develop such a proposed press release for the review and approval of the two Representatives.

3. I also propose that the Republic of Korea and United States Representatives participate in a joint television program on the American Forces Korea Network which would be designed primarily to inform the American serviceman about the Status of Forces Agreement and some of the significant activities of the Joint Committee in connection with the fifth anniversary of the Status of Forces Agreement.

(4. FOR YOUR INFORMATION: The ROK Representative reportedly will concur in the US Representative's suggestion about a TV program on AFKN. In connection with the proposed press release, a proposed draft of such a press release was developed by J5 for the assistance of appropriate Korean and American authorities in preparing a mutually agreeable press release for presentation to the respective ROK and US Representatives.)

2

20

(1. FOR YOUR INFORMATION: In accordance with the new procedure for designating the date of the next Joint Committee meeting,
the ROK Representative will ask the US Representative if he would
like to propose the date, time, and place for the next meeting. Since
it is planned that the US Representative will host a luncheon honoring
the new ROK Representative just prior to the next Joint Committee
meeting, it is proposed that the next meeting start at 1400 hours on
24 February, immediately after the luncheon.)

2. The United States Representative would like to propose that the
seventy-first meeting of the Joint Committee be held in the United
States Status of Forces Agreement Conference Room on Thursday,
24 February 1972, at 1400 hours.

(3. FOR YOUR INFORMATION: The ROK SOFA Secretary has
indicated that the ROK Representative will concur in the proposed date,
time, and place for the seventy-first Joint Committee meeting.)

21

AGENDA ITEM XIII   ROK PRESENTATION

(1. FOR YOUR INFORMATION: The ROK Representative will propose approval of the joint press release as drafted by the two SOFA Secretaries and as distributed in advance.)

2. The United States Representative is happy to approve the joint press release for the seventieth Joint Committee meeting as distributed in advance.

22

(1. FOR YOUR INFORMATION: The ROK Representative will ask
the US Representative if he has any further items to present at the
seventieth Joint Committee meeting.)

2. The United States Representative has no further items to
present at this time.

(3. FOR YOUR INFORMATION: The ROK Representative will
indicated that, since there is no further business to come before this
meeting, he will declare the seventieth meeting of the Joint Committee
adjourned.)

23

AGENDA FOR THE SEVENTIETH MEETING
OF THE ROK-US JOINT COMMITTEE
1530 HOURS, 28 JANUARY 1972, ROK CAPITOL BUILDING

I.   Presentation of Credentials by the ROK Representative.

II.   Assignment of Tasks to Facilities and Areas Subcommittee - US Presentation.

III.   Assignment of Task to Transportation Subcommittee - ROK Presentation.

IV.   Recommendations of Facilities and Areas Subcommittee - US Presentation.

V.   Recommendation of Transportation Subcommittee - US Presentation.

VI.   Consideration of Fifth Report and Recommendations of Ad Hoc Subcommittee on Civil-Military Relations - ROK and US Presentations.

VII.   Memorandum of Understanding of 24 December 1971, which Resolved Two Labor Disputes in Accordance with the Procedures of SOFA Article XVII - US Presentation.

VIII.   Memoranda on the Designation of US Invited Contractors - US Presentation.

~~IX.   Memorandum on the Withdrawal of Designation of US Invited Contractor - US Presentation.~~ *Record*

IX. ~~X.~~   Memoranda Presented to the ROK Government by the US in the Implementation of the SOFA - US Presentation.

X. ~~XI.~~   Publicity Relating to Fifth Anniversary of SOFA - ROK and US Presentations.

XI. ~~XII.~~   Proposed Time of Next Meeting - 1400 Hours, Thursday, 24 February 1972, in the US SOFA Conference Room.

XII. ~~XIII.~~   Agreement on Joint Press Release.

XIV. ~~XIII.~~   Adjourn.

24

27 January 1972

MEMORANDUM FOR: Chairmen, Facilities and Areas Subcommittee

SUBJECT: Request for Acquisition of Real Estate

1. SOFA provides in Article II, paragraph 2, that the Governments of the Republic of Korea and the United States may agree that facilities and areas or portions thereof shall be returned to the Republic of Korea or that additional facilities and areas may be provided.

2. Pursuant to paragraph 1 above, it is requested that a recommendation be presented to the Joint Committee concerning a request for the acquisition of a total of 30.33 acres of land located in Yangju-gun, Kyonggi-do. Of this acreage, 30 acres located in two noncontiguous areas are required on a permanent use basis, and the remaining 0.33 acre is required on a perpetual restrictive easement basis. This land is required as a source of crushed road products and for an access road to the crushing site.

KIM DONG WHIE
Republic of Korea
Representative

ROBERT N. SMITH
Lieutenant General
United States Air Force
United States Representative

2₅

27 January 1972

MEMORANDUM FOR: Chairmen, Facilities and Areas Subcommittee

SUBJECT: Requests for Release of Real Estate

1. SOFA provides in Article II, paragraph 2, that the Governments of the Republic of Korea and the United States may agree that facilities and areas or portions thereof shall be returned to the Republic of Korea or that additional facilities and areas may be provided.

2. Pursuant to paragraph 1 above, it is requested that recommendations be presented to the Joint Committee concerning requests for the following actions:

a. Release of 505.517 acres of land, constituting the Hyongga-Ri Tank Range, currently held under Acquisition No. 7X-5, located in Yonchon-gun, Kyonggi-do, subject to the conditions specified below. This request for release includes a total of four buildings and facilities located on the installation. The conditions attached to this request for release are that: (1) The I Corps (ROK/US) Group retain scheduling control over the range area activities; (2) The Republic of Korea Ministry of National Defense insure that this range will be made available only for the use and occupancy of the VI ROK Army Corps element solely for training range purposes; and (3) The VI ROK Army Corps element be solely responsible for the security and operational maintenance of all of the real property located at the Hyonggi-Ri Tank Range.

b. Release of 21.039 acres of land, constituting a portion of Camp Richmond installation held under Acquisition Nos. ACS-300 and AAC-391, and located in Buchon-gun, Kyonggi-do. This request for release includes a total of 83 buildings and facilities, of which 55 are USFK-constructed and 28 are Korean-constructed. Excluded from this request for release are an overhead electric power line, three 25-KVA transformers, a water pipeline, and one water storage tank, with unrestricted right of entry/exit thereto, as well as 0.604 acre of easement land and 0.36 acre of land held on an exclusive use basis, as shown on maps in the possession of the Republic of Korea Ministry of National Defense and the Engineer, USFK.

26

c. Release of 12.07 acres of land, constituting Tracy Installation held under Acquisition No. SAC-673, and located in Seoul City. This request for release includes 80 USFK-constructed buildings and facilities and two Korean-constructed facilities. This real estate has become excess to USFK requirements.

d. Release of 2.58 acres of land, constituting a portion of Yuma Installation held under Acquisition No. AAC-397, and located in Inchon City, Kyonggi-do. This request for release includes 5,559 linear feet of 8-inch underground POL pipeline and one 570 square foot pump house. This real estate has become excess to USFK requirements.

e. Release of 6.635 acres of land, constituting a portion of Alamo Installation held under Acquisition Nos. 7X-13 and 7X-174, and located in Yonchon-gun, Kyonggi-do. This request for release includes a total of 29 USFK-constructed buildings and facilities located on the Installation. This real estate has become excess to USFK requirements.

f. Release of 15.72 acres of land, constituting a portion of Camp Mercer Installation held under Acquisition No. ASCOM-378, and located in Kimpo-gun, Kyonggi-do. This request for release includes a total of 17 USFK-constructed buildings and facilities located on the Installation. This real estate has become excess to USFK requirements.

g. Release of 45.757 acres of land, constituting a portion of ASP #46 Installation held under Acquisition No. SAC-715, and located in Seoul City. This request for release includes a total of 84 USFK-constructed buildings and facilities, and a total of 10 Korean-constructed buildings and facilities. This request for release is contingent upon the provision by the Republic of Korea Ministry of National Defense, without cost to the US Government, of the following activities: (1) Construction of approximately 460 linear feet of barbed wire security fencing at a specified location; (2) Construction of approximately 1,585 linear feet of barbed wire security fencing with one vehicle gate, at another location; (3) The relocation of Bldg. No. T-181 to the USFK-retained communication area; and (4) The installation of water and electric meters. The locations involved in activities (1) through (3) above are indicated on a map in possession of the Republic of Korea Ministry of National Defense and the USFK Engineer.

KIM DONG WHIE
Republic of Korea
Representative

ROBERT N. SMITH
Lieutenant General
United States Air Force
United States Representative

27

28 January 1972

MEMORANDUM FOR: Chairmen, Facilities and Areas Subcommittee

SUBJECT: Request for Acquisition of Easement

1. SOFA provides in Article II, paragraph 2, that the Governments of the Republic of Korea and the United States may agree that facilities and areas or portions thereof, shall be returned to the Republic of Korea or that additional facilities and areas may be provided.

2. Pursuant to paragraph 1 above, it is requested that a recommendation be presented to the Joint Committee concerning a request for the acquisition, on a perpetual restrictive easement basis, of 4.17 acres of land located in Kwangju-gun, Kyonggi-do, for the installation of underground communication cables.

KIM DONG WHIE
Republic of Korea
Representative

ROBERT N. SMITH
Lieutenant General
United States Air Force
United States Representative

28

28 January 1972

MEMORANDUM FOR: Chairmen, Facilities and Areas Subcommittee

SUBJECT: Request for Acquisition of Real Estate

1. SOFA provides in Article II, paragraph 2, that the Governments of the Republic of Korea and the United States may agree that facilities and areas or portions thereof, shall be returned to the Republic of Korea or that additional facilities and areas may be provided.

2. Pursuant to paragraph 1 above, it is requested that a recommendation be presented to the Joint Committee concerning a request for the acquisition of a total of 114 square feet of building space on a permanent use basis, located in Chinhae City, Kyongsangnam-do. This real estate is required to expand a bunker operation at that location, which is currently held under Acquisition No. PAC-185.

KIM DONG WHIE
Republic of Korea
Representative

ROBERT N. SMITH
Lieutenant General
United States Air Force
United States Representative

29

13 January 1972

MEMORANDUM FOR: Chairmen, Transportation Subcommittee

SUBJECT: Applicability of Certain Provisions of Ministry of Transportation Instruction #335 to USFK Personnel Departing the Republic of Korea in a Leave Status

1. Mutual consultations are requested concerning whether paragraph 4, Item 5, of Article 12 of the Ministry of Transportation Instruction #335 of 8 July 1969, relating to avionics facility management, pertains to those persons who are subject to the Republic of Korea-United States Status of Forces Agreement and who depart the Republic of Korea via commercial aircraft utilizing a commercial airport terminal facility, and whose travel is in a leave status.

2. It is further requested that upon completion of such consultations a recommendation on this subject be transmitted to the Joint Committee.

ROBERT N. SMITH
Lieutenant General
United States Air Force
United States Representative

KIM DONG WHIE
Republic of Korea
Representative

30

REPUBLIC OF KOREA - UNITED STATES
FACILITIES AND AREAS SUBCOMMITTEE

19 January 1972

MEMORANDUM FOR: THE JOINT COMMITTEE

1. Subcommittee Members:

United States

BG Philip T. Boerger, Chairman
COL Leonard Edelstein, Alt. Chairman
COL Eugene T. Blanton, USAF
MAJ William S. Littlefield, J4, USFK
MAJ Allen D. Adams, USAFCS, K
CPT James H. Smith, USAF
Mr. Francis K. Cook, J5, USFK
Mr. S. F. O'Hop, ENJ-RE, Secty
Mr. E. H. Brummett, ENJ-RE,
    Alt. Secty

Republic of Korea

BG PAK Woo Bum, Chairman
Mr. MIN Won Sik, Secty
Mr. KANG Hong Suk, Asst Secty
LTC SHIN Sang Pil
Mr. KIM Young Sup
Mr. PAK Bung Hun
Mr. RHO Won Tae
Mr. SOUNG Baek Jon
Mr. DO Tae Ku
Mr. SUH Chin Hwan
Mr. LEE Soung Woo
Mr. PARK Dahl Young
Mr. BAE Jeung Sun

2. Subject of Recommendation: Request for Conversion of Real Estate, Joint Committee memorandum dated 22 April 1971.

3. Recommendation: Task 976 The request for the conversion from the temporary use to permanent use land of 4,446 acres of land out of the 120,571.20 acres of land currently held under Acq. No. CAV-T-16, located in Changdan-gun, Kyonggi-do, to provide an adequate and unobstructed maneuver area and firing range for the US 2d Infantry Division, has been withdrawn by the US requesting agency upon the assurance of the Ministry of National Defense that the Republic

31

<u>Task 976</u>

of Korea Government will prohibit any construction, farming, or encroachments on this land, per letter RE: 947.01-2670, dated 9 September 1971, Ministry of National Defense. It is recommended therefore that no further action be taken on this task.

4. Security Classification: Unclassified.

Brigadier General PAK Woo Bum
Chairman, ROK Component
Facilities and Areas Subcommittee

Brigadier General Philip T. Boerger
Chairman, US Component
Facilities and Areas Subcommittee

2

32

REPUBLIC OF KOREA - UNITED STATES
FACILITIES AND AREAS SUBCOMMITTEE

14 January 1971

MEMORANDUM FOR: THE JOINT COMMITTEE

1. Subcommittee Members:

United States

BG Philip T. Boerger, Chairman
COL Leonard Edelstein, Alt. Chairman
LTC Edward W. Lingel, USAF
MAJ William S. Littlefield, J4, USFK
MAJ Allen D. Adams, USAFCS, K
CPT James H. Smith, USAF
Mr. Francis K. Cook, J5, USFK
Mr. S. F. O'Hop, ENJ-RE, Secty
Mr. E. H. Brummett, ENJ-RE,
   Alt. Secty

Republic of Korea

BG PAK Woo Bum, Chairman
Mr. MIN Won Sik, Secty
Mr. KANG Hong Suk, Asst Secty
LTC SHIN Sang Pil
Mr. KIM Hyung Kun
Mr. PAK Bung Hun
Mr. NOE Won Tae
Mr. PARK Byong Yong
Mr. DO Tae Ku
Mr. SUH Chin Hwan
Mr. LEE Soung Woo
Mr. PARK Dahl Young
Mr. BAE Jeung Sun

2. Subject of Recommendation: Request for Acquisition of Real Estate,
Joint Committee memorandum dated 24 November 1971.

3. Recommendation: Task 1115   The request for the acquisition, on a
permanent use basis, of a total of 0.09 acre of land, comprising 3,938 square
feet, located at the Tong-Taegu Railroad Station in Taegu City, Kyongsangbuk-
do, has been approved by the Ministry of National Defense. Of this area,
2,871 square feet are required for office space and the remaining 1,067
square feet are required as a vehicle parking area. This real estate is in
lieu of the existing Taegu RTO, which will be requested for release upon
completion of the acquisition of the above-referenced 0.09 acre. The Ministry
of National Defense and the USFK Engineer will prepare the necessary documents. It is recommended that the Joint Committee, SOFA, approve this
acquisition request.

33

Task 1115

4. Security Classification: Unclassified.

_____
Brigadier General PAK Woo Bum
Chairman, ROK Component
Facilities and Areas Subcommittee

_____
Brigadier General Philip T. Boerger
Chairman, US Component
Facilities and Areas Subcommittee

2

34

REPUBLIC OF KOREA - UNITED STATES
FACILITIES AND AREAS SUBCOMMITTEE

19 January 1972

MEMORANDUM FOR: THE JOINT COMMITTEE

1. Subcommittee Members:

United States	Republic of Korea
BG Philip T. Boerger, Chairman	BG PAK Woo Bum, Chairman
COL Leonard Edelstein, Alt. Chairman	Mr. MIN Won Sik, Secty
COL Eugene T. Blanton, USAF	Mr. KANG Hong Suk, Asst Secty
MAJ William S. Littlefield, J4, USFK	LTC SHIN Sang Pil
MAJ Allen D. Adams, USAFCS, K	Mr. KIM Young Sup
CPT James H. Smith, USAF	Mr. PAK Bung Hun
Mr. Francis K. Cook, J5, USFK	Mr. RHO Won Tae
Mr. S. F. O'Hop, ENJ-RE, Secty	Mr. SOUNG Baek Jon
Mr. E. H. Brummett, EMJ-RE,	Mr. DO Tae Ku
Alt. Secty	Mr. SUH Chin Hwan
	Mr. LEE Soung Woo
	Mr. PARK Dahl Young
	Mr. BAE Jeung Sun

2. Subject of Recommendation: Requests for Acquisition of Real Estate, Joint
Committee memorandum dated 24 November 1971.

3. Recommendation: Task 1116   The request for acquisition of a total of 0.212
acre of land located in the Han River bed, Seoul City (0.014 acre, consisting of
six non-contiguous areas required on a permanent use basis for the erection of
six power poles, and the remaining 0.198 acre required on a perpetual restrictive
easement basis for the installation of overhead power and communication lines),

35

<u>Task 1116</u>

has been accepted by the Ministry of National Defense. The Ministry of
National Defense and the USFK Engineer will prepare the necessary documents.
It is recommended that the Joint Committee, SOFA, approve the attached
proposed agreement.

4. Security Classification: Unclassified.

_____   _____
Brigadier General PAK Woo Bum   Brigadier General Philip T. Boerger
Chairman, ROK Component   Chairman, US Component
Facilities and Areas Subcommittee   Facilities and Areas Subcommittee

2

36

REPUBLIC OF KOREA - UNITED STATES
FACILITIES AND AREAS SUBCOMMITTEE

19 January 1972

MEMORANDUM FOR: THE JOINT COMMITTEE

1. Subcommittee Members:

United States	Republic of Korea
BG Philip T. Boerger, Chairman	BG PAK Woo Bum, Chairman
COL Leonard Edelstein, Alt. Chairman	Mr. MIN Won Sik, Secty
COL Eugene T. Blanton, USAF	Mr. KANG Hong Suk, Asst Secty
MAJ William S. Littlefield, J4, USFK	LTC SHIN Sang Pil
MAJ Allen D. Adams, USAFCS, K	Mr. KIM Young Sup
CPT James H. Smith, USAF	Mr. PAK Bung Hun
Mr. Francis K. Cook, J5, USFK	Mr. RHO Won Tae
Mr. S. F. O'Hop, ENJ-RE, Secty	Mr. SOUNG Baek Jon
Mr. E. H. Brummett, ENJ-RE,	Mr. DO Tae Ku
Alt. Secty	Mr. SUH Chin Hwan
	Mr. LEE Soung Woo
	Mr. PARK Dahl Young
	Mr. BAE Jeung Sun

2. Subject of Recommendation: Request for Extension of Temporary Use
Permit, Joint Committee memorandum dated 24 November 1971.

3. Recommendation: Tasks 1125-1126 The following requests for Extension
of Temporary Use Permits were accepted by the Ministry of National Defense.

    a. Task 1125 Extension of Temporary Use Permit K-F-T-58, involving
31.0 acres of land located in Pyongtaek-gun, Kyonggi-do, from 1 December
1971 through 31 May 1972. Continued use of this land is required as a source
of obtaining select material in troop housing construction at Camp Humphreys
Installation.

37

b. **Task 1126** Extension of Temporary Use Permit K-G-T-15, involving 8.25 acres of riverbed located in Chilkok-gun, Kyongsangbuk-do, from 1 December through 30 November 1972. This land has been utilized as a source area for filling operations at Camp Carroll and there is a continuing need for its use for that purpose.

The Ministry of National Defense and the USFK Engineer will prepare the necessary documents. It is recommended that these two requests for extension of temporary use permits be approved by the Joint Committee, SOFA.

4. Security Classification: Unclassified.

Brigadier General PAK Woo Bum
Chairman, ROK Component
Facilities and Areas Subcommittee

Brigadier General Philip T. Boerger
Chairman, US Component
Facilities and Areas Subcommittee

38

2

REPUBLIC OF KOREA - UNITED STATES
FACILITIES AND AREAS SUBCOMMITTEE

19 January 1972

MEMORANDUM FOR: THE JOINT COMMITTEE

1. Subcommittee Members:

United States	Republic of Korea
BG Philip T. Boerger, Chairman	BG PAK Woo Bum, Chairman
COL Leonard Edelstein, Alt. Chairman	Mr. MIN Won Sik, Secty
LTC Edward W. Lingel, USAF	Mr. KANG Hong Suk, Asst Secty
MAJ William S. Littlefield, J4, USFK	LTC SHIN Sang Pil
MAJ Allen D. Adams, USAFCS, K	Mr. KIM Young Sup
CPT James H. Smith, USAF	Mr. PAK Bung Hun
Mr. Francis K. Cook, J5, USFK	Mr. NOE Won Tae
Mr. S. F. O'Hop, ENJ-RE, Secty	Mr. PARK Byong Yong
Mr. E. H. Brummett, ENJ-RE,	Mr. DO Tae Ku
Alt. Secty	Mr. SUH Chin Hwan
	Mr. LEE Soung Woo
	Mr. PARK Dahl Young
	Mr. BAE Jeung Sun

2. Subject of Recommendation: Request for Release of Real Estate, Joint Committee memorandum dated 16 December 1971.

3. Recommendation: Task 1127 The request for release of 10.48 acres of land, constituting Thor Echo Installation currently held under Acq. No. IC-148, and located in Uijongbu-si, Kyonggi-do, has been approved by the Ministry of National Defense. This real estate contains a total of 48 buildings and facilities which will be released upon the release of the land. The Ministry of National Defense and the USFK Engineer will prepare the necessary documents. It is recommended that the Joint Committee, SOFA, approve this release request.

39

<u>Task 1127</u>

4. Security Classification: Unclassified.

_____
Brigadier General PAK Woo Bum
Chairman, ROK Component
Facilities and Areas Subcommittee

_____
Brigadier General Philip T. Boerger
Chairman, US Component
Facilities and Areas Subcommittee

2

40

REPUBLIC OF KOREA - UNITED STATES
FACILITIES AND AREAS SUBCOMMITTEE

19 January 1972

MEMORANDUM FOR: THE JOINT COMMITTEE

1. Subcommittee Members:

United States

BG Philip T. Boerger, Chairman
COL Leonard Edelstein, Alt. Chairman
LTC Edward W. Lingel, USAF
MAJ William S. Littlefield, J4, USFK
MAJ Allen D. Adams, USAFCS, K
CPT James H. Smith, USAF
Mr. Francis K. Cook, J5, USFK
Mr. S. F. O'Hop, ENJ-RE, Secty
Mr. E. H. Brummett, ENJ-RE,
    Alt. Secty

Republic of Korea

BG PAK Woo Bum, Chairman
Mr. MIN Won Sik, Secty
Mr. KANG Hong Suk, Asst Secty
LTC SHIN Sang Pil
Mr. KIM Young Sup
Mr. PAK Bung Hun
Mr. NOE Won Tae
Mr. PARK Byong Yong
Mr. DO Tae Ku
Mr. SUH Chin Hwan
Mr. LEE Soung Woo
Mr. PARK Dahl Young
Mr. BAE Jeung Sun

2. Subject of Recommendation: Requests for Release of Real Estate

3. Recommendation: Tasks 1128-1129   The following requests for release
of real estate have been accepted by the Ministry of National Defense and
the United States Forces, Korea.

    a. Task 1128   Release of 0.12 acre of land, currently held as a portion
of the area held under Acq. No. IC-207, and located in Uijongbu-si, Kyonggi-
do. This real estate has become excess to USFK requirements.

    b. Task 1129   Release of 0.11 acre of land, currently held as a portion
of the area held under Acq. No. IC-168, and located in Uijongbu-si, Kyonggi-
do. This real estate has become excess to USFK requirements.

4|

Tasks 1128-1129

The Ministry of National Defense and the USFK Engineer will prepare the necessary documents. It is recommended that the Joint Committee, SOFA, approve these two release requests.

4. Security Classification: Unclassified.

Brigadier General PAK Woo Bum
Chairman, ROK Component
Facilities and Areas Subcommittee

Brigadier General Philip T. Boerger
Chairman, US Component
Facilities and Areas Subcommittee

2

US-ROK Transportation Subcommittee
Under the
US-ROK Joint Committee
Established by Article XXVIII of the
Status of Forces Agreement (SOFA)

20 December 1971

MEMORANDUM FOR: The Joint Committee

1. Subcommittee Members:

COL Maurice A. Gainey, Jr., Chairman	Mr. SUH In Soo, Chairman
LTC William W. Raitt, USAF	Mr. KIM Doo Bang
LTC Alan B. Cayo, USA	Mr. PARK Byung Sun
LTC Richard D. Le Doux, USAF	Mr. SHIN Young Kook
LTC Robert A. Neff, USAF	Mr. HWANG Sun Ku
LTC Robert B. Claypool, USAF	Mr. KIM Mun Sun
LTC Ralph E. Fisher, USAF	Mr. KIM Byung Yoon
LTC Charles W. Johns, USAF	Mr. LEE Yong Hoi
LTC Donald E. Lockstrom, USAF	Mr. LIM Uoo Soon
LCDR Robert E. Spydell, USN	Mr. BAK Yong Chun
MAJ Hames J. Hallihan, USA	Mr. PARK Hyung Hee
MAJ Dick J. Petersen, USAF	COL YOO Choong Hyeun
Mr. Sam Pollack, USFK	Mr. NOH Sung Ho
	LTC SUH Sang Ho

2. Subject of Recommendation: Distinctive License Plates for Privately-Owned Vehicles of USFK Personnel and Invited Contractors.

3. Recommendation: The first sentence of paragraph two of the Agreed Procedures for licensing and registration of privately-owned vehicles of United States Forces, Korea personnel and United States armed forces invited contractors approved by the Joint Committee at its twenty-eighth and thirty-second meetings on 3 July 1968 and 7 November 1968 respectively, be deleted and replaced with the following sentences:

43

"The Government of the Republic of Korea will produce a requisite number of license plates and seals of a distinctive design and specification after consultations between the vehicle registration authorities of the United States Forces, Korea and the Republic of Korea.

"Revalidation of registration and issuance of license plates will be accomplished on an annual basis."

4. Security Classification: Unclassified.

SUH IN SOO
Chairman, ROK Component
Transportation Subcommittee

MAURICE A. GAINEY, JR, COL, USA
Chairman, US Component
Transportation Subcommittee

APPROVED BY THE JOINT COMMITTEE ON
30 DECEMBER 1971

KOO CHOONG WHAY
Republic of Korea
Representative

ROBERT N. SMITH
Lieutenant General
United States Air Force
United States Representative

44

공   란

공   란

공 란

공 란

공   란

공   란

공   란

공   란

공 란

공　　　란

공   란

MEMORANDUM OF UNDERSTANDING

1. The Foreign Organizations Employees Union (FOEU) accepts recently approved wage schedules (Inclosure 1) by USARPAC to be effective 1 January 1972. These schedules are applicable to all USFK Korean employees, including Korean Service Corps personnel. (Korean contractor and personal hire employees are not USFK employees.)

2. USFK agrees to reassess the Mess Attendant grade level during the course of CY 72 locality wage survey to determine pay comparability with prevailing wages.

3. USFK severance pay plan is adjusted (Inclosure 2) in part for short tenure employees to meet requirements of the Korean Labor Standards Law, and will be effective 1 January 1972.

4. The official labor disputes filed by FOEU on 26 November 1971 and 11 August 1970 with the Office of Labor Affairs (OLA) are terminated.

5. The FOEU and USFK agree that joint efforts will be made to improve long range planning for specialized training and outplacement actions under Korean Nationals Outplacement Program (KNOP).

FOR UNITED STATES FORCES,
KOREA:

FOR FOREIGN ORGANIZATIONS
EMPLOYEES UNION:

FREDRIC NEWMAN
Chairman
Joint Labor Affairs Committee

KANG CHU WON
President

CARL J. BENDER, JR.
Executive Secretary
Joint Labor Affairs Committee

CHANG SU TOK
Secretary General

HAN CHIN HUI
Director
Labor Affairs Bureau
Office of Labor Affairs

US FORCES WAGE SCHEDULE

KOREA
MANUAL (KWB) WAGE SCHEDULE
LOCALLY HIRED, NON-US CITIZEN EMPLOYEES

HOURLY STEP RATES (KOREAN WON)

KWB GRADE	STEP A	STEP B	STEP C	STEP D	STEP E	STEP F	STEP G	STEP H	STEP I	STEP J
1	93	98	102	107	111	115	120	124	129	133
2	116	121	127	132	138	144	149	155	160	166
3	139	145	152	158	165	172	178	185	191	198
4	160	168	176	183	191	199	206	214	222	229
5	183	192	201	209	218	227	235	244	253	262
6	206	216	225	235	245	255	265	274	284	294
7	228	238	249	260	271	282	293	304	314	325
8	250	262	274	286	298	310	322	334	346	358
9	272	285	298	311	324	337	350	363	376	389
10	295	309	323	337	351	365	379	393	407	421
11	360	378	395	412	429	446	463	480	498	515
12	423	444	464	484	504	524	544	564	585	605
13	486	510	533	556	579	602	625	648	672	695

Effective date: No earlier than 1 January 1972

BEN B BEESON
Asst DCSPER (Civ Per)
US Army, Pacific

JOHN E. TAYLOR
Director Civilian Personnel
US Pacific Air Forces

WILLIAM M. MEAUT
Fleet Civilian Personnel
Director
US Pacific Fleet

Inclosure 1

57

US FORCES WAGE SCHEDULE

KOREA
NON-MANUAL (KGS) WAGE SCHEDULE
LOCALLY HIRED, NON-US CITIZEN EMPLOYEES

HOURLY STEP RATES (KOREAN WON)

KGS GRADE	STEP A	STEP B	STEP C	STEP D	STEP E	STEP F	STEP G	STEP H	STEP I	STEP J
1	100	105	109	114	119	124	129	133	138	143
2	133	139	145	152	158	164	171	177	183	190
3	165	172	180	188	196	204	212	220	227	235
4	197	206	215	225	234	243	253	262	271	281
5	228	239	250	261	272	283	294	305	316	326
6	260	273	285	298	310	322	335	347	360	372
7	292	306	320	334	348	362	376	390	404	418
8	324	340	355	371	386	401	417	432	448	463
9	375	392	410	428	446	464	482	500	517	535
10	425	445	466	486	506	526	546	567	587	607
11	475	498	521	543	566	589	611	634	657	679
12	553	579	605	632	658	684	711	737	763	790
13	630	660	690	720	750	780	810	840	870	900

Effective date: No earlier than 1 January 1972

BEN B BEESON
Asst DCSPER (Civ Per)
US Army, Pacific

JOHN E. TAYLOR
Director Civilian Personnel
US Pacific Air Forces

WILLIAM M. MEAUT
Fleet Civilian Personnel
Director
US Pacific Fleet

US FORCES WAGE SCHEDULE

KOREA
MARINE (KM) WAGE SCHEDULE
LOCALLY HIRED, NON-US CITIZEN EMPLOYEES

HOURLY STEP RATES (KOREAN WON)

KM GRADE	STEP A	STEP B	STEP C	STEP D	STEP E	STEP F	STEP G	STEP H	STEP I	STEP J
1	139	146	153	159	166	173	179	186	193	199
2	155	162	169	177	184	191	199	206	213	221
3	173	181	190	198	206	214	222	231	239	247
4	189	198	207	216	225	234	243	252	261	270
5	221	231	242	252	263	274	284	295	305	316
6	249	261	273	285	297	309	321	333	345	356
7	296	310	324	338	352	366	380	394	408	422
8	343	359	375	392	408	424	441	457	473	490
9	449	470	491	513	534	555	577	598	619	641
10	512	537	561	586	610	634	659	683	708	732

Effective date: No earlier than 1 January 1972

BEN B BEESON
Asst DCSPER (Civ Per)
US Army, Pacific

JOHN E. TAYLOR
Director Civilian Personnel
US Pacific Air Forces

WILLIAM M. MEAUT
Fleet Civilian Personnel
Director
US Pacific Fleet

59

Revised Provisions to Bring Lower Tenure Service to ROK Legal Minimum

EA CPR 690-1, Extract

"60. c. Computation. Payment will be either the amount computed in (1) or (2) below whichever is the greater.

(1) Divide by three (3) the employee's total normal wages for (a) the 3-month period immediately preceding the date of separation or (b) any three (3) consecutive full month period which represents the highest wages earned; multiply the result of (a) or (b) whichever provides the greater base by the number of credit-months applicable to the type of separation and amount of creditable services as provided in Appendix E.

(2) Divide by three (3) the employee's total wages (including premium pay, allowances and prorated bonus) for the 3-month period immediately preceding the date of separation; multiply the result by the number of _full years_ of continuous service.

(3) The following guidance pertains: The 3-month period immediately prior to effective date of separation is three (3) calendar months (e.g., from 15 July thru 14 October, if separation is effective 15 October) and any three (3) consecutive full months are in terms of full months (e.g., from 1 January thru 31 March or 1 February thru 30 April). Normal wage includes extended workweek, but is exclusive of all overtime, holiday pay, night differential, allowances and bonuses; non-pay status during the 3-month period is included as if the employee had received his normal basic pay for the period of non-pay status. Total wages include overtime pay, night differential, holiday pay, remote area allowance, subsistence allowance and the prorated bonuses received by the employee during 3-month period. Remote area allowance will be calculated based on number of full weeks (7 days) during the period multiplied by 600 won. Subsistence allowance of 230 won daily will be credited for each work day to those employees who were provided meals during the 3-month period. Prorated bonuses will be 25% of the normal wages earned during the period. Thus the format for deriving monthly base for severance pay computation is as follows:

Normal Wage + OT Pay + ND + HW Pay + Remote Area All + Sub All + Bonus (Nor Wx25%)"

3

Inclosure 2

60

**JOINT COMMITTEE
UNDER
THE REPUBLIC OF KOREA AND THE UNITED STATES
STATUS OF FORCES AGREEMENT**

MEMORANDUM FOR: THE JOINT COMMITTEE   11 JAN 1972

SUBJECT: Designation of US Invited Contractor under Article XV, Status
          of Forces Agreement

1. References:

    a. Paragraph 2, Article XV, Status of Forces Agreement.

    b. US Chairman, Commerce Subcommittee letter, dated 25 Feb 1971,
subject as above (Incl 1).

    c. ROK Chairman, Commerce Subcommittee letter, dated 5 Mar 1971,
subject as above (Incl 2).

2. The United States, after consultation with the ROK Commerce Subcommittee and having duly considered their views, has designated Associated
American Engineers Overseas, Inc., as a US invited contractor, in joint
venture with a Korean firm, for execution of contract F62087-72-C-0054 for
operation and maintenance services for Air Force installations, Korea.

3. Pertinent data concerning US or third country national employees will
be provided to the Joint Secretariat by established reporting procedures.

2 Incl   ROBERT N. SMITH
as   Lieutenant General, USAF
                                 United States Representative
                                 Joint Committee

61

REPUBLIC OF KOREA - UNITED STATES
COMMERCE SUBCOMMITTEE

25 February 1971

SUBJECT: Designation of US Invited Contractor Under Article XV,
Status of Forces Agreement

ROK Chairman, Commerce Subcommittee

1. Reference Paragraph 2, Article XV of the Status of Forces Agreement.

2. The Government of the Republic of Korea is informed through this written consultative process that the United States Forces, Korea, proposes to extend invited contractor status to the US member of the successful negotiated bidder among qualified joint venture firms for the forthcoming Facilities Engineering Services Contract for the US Air Force Bases and sites in Korea. This new contract will replace contract DAJB03-67-C-0592.

3. The following data are provided:

a. Company Name: The list of contractors being considered is attached as inclosure 1.

b. Local Address: To be supplied upon designation.

c. Identification of US Citizen Employees: To be supplied upon designation.

d. Number of US and ROK Employees: It is estimated that 14 US citizens and 466 Koreans will be employed under the contract.

e. Reason for Designation of a Joint Venture Contractor: Open competitive bidding is not practicable due to the following:

(1) A contract utilizing ROK contractor only would not be feasible due to the extensive security requirements demanded by the US Air Force. The contractor will be involved in the operations and maintenance of critical support facilities which directly affect the mission capabilities of the US Air Force. He will be involved with programming actions which may be classified and contain information not releasable to foreign nationals.

62

SUBJECT: Designation of US Invited Contractor Under Article XV,
Status of Forces Agreement

(2) Fully qualified and trained managers and supervisors are essential to meet civil engineering requirements. The management of government resources placed in the hands of the contractor such as supplies, equipment, tools, and vehicles require that the contractor be responsible for and responsive to USAF policies and requirements. Fire Department operations require personnel familiar with aircraft fire protection and crash rescue procedures and equipment.

(3) The contractor is required to comply with various Air Force manuals and regulations and other applicable publications which are technical in nature. The facilities and technical equipment are US design and manufacture and must be maintained to USAF standards which in most cases is above that of local standards and beyond the capability of local national personnel without US supervision.

f. Location of Contract: US Air Force Korea.

g. Type of Contracts: Award of a single contract for the management, operation, maintenance and repair of real property facilities, to include fire protection and crash rescue service is contemplated.

h. Length of Contract: 1 July 1971 through 30 June 1972 with an option to extend the contract up to two additional years. The contract will also provide for a 30-day transition period at the end of the contract to assist a successor contractor. Total duration of the contract, including options and period of transition, will not exceed thirty-seven (37) months.

i. Sponsoring Component Commander: Commander, Air Forces, Korea.

1 Incl
as

RICHARD T. CANN
Colonel, U.S. Army
ACofS, J4

2

MINISTRY OF COMMERCE AND INDUSTRY
REPUBLIC OF KOREA
SEOUL, KOREA

5 March 1971

Subject: Designation of US Invited Contractor under Article XV
          Status of Forces Agreement

US Chairman, Commerce Subcommittee

1. Reference:

    a. Paragraph 2, Article XV, Status of Forces Agreement

    b. US Commerce Subcommittee Memorandum of Consultation, dated
25 February 1971, subject as above, pertaining to joint venture
contract for Facilities Engineering Services for the US Air Base, Korea.

2. The US memorandum reference 1b above, has been reviewed and the
Government of the Republic of Korea understands the requirement for
invitied contractor status to the US member of ROK/US joint venture
contract firm in this instance.

3. The list of qualified Korean contractors to be considered for
joint venture with US firms for the above contract is attached herewith.

                                Chung Min Kil
                                Chairman
                                Commerce Subcommittee, ROK

64

21 DEC 1971

MEMORANDUM FOR: THE JOINT COMMITTEE

SUBJECT: Designation of US Invited Contractor under Article XV, Status of Forces Agreement

1.   References:

    a.   Paragraph 2, Article XV, Status of Forces Agreement.

    b.   US Chairman, Commerce Subcommittee letter, dated 10 Sep 1971, subject as above (Incl 1).

    c.   ROK Chairman, Commerce Subcommittee letter, dated 15 Sep 1971, subject as above (Incl 2).

2.   The United States, after consultation with the ROK Commerce Subcommittee and having duly considered their views, has designated Trans Asia Engineering Company as a US invited contractor for execution of contract DACA79-72-C-0038 for design of POL systems, Osan, Suwon, Taegu, Kwangju and Kunsan.

3.   Pertinent data concerning US or third country national employees will be provided to the Joint Secretariat by established reporting procedures.

2 Incl
as

ROBERT N. SMITH
Lieutenant General, USAF
United States Representative
Joint Committee

65

REPUBLIC OF KOREA - UNITED STATES
COMMERCE SUBCOMMITTEE   10 September 1971

SUBJECT: Designation of US Invited Contractor Under Article
           XV, Status of Forces Agreement

ROK Chairman, Commerce Subcommittee

1.   Reference paragraph 2, Article XV of the Status of Forces
Agreement.

2.   The Government of the Republic of Korea is informed
through this written consultative process that the United
States Forces, Korea, proposes to extend invited contractor
status to the qualified US firm awarded the contract for
design of POL systems, Osan, Suwon, Taegu, Kwangju and
Kunsan Air Bases.

3.   The following data are provided:

     a.   Company Name:

          (1)   Trans Asia Engineering Associates, APO 96301
          (2)   The Hinchman Company, Detroit, Michigan
          (3)   Harco Corporation, Cleveland, Ohio

     b.   Local Address of each firm:

          (1)   Trans Asia Engineering Associates: APO 96301
          (2)   The Hinchman Company: None
          (3)   Harco Corporation: None

     c.   Identification of US Citizen Employees: To be
provided after contract award.

     d.   Number of US and ROK Employees: To be provided
after contract award.

     e.   Reasons for Designation of an Invited Contractor:

          (1)   Contracting Officer is bound by US law to select
architect-engineer firms for professional services contracts
in strict accordance with the procedures set forth in paragraph 18-402 of the Armed Services Procurement Regulation
(ASPR).   Such selection is not based upon competitive bidding

procedures, but rather upon the professional qualifications necessary for the satisfactory performance of the services required, subject to additional considerations such as required specialized experience, demonstrated performance, and security qualifications. The Contracting Officer is prohibited from selecting from among other than those firms who have properly filed GSA Standard Form 251, "U.S. Government Architect-Engineer Questionnaire", and have been declared qualified to perform such services for the US Government under procedures prescribed in the ASPR. All firms listed in paragraph 2a, above, have properly filed qualification data in accordance with the procedures described above; have been declared fully qualified to perform such services, and therefore, are eligible to be selected by Contracting Officer for professional services contracts. None other than U.S. Firms have thus far filed qualification data and met the prerequisities for selection. Accordingly, designation of US Invited Contractor is required for the performance of this work under the applicable terms of SOFA.

(2) "A" recognized expert in the field of Cathodic Protection is required, the design per usual American Practices is needed to facilitate later maintenance.

f. <u>Location of Contract:</u> Osan, Suwon, Taegu, Kwangju and Kunsan

g. <u>Type of Contract:</u> Fixed Price, Type B

h. <u>Length of Contract:</u> To be provided after contract award.

i. <u>USFK Sponsor:</u> Far East District, Corps of Engineers

RICHARD T. CANN
Colonel, U.S. Army
United States Chairman
Commerce Subcommittee

2

67

MINISTRY OF COMMERCE AND INDUSTRY
REPUBLIC OF KOREA
SEOUL, KOREA

15 September 1971

Subject: Designation of US Invited Contractor under Article XV, Status of Forces Agreement

US Chairman, Commerce Subcommittee

1. Reference:

    a. Paragraph 2, Article XV, Status of Forces Agreement

    b. US Commerce Subcommittee Memorandum of Consultation, dated 10 September 1971 subject as above, pertaining to contract for design of POL systems, Osan, Suwon, Taegu, Kwangju and Kunsan Air Bases, Korea.

2. The US memorandum, reference 1b above, has been reviewed and the government of the Republic of Korea understands the requirement for an invited contractor in this instance.

Chung Min Kil
Chairman
Commerce Subcommittee, ROK

68

21 DEC 1971

MEMORANDUM FOR: THE JOINT COMMITTEE

SUBJECT: Designation of US Invited Contractor under Article XV, Status of Forces Agreement

1. References:

   a. Paragraph 2, Article XV, Status of Forces Agreement.

   b. US Chairman, Commerce Subcommittee letter, dated 1 Sep 1971, subject as above (Incl 1).

   c. ROK Chairman, Commerce Subcommittee letter, dated 8 Sep 1971, subject as above (Incl 2).

2. The United States, after consultation with the ROK Commerce Subcommittee and having duly considered their views, has designated the National Cash Register Company as a US invited contractor for execution of contract DAJB03-72-C-3033 for maintenance of National Cash Register and Multilith machines.

3. Pertinent data concerning US or third country national employees will be provided to the Joint Secretariat by established reporting procedures.

2 Incl
as

ROBERT N. SMITH
Lieutenant General, USAF
United States Representative
Joint Committee

69

1 September 1971

SUBJECT: Designation of US Invited Contractor under Article XV Status of
Forces Agreement

ROK Chairman, Commerce Subcommittee

1. Reference: Para 2, Article XV, Status of Forces Agreement.

2. The Government of the Republic of Korea is informed through this
written consultative process that the United States Forces, Korea, proposes to extend invited contractor status to the National Cash Register
Company, Korea Branch, for maintenance and repair of NCR machines and
multilith duplicating machines at various Eighth Army activities.

3. The following data are provided:

    a. Company Name: National Cash Register Company, Korea Branch.

    b. Local Address: APO 96301.

    c. Identification of US Citizen Employee: Mr. E. A. Potter.

    d. Number of US and ROK Employees: It is anticipated that one (1)
US and thirty (30) Korean personnel will be employed.

    e. Reasons for Designation of a US Invited Contractor: Open com-
petitive bidding is not practicable due to local unavailability of materials
or services required by US standards as explained below:

    (1) NCR factory-made spare parts are available only from bonafide NCR Company
operation. No other US or Korean firm can furnish NCR parts.

    (2) NCR provides guarantee and warranty services. NCR guarantees
that all equipment delivered in Korea shall be in good operating condition
and it shall replace free of charge during the first year any defective
parts and it will make any other repairs and adjustments required during
the one year guarantee period free of charge.

    (3) The NCR warranty is automatically voided if the equipment is
serviced by other than a certified NCR employee.

70

SUBJECT: Designation of US Invited Contractor under Article XV Status of
Forces Agreement

(4) NCR furnishes for the initial training period, supervised equipment operator training and instruction of USFK employees.

f. Location of Contract: Eighth US Army installations throughout
the Republic of Korea.

g. Type of Contract: Fixed Price contract for maintenance and repair
of NCR machines and duplicating machines.

h. Length of Contract: 12 months.

i. Sponsoring Component Commander: US Army Korea Procurement Agency.

RICHARD X. CANN
Colonel, U.S. Army
United States Chairman
Commerce Subcommittee

2

MINISTRY OF COMMERCE AND INDUSTRY
REPUBLIC OF KOREA
SEOUL, KOREA

8 September 1971

Subject: Designation of US Invited Contractor under Article XV, Status of Forces Agreement

US Chairman, Commerce Subcommittee

1. Reference:

    a. Paragraph 2, Article XV, Status of Forces Agreement

    b. US Commerce Subcommittee Memorandum of Consultation, dated 1 September 1971 subject as above, pertaining to contract for maintenance and repair of NCR machines and duplicating machines at various Eighth Army activities.

2. The US memorandum, reference 1b above, has been reviewed and the government of the Republic of Korea understands the requirement for an invited contractor in this instance.

for *Changsulk Chu*
Chung Min Kil
Chairman
Commerce Subcommittee, ROK

72

JOINT COMMITTEE
UNDER
THE REPUBLIC OF KOREA AND THE UNITED STATES
STATUS OF FORCES AGREEMENT

21 DEC 1971

MEMORANDUM FOR: THE JOINT COMMITTEE

SUBJECT: Designation of US Invited Contractor under Article XV, Status of Forces Agreement

1. References:

    a. Paragraph 2, Article XV, Status of Forces Agreement.

    b. US Chairman, Commerce Subcommittee letter, dated 1 Sep 1971, subject as above (Incl 1).

    c. ROK Chairman, Commerce Subcommittee letter, dated 8 Sep 1971, subject as above (Incl 2).

2. The United States, after consultation with the ROK Commerce Sub-committee and having duly considered their views, has designated the National Cash Register Company as a US invited contractor for execution of contract BK-71-0104 for maintenance of NCR machines for the Korea Regional Exchange.

3. Pertinent data concerning US or third country national employees will be provided to the Joint Secretariat by established reporting procedures.

2 Incl
as

ROBERT N. SMITH
Lieutenant General, USAF
United States Representative
Joint Committee

REPUBLIC OF KOREA - UNITED STATES
COMMERCE SUBCOMMITTEE

1 September 1971

SUBJECT: Designation of US Invited Contractor under Article XV, Status of Forces Agreement

ROK Chairman, Commerce Subcommittee

1. Reference: Para 2, Article XV, Status of Forces Agreement.

2. The Government of the Republic of Korea is informed through this written consultative process that the United States Forces, Korea, proposes to extend invited contractor status to the National Cash Register Company, Korea Branch, for maintenance and repair of NCR machines for the Korea Regional Exchange.

2. The following data are provided:

   a. Company Name: National Cash Register Company, Korea Branch.

   b. Local Address: #24-738, Hanam-dong, Yongsan-ku, Seoul, Korea.

   c. Identification of US Citizen Employee: Mr. Edmond A. Potter.

   d. Number of US and ROK Employees: It is anticipated that one (1) US and thirty (30) Korean personnel will be employed under this contract.

   e. Reason for Designation of US Invited Contractor: Open competitive bidding is not practical due to local unavailability of materials or services required by US standards as explained below:

   (1) NCR factory-made spare parts are available only from bonafide NCR Company operation. No other US or Korean firm can furnish NCR parts.

   (2) NCR provides guarantee and warranty services. NCR guarantees that all equipment delivered in Korea shall be in good operating condition and it shall replace free of charge during the first year any defective parts and it will make any other repairs and adjustments required during the one (1) year guarantee period free of charge.

   (3) The NCR warranty is automatically voided if the equipment is serviced by other than a certified NCR employee.

SUBJECT: Designation of US Invited Contractor under Article XV Status of
Forces Agreement

(4) NCR furnishes for the initial training period, supervised equipment operator training and instruction of USFK employees.

f. **Location of Contract**: Korea Regional Exchange installations throughout the Republic of Korea.

g. **Type of Contract**: Fixed price contract for maintenance and repair of NCR machines.

h. **Length of Contract**: Two years with three (3) one year renewal options.

i. **Sponsoring Component Command**: PACEX Procurement Office - Korea.

RICHARD T. CANN
Colonel, U.S. Army
United States Chairman
Commerce Subcommittee

2

75

MINISTRY OF COMMERCE AND INDUSTRY
REPUBLIC OF KOREA
SEOUL, KOREA

8 September 1971

Subject: Designation of US Invited Contractor under Article XV,
Status of Forces Agreement

US Chairman, Commerce Subcommittee

1. Reference:

   a. Paragraph 2, Article XV, Status of Forces Agreement

   b. US Commerce Subcommittee Memorandum of Consultation, dated
1 September 1971 subject as above, pertaining to contract for
maintenance and repair of NCR machines for the Korea Regional
Exchange-PACEX.

2. The US memorandum, reference 1b above, has been reviewed and
the government of the Republic of Korea understands the requirement
for an invited contractor in this instance.

for Chung Min Kil
     Chairman
     Commerce Subcommittee, ROK

MEMORANDUM FOR: THE JOINT COMMITTEE

SUBJECT: Designation of US Invited Contractor under Article XV, Status of Forces Agreement

1. References:

    a. Paragraph 2, Article XV, Status of Forces Agreement.

    b. US Chairman, Commerce Subcommittee letter, dated 10 Sep 1971, subject as above (Incl 1).

    c. ROK Chairman, Commerce Subcommittee letter, dated 15 Sep 1971, subject as above (Incl 2).

2. The United States, after consultation with the ROK Commerce Sub-committee and having duly considered their views, has designated Trans Asia Engineering Company as a US invited contractor for execution of contract DACA79-72-C-0038 for design of POL systems, Osan, Suwon, Taegu, Kwangju and Kunsan.

3. Pertinent data concerning US or third country national employees will be provided to the Joint Secretariat by established reporting procedures.

2 Incl   ROBERT N. SMITH
as   Lieutenant General, USAF
                              United States Representative
                              Joint Committee

77

JOINT COMMITTEE
UNDER
THE REPUBLIC OF KOREA AND THE UNITED STATES
STATUS OF FORCES AGREEMENT

MEMORANDUM FOR: THE JOINT COMMITTEE   30 DEC 1971

SUBJECT: Designation of US Invited Contractor under Article XV, Status of Forces Agreement

1. References:

    a. Paragraph 2, Article XV, Status of Forces Agreement.

    b. US Chairman, Commerce Subcommittee letter, dated 19 August 1971, subject as above (Incl 1).

    c. ROK Chairman, Commerce Subcommittee letter, dated 23 August 1971, subuect as above (Incl 2).

2. The United States, after consultation with the ROK Commerce Subcommittee and having duly considered their views, has designated Lyon Associates as a US invited contractor for execution of contract DACA 79-72-C-0040 for design of Phase II, Army Security Agency (ASA) Project Adventure, various locations, Korea.

3. Pertinent data concerning US or third country national employees will be provided to the Joint Secretariat by established reporting procedures.

2 Incl
as

                ROBERT N. SMITH
                Lieutenant General, USAF
                United States Representative
                Joint Committee

78

REPUBLIC OF KOREA - UNITED STATES
COMMERCE SUBCOMMITTEE

19 August 1971

SUBJECT: Designation of US Invited Contractor Under Article XV,
Status of Forces Agreement

Republic of Korea Chairman, Commerce Subcommittee

1. Reference: Paragraph 2, Article XV of the Status of Forces Agreement.

2. The Government of the Republic of Korea is informed through this written consultative process that the United States Forces Korea proposes to extend invited contractor status to the qualified US firm on the contract for the design of Phase II, Army Security Agency (ASA) Project Adventure, various locations throughout Korea.

3. The following data are provided:

   a. Company name:

   (1) Lyon Associates

   (2) Adrian Wilson Associates

   (3) Daniel, Mann, Johnson and Mendenhall

   b. Local address: APO 96301

   c. Identification of US citizen employees: To be provided later.

   d. Number of US and ROK employees: To be provided later.

   e. Reasons for designation as an invited contractor: Contracting officer is bound by US law to select architect-engineer firms for professional services contracts in strict accordance with the procedures set forth in paragraph 18-402 of the Armed Services Procurement Regulation (ASPR). Such selection is not based upon competitive bidding procedures, but rather upon the professional qualifications necessary for the satisfactory performance of the services required, subject to additional

SUBJECT: Designation of US Invited Contractor Under Article XV,
            Status of Forces Agreement

considerations such as required specialized experience, demonstrated
performance, and security qualifications. The contracting officer is
prohibited from selecting from among other than those firms who have
properly filed GSA Standard Form 251, "U.S. Government Architect-
Engineer Questionnaire," and have been declared qualified to perform
such services for the US Government under procedures prescribed in the
ASPR. All firms listed in paragraph 2a, above, have properly filed
qualification data in accordance with the procedures described above;
have been declared fully qualified to perform such services and, therefore, are eligible to be selected by contracting officer for
professional services contracts. None other than US firms have thus
far filed qualification data and met the prerequisites for selection.
Accordingly, designation of US Invited Contractor is required for the
performance of this work under the applicable terms of SOFA.

    f. Location of contract: Various locations throughout Korea.

    g. Type of contract: Firm, fixed price, A&E Services, type B.

    h. Length of contract: To be provided.

    i. Sponsoring component commander: US Army Engineer District,
Far East.

RICHARD Z. CANN
Colonel, US Army
United States Chairman
Commerce Subcommittee

2

80

MINISTRY OF COMMERCE AND INDUSTRY
REPUBLIC OF KOREA
SEOUL, KOREA

23 August 1971

Subject: Designation of US Invited Contractor under Article XV,
Status of Forces Agreement

US Chairman, Commerce Subcommittee

1.   Reference:

a.   Paragraph 2, Article XV, Status of Forces Agreement

b.   US Commerce Subcommittee Memorandum of Consultation, dated
19 August 1971 subject as above, pertaining to contract for the
desugn of Phase II, Army Security Agency (ASA) Project Adventure,
Various locations throughout Korea.

2.   The US memorandum, reference 1b above, has been reviewed and
the government of the Republic of Korea understands the requirement
for an invited contractor in this instance.

Chung Jin Kil
Chairman
Commerce Subcommittee, ROK

81

JOINT COMMITTEE
UNDER
THE REPUBLIC OF KOREA AND THE UNITED STATES
STATUS OF FORCES AGREEMENT

MEMORANDUM FOR: THE JOINT COMMITTEE   6 JAN 1972

SUBJECT: Designation of US Invited Contractor under Article XV, Status
of Forces Agreement

1. References:

a. Paragraph 2, Article XV, Status of Forces Agreement.

b. US Chairman, Commerce Subcommittee letter, dated 29 Sep 1971,
subject as above (Incl 1).

c. ROK Chairman, Commerce Subcommittee letter, dated 4 Oct 1971,
subject as above (Incl 2).

2. The United States, after consultation with the ROK Commerce Subcommittee and having duly considered their views, has designated Daniel,
Mann, Johnson and Mendenhall as a US invited contractor for execution of
contract DACA 79-72-C-0042 for design of Autodin Switching Center, Camp
Walker, Taegu.

3. Pertinent data concerning US or third country national employees will
be provided to the Joint Secretariat by established reporting procedures.

2 Incl   ROBERT N. SMITH
as   Lieutenant General, USAF
                                       United States Representative
                                       Joint Committee

REPUBLIC OF KOREA - UNITED STATES
COMMERCE SUBCOMMITTEE

29 September 1971

SUBJECT: Designation of US Invited Contractor Under Article XV, Status
of Forces Agreement

ROK Chairman, Commerce Subcommittee

1. Reference paragraph 2, Article XV of the Status of Forces Agreement.

2. The Government of the Republic of Korea is informed through this
written consultative process that the United States Forces, Korea, proposes to extend invited contractor status to the qualified US firms
awarded the contract for design of Autodin Switching Center, Camp Walker,
Korea.

3. The following data are provided:

a. <u>Company Name</u>:

   (1) Adrian Wilson Associates
   (2) Associated American Engineers, Inc.
   (3) Daniel, Mann, Johnson & Mendenhall
   (4) Lyon Associates, Inc.
   (5) Pacific Architects & Engineers, Inc.

b. <u>Local Address</u>:

   (1) Adrian Wilson Associates, APO 96301
   (2) Associated American Engineers, Inc., APO 96301
   (3) Daniel, Mann, Johnson & Mendenhall (None)
   (4) Lyon Associates, Inc., APO 96301
   (5) Pacific Architects & Engineers, Inc. (None)

   c. <u>Identification of US Citizen Employees</u>: To be provided after
contract award.

   d. <u>Number of US and ROK Employees</u>: To be provided after contract
award.

   e. <u>Reasons for Designation of an Invited Contractor</u>: Contracting
Officer is bound by US law to select architect-engineer firms for professional services contracts in strict accordance with the procedures set

forth in paragraph 18-402 of the Armed Services Procurement Regulation (ASPR). Such selection is not based upon competitive bidding procedures, but rather upon the professional qualifications necessary for the satisfactory performance of the services required, subject to additional considerations such as required specialized experience, demonstrated performance, and security qualifications. The Contracting Officer is prohibited from selecting from among other than those firms who have properly filed GSA Standard Form 251, "U. S. Government Architect-Engineer Questionnaire", and have been declared qualified to perform such services for the US Government under procedures prescribed in the ASPR. All firms listed in paragraph 3a above have properly filed qualification data in accordance with the procedures described above; have been declared fully qualified to perform such services, and, therefore, are eligible to be selected by Contracting Officer for professional services contracts. None other than U.S. firms have thus far filed qualification data and met the prerequisites for selection. Accordingly, designation of US Invited Contractor is required for the performance of this work under the applicable terms of SOFA.

    f. **Location of Contract:** Taegu, Korea.

    g. **Type of Contract:** Fixed Price, Type B contract for architect-engineer services to design an Autodin Switching Center, for relocation to Camp Walker. The Autodin Switching Center includes a pre-engineered building with extensive air conditioning and environmental control for communications equipment. The work will include the design of drainage structures, access road, standby power, heating, air conditioning, utilities and related aspects to provide a complete facility ready for installation of communication equipment.

    h. **Length of Contract:** To be provided after contract award.

    i. **USFK Sponsor:** District Engineer.

RICHARD T. CANN
Colonel, US Army
United States Chairman
Commerce Subcommittee

84

2

MINISTRY OF COMMERCE AND INDUSTRY
REPUBLIC OF KOREA
SEOUL, KOREA

4 October 1971

Subject: Designation of US Invited Contractor under Article XV,
Status of Forces Agreement

US Chairman, Commerce Subcommittee

1. Reference:

    a. Paragraph 2, Article XV, Status of Forces Agreement

    b. US Commerce Subcommittee Memorandum of Consultation, dated
29 September 1971 subject as above, pertaining to contract for
design of Autodin Switching Center, Camp Walker, Korea.

2. The US memorandum, reference 1b above, has been reviewed and
the government of the Republic of Korea understands the requirement
for an invited contractor in this instance.

Chung Min Kil
Chairman
Commerce Subcommittee, ROK

JOINT COMMITTEE
UNDER
THE REPUBLIC OF KOREA AND THE UNITED STATES
STATUS OF FORCES AGREEMENT

MEMORANDUM FOR: The Joint Committee   19 January 1972

SUBJECT: Designation of US Invited Contractor Under Article XV, Status
of Forces Agreement

1. References:

a. Paragraph 2, Article XV, Status of Forces Agreement.

b. US Chairman, Commerce Subcommittee letter, dated 22 June 1971,
subject as above (Inclosure 1).

c. ROK Chairman, Commerce Subcommittee letter, dated 24 August 1971,
subject as above (Inclosure 2).

2. The United States, after consultation with the ROK Commerce Subcommittee, and having duly considered their views, has designated Collins
Radio Company as a US invited contractor for execution of Contract DAAB 07-
72-C-0010 for a new 60 channel add-on to the existing ROKA Backbone
Microwave System.

3. Pertinent data concerning US citizen employees will be provided to the
Joint Secretariat in the established format.

2 Incl
as
                                         ROBERT N. SMITH
                                         Lieutenant General, USAF
                                         United States Representative
                                         Joint Committee

REPUBLIC OF KOREA – UNITED STATES
COMMERCE SUBCOMMITTEE

22 June 1971

SUBJECT: Designation of US Invited Contractor Under Article XV,
Status of Forces Agreement

ROK Chairman, Commerce Subcommittee

1. Reference: Paragraph 2, Article XV, of the Status of Forces
Agreement.

2. The Government of the Republic of Korea is informed through this
written consultative process that the United States Forces, Korea,
proposes to extend invited contractor status to the Collins Radio
Company to develop an engineering plan, provide and install associated
radio and multiplex equipment, and perform all system tests and
alignments for a new 60 channel add-on to the existing ROKA Backbone
Microwave System.

3. The following data are provided:

    a. Company Name: Collins Radio Company

    b. Local Address: Office #1113, Ko-Ryo Building, 24, 1-Ka,
        Shin Moon-Ro, Chongro-ku, Seoul, Korea

    c. Identification of US Citizen Employees: To be supplied upon
award of contract.

    d. Number of US and ROK Employees: The number of US citizens
and Korean employees is not known at this time and will be supplied
upon conclusion of negotiations.

    e. Reasons for Designation of an Invited Contractor: Open
competitive bidding is not practicable due to the exclusive type US
Manufactured equipments to be installed on a now-existing system.
This equipment must be manufactured by the Collins Radio Company, as
specified in Article VII of the Memorandum of Agreement, SUBJECT:
Utilization of the Republic of Korea Army (ROKA) Microwave (M/W) System

87

SUBJECT: Designation of US Invited Contractor Under Article XV,
         Status of Forces Agreement

by the United Nations Command/United States Forces, Korea, dated 5 June
1970. This Memorandum of Agreement was agreed to and authorized in
accordance with Article III, paragraph 2(8), of the United States of
America and the Republic of Korea Status of Forces Agreement, third
edition dated July 1969.

  (1) Invited Contractor Status is considered necessary to insure
that the US equipment provided will be installed, tested, and placed in
operation so as to meet all specifications as stated in the Memorandum
of Agreement. This is addressed in paragraph g, Article VII of the
Memorandum of Agreement which states: "g. ROKA will authorize access
to ROKA microwave sites of US personnel as required to conduct joint
surveys, path profiles, installation and maintenance necessary to engineer
and install the expanded R/F path and 60-channel supergroup on the ROKA
microwave system. If Korean technicians, in US employ, are required,
their clearance will be subject to approval by ROK security agency."
This clearly identifies that the award will be to a US Contractor who
gains the option to use Korean Technicians, if required.

  (2) End to end telecommunications utilizing media from two countries,
as stated in the Memorandum of Agreement, is required. To meet operational
standards it is essential that only one firm be held responsible to insure
that they are met over the entire system. To achieve this, the procurement, installation, and testing cannot be subdivided or piece-mealed out.

  f. Location of Contract: Contract installation work will be performed at the following ROKA microwave sites:

  (1) Seoul

  (2) Mangyung-dae

  (3) Paegunsan

  (4) Yongwhabong

  (5) Hakkasan

  (6) Palgongsan

  (7) Taegu

  (8) Pulmosan

  (9) Changsan   )

                                                    2

22 June 1971

SUBJECT: Designation of US Invited Contractor Under Article XV,
Status of Forces Agreement

g. Type of Contract: The contactor will provide system engineering,
equipment installation and testing for a 60-channel add-on to the ROKA
Backbone Microwave System.

h. Length of Contract: Approximately 10 months.

i. Sponsoring Component Command: Commanding General, Eighth United
States Army.

Norman W. Hammes, COL
RICHARD T. CANN
Colonel, US Army
United States Chairman
Commerce Subcommittee

3

MINISTRY OF COMMERCE AND INDUSTRY
REPUBLIC OF KOREA
SEOUL, KOREA

24 August 1971

Subject: Designation of US Invited Contractor under Article XV,
Status of Forces Agreement

US Chairman, Commerce Subcommittee

1. Reference:

a. Paragrph 2, Article XV, Status of Forces Agreement

b. US Commerce Subcommittee Memorandum of Consultation, dated
22 June 1971 subject as above, pertaining to contract for a new 60
channel add-on to the existing ROKA Backbone Microwave System, Korea.

2. The US memorandum, reference 1b above, has been reviewed and
the government of the Republic of Korea understands the requirement
for an invited contractor in this instance.

Chung Min Kil
Chairman
Commerce Subcommittee, ROK

90

JOINT COMMITTEE
UNDER
THE REPUBLIC OF KOREA AND THE UNITED STATES
STATUS OF FORCES AGREEMENT

2 JAN 1972

MEMORANDUM FOR: THE JOINT COMMITTEE

SUBJECT: SOFA Status of the University of Maryland Personnel

1. Reference: Article I and Article XV, Status of Forces Agreement.

2. The status of the University of Maryland personnel has been a matter of review with the officials of the Republic of Korea. In accord with the review, the United States Forces Korea is withdrawing the designation of invited contractor from the University of Maryland and will consider the personnel of this organization henceforth as members of the civilian component.

ROBERT N. SMITH
Lieutenant General
United States Forces Korea
United States Representative

91

JOINT ROK-US PRESS RELEASE
SEVENTIETH ROK-US JOINT COMMITTEE MEETING
28 JANUARY 1972

The ROK-US Joint Committee completed its first five years of work in implementation of the Status of Forces Agreement with the holding of the seventieth meeting at the Foreign Ministry Conference Room in the ROK Capitol Building on 28 January. The new ROK Government Representative, Mr. KIM Dong Whie, who recently was named Director of the Europe and America Bureau of the Foreign Ministry, presided at the meeting which included fourteen agenda items.

The Joint Committee approved the fifth report of its Ad Hoc Sub-committee on Civil-Military Relations, including a total of five recommendations from its Panels on Health and Sanitation, Narcotics and Drug Control, and Race Relations and Equality of Treatment. This brings to nineteen the number of recommendations of the Ad Hoc Sub-committee on Civil-Military Relations which have been approved by the Joint Committee and reflects the increasing emphasis of both Governments in improving civil-military relations in the Korean communities adjacent to US military installations in the ROK.

The Joint Committee also approved ten recommendations of its Facilities and Areas Subcommittee and noted for the record the earlier exigent approval of a recommendation of its Transportation Subcommittee which has enabled the re-registration and licensing of the privately

92

owned vehicles of United States Forces Korea personnel to begin this week.

Among the other actions of the Joint Committee at its seventieth meeting were the assignment of ten additional tasks to its Facilities and Areas Subcommittee, one task to its Transportation Subcommittee, designation of six new US invited contractors, the withdrawal of the designation of one US invited contractor, and the noting for the record of the recent resolution of two labor disputes in accordance with the procedures of the SOFA Labor Article.

The Joint Committee also approved plans for observation of the fifth anniversary of the entering into force of the SOFA which comes on 9 February 1972. The next meeting of the Joint Committee is scheduled for 24 February in the US SOFA Conference Room.

93

공   란

공   란

공   란

공   란

공   란

공　　　란

공　　　　란

공   란

공   란

공 란

공   란

공   란

공   란

공   란

공 란

공   란

공   란

ROK-US Joint Committee Press Release
Fifth Anniversary of Entry into Force of SOFA
9 February 1972

The fifth anniversary of the entry into force of the ROK-US Status of Forces Agreement (SOFA) is being observed on 9 February 1972. The ROK-US SOFA is a comprehensive agreement containing 31 articles covering almost all facets of the relations between the ROK and US Governments relating to the presence of US military forces in Korea. The SOFA provides that this agreement will remain in force while the 1954 ROK-US Defense Treaty remains in force unless terminated earlier by agreement between the two Governments.

The successful implementation of the SOFA during its first five years has been the work of the ROK-US Joint Committee which was established in accordance with SOFA provisions to implement this Agreement and to deal with all problems except those concerning telecommunications. This Government-to-Government body, which includes a ROK Representative who is the Director of the Bureau of European and American Affairs and a US Representative who is the Chief of Staff, United States Forces, Korea, has held seventy formal meetings and innumerable other conferences in the last five years, and has taken up hundreds of topics relating to the implementation of the ROK-US SOFA. The current ROK Representative, Mr. KIM Dong-Whie, Director of the European and American Bureau of the Foreign Ministry, is

//)

assisted on the Joint Committee by eight senior Bureau directors from six major Ministries as well as by a SOFA Secretariat which is headed by the Chief of the North America Second Section of the MOFA, Mr. KIM Young Sup. The US Representative who, for the past 34 months, has been Lieutenant General Robert N. Smith, Chief of Staff, USFK, is supported on the US component of the Joint Committee, by representatives of all the major components of USFK as well as by the USFK Staff Judge Advocate, an Embassy SOFA Political Advisor, and a US SOFA Secretariat which is headed by the senior American civilian officer in USFK, Mr. Robert A. Kinney.

Since the Joint Committee deals with all problems relating to the presence of US forces in the ROK, it has organized 12 joint ROK-US Subcommittees for the purpose of giving advice and making recommendations to the Joint Committee. During the first five years of operations, the Joint Committee has assigned a total of 1212 tasks to these Subcommittees. The Subcommittees have submitted mutually agreed recommendations on 1176 of these tasks, which, in turn, have been approved by the ROK-US Joint Committee. Many of the 36 tasks outstanding at this time were recently assigned to the respective Subcommittees for deliberation and recommendation. The SOFA provides that in the event the Joint Committee cannot resolve a problem, the problem shall be referred to the respective Governments. Thus far, in its

2

112

(4) 나머지 (제1) 충분히

first five years of operations, the Joint Committee has not referred any problems to higher levels of their Governments for it has either resolved them on a mutually satisfactory basis, or is still working on them.

One of the busiest of the twelve Joint Committee Subcommittees is its Facilities and Areas Subcommittee, which deals with the acquisition and release of facilities and areas required by the United States military forces in the ROK. During the first five years of the SOFA, the Joint Committee has assigned 1139 tasks to this Subcommittee, and the Subcommittee, in turn, has submitted 1113 recommendations which have been accepted by the Joint Committee. Only 26 tasks are outstanding in this Subcommittee as of the end of the first five years of the SOFA, ten of which were assigned within the past two weeks.

The SOFA provides that the ROK Government may assume criminal jurisdiction over USFK personnel under certain circumstances, in accordance with the provisions of the SOFA Criminal Jurisdiction Article (XXII). From 1967 through 30 January 1972, the ROK Government had assumed jurisdiction over US personnel in 191 cases with 157 convictions and three acquittals thus far. Of the 157 personnel convicted, 114 were fined, 36 had confinement suspended, and seven were sent to the ROK prison at Suwon. At present, only one US citizen who is in Korea under the SOFA is serving his term in a ROK

3

prison. Many of the cases involving US personnel in Korea, over which the US military authorities have jurisdiction in accordance with SOFA provisions, have been tried by US military courts martial. The ROK Government, however, assumes jurisdiction over cases "of particular importance" to the Republic of Korea.

The SOFA Labor Article (XVII) has exerted a positive influence in developing stable and effective labor relations between the USFK and its more than 27,000 Korean direct-hire and US invited contractor employees. Provisions of Article XVII relating to mediation of disputes has provided an effective instrument for resolution of disputes between the Foreign Organizations Employees Union (FOEU) and the USFK. USFK wage levels for its Korean employees are established on the basis of periodic wage surveys in the ROK. The enlightened labor relations policies of the USFK, coupled with   close cooperation of the FOEU and the ROK Government have resulted in continuing improvement in the generally favorable labor relations between the Korean nationals working for USFK and the US command in Korea. In the first five years of the SOFA, all labor disputes have been settled in accordance with provisions of the SOFA.

The SOFA has assigned the responsibility for the settlement of most claims involving USFK personnel to the ROK Government, and through 31 January 1972, a total of 3664 claims have been processed

4

under Article XXIII of the SOFA. Of these claims, a total of 2268
have been paid on the agreed basis of 75 percent by the United States
and 25 percent by the Republic of Korea. A total of 149 claims out
of the 3664 submitted have been disallowed.

In its operation, the Joint Committee has met the changing situations confronting it and it has provided that in urgent situations, exigent action can be taken by the US and ROK Representatives without
formally convening a Joint Committee meeting. A recent illustration
of the dynamic operation of the Joint Committee is its establishment of
an Ad Hoc Subcommittee on Civil-Military Relations in September 1971
in order to deal more effectively with problems in civil-military relations in the Korean communities adjacent to US military installations.
This Subcommittee has made information gathering field trips to almost
all the major US bases and adjacent Korean communities in Korea, and
thus far has submitted a series of 19 recommendations, all of which
were approved by the Joint Committee, to improve relations between
US military personnel and the Korean people. The US-ROK Ad Hoc
Subcommittee has supported the current program of the ROK Government to improve the conditions in these camp communities through the
ROK inter-ministerial "Base Community Clean-Up Committee."

The Ad Hoc Subcommittee on Civil-Military Relations has seven
panels which work on specific areas of civil-military relations, inclu-

5

115

ding local community and governmental relations, ROK police-US military police cooperation and coordination, health and sanitation, narcotics and drug control, larceny and black marketing, race relations and equality of treatment, and people-to-people projects. It is anticipated that the camp communities will be better and more comfortable for all concerned as a result of these activities.

Other Joint Committee subcommittees have been organized to function in various areas of SOFA responsibility, including Criminal Jurisdiction, Civil Jurisdiction, Finance, Commerce, Transportation, Entry and Exit, and Labor, respectively. Only the Joint Committee, however, can make decisions; the Subcommittees only give advice and make reccommendations.

During its first five years of operation, the ROK-US Joint Committee has demonstrated that the ROK-US SOFA is a living and vital agreement which has exerted a positive influence in the promotion of continued ROK-US friendship and strengthening our mutual defense against Communist aggression.

6

116

기 안 용 지

분류기호 문서번호	미이 720 -	(전화번호)	전결규정 조 항 **국장** 전결사항
처 리 기 간			
시 행 일 자			
보 존 년 한			

보 조 기 관	북미 2 과장		협
기 안 책 임 자	정대익 북미 2 과 (72. 2. 10)		
경 유			
수 신	수신처 참조		
참 조			
제 목	한.미 합동위원회 회의록 송부		

1712
1972 2 11
외 무 부

감 여
1972. 2. 11.

1. 한.미간 군대지위협정에 따른 한.미 합동위원회 제 70 차회의 가

72. 1. 28. 개최되었는 바, 동 회의 회의록을 별첨 송부하오니 참조하시고

바랍니다. 함께 결과사항중 거부조판사항을 시행하시고 그 결과를
 양부에 통보하여 주시기 바랍니다.

2. 본 회의록은 한.미 양측의 합의에 의하여서만 공개할수 있는

문서이오니 유념하시기 바랍니다.   정서

첨부 : 합동위원회 70 차 회의록   부.끕.

관 인

(수신처): 법무부장관 (법무실장, 검찰국장, 출입국관리국장),

국방부장관 (기획국장, 시설국장), 재무부장관 (세관국장,

세제국장), 상공부장관 (상역국장), 노동청장 (노정국장),   발송

교통부장관 (종합수송관), 내무부장관 (치안국장),

경제기획원장관 (물가정책관), 주미, 주일, 주중, 주비대사.

**JOINT COMMITTEE
UNDER
THE REPUBLIC OF KOREA AND THE UNITED STATES
STATUS OF FORCES AGREEMENT**

MINUTES OF THE SEVENTIETH MEETING

28 January 1972
Capitol Building
Republic of Korea
Seoul, Korea

1. The meeting was convened at 1530 hours by Mr. KIM Dong-Whie, the ROK Representative, who presided at the meeting. A copy of the agenda is attached as Inclosure 1.

2. The following were in attendance:

ROK	US
Mr. KIM Dong-Whie	LTG Robert N. Smith, USAF
Mr. KIM Chong Kyung	Captain Frank M. Romanick, USN
Mr. LEE Chong Won	COL David P. Heekin, USA
MG CHO Jae Joon	COL Carl G. Schneider, USAF
BG PAK Woo Bum	COL Bruce T. Coggins, USA
Mr. JUNG Ik Won	Mr. Richard W. Finch, US Embassy
Mr. HAN Jin Hee	Mr. Robert A. Kinney, USFK
Mr. KIM Young Sup	MAJ Dick J. Petersen, USAF
Mr. KIM Kee Joe	Mr. Francis K. Cook, USFK
Mr. CHUNG Tai Ik	
Mr. KWON Chan	

3. The ROK Representative submitted for the record a copy of an official notification from the ROK Ministry of Foreign Affairs to the US Embassy in Seoul, dated 4 January 1972, informing the US Government of his appointment as the new ROK Representative to the Joint Committee, succeeding his predecessor, Mr. KOO Choong Whay (Inclosure 2).

4. The US Representative, Lieutenant General Robert N. Smith, accepted a copy of the ROK Representative's credentials and made the following statement:

0568

70th JC
28 Jan 72

These minutes are considered as official documents pertaining to both Governments and will ● ot be released without mutual ● reement.

"Mr. Kim, I am very happy to accept a copy of your credentials informing my Government of your appointment as the ROK Representative to the ROK-US Joint Committee. On behalf of my Government and the US component of the Joint Committee, I wish to extend to you a warm and hearty welcome in your important new post.

"I have been informed that you had an important part in the negotiation of the ROK-US SOFA while you were serving as the Chief of the Treaty Section in the Ministry of Foreign Affairs during the years 1965-1966. It is indeed a pleasure to have you return as your Government's Representative to work on the implementation of this important agreement which you helped negotiate. The SOFA will have been in effect for five years on 9 February 1972. Through the friendly cooperation and diligent work of officials of our two Governments, this important Agreement has been implemented effectively, thereby promoting our mutual defense interests and enhancing the traditional friendship between our two peoples.

"As you assume the position of the ROK Representative to the Joint Committee, Mr. Kim, I wish to assure you of our desire to continue to work together with you and your colleagues on our common tasks in the Joint Committee in a spirit of close and friendly cooperation and mutual understanding of our defense objectives. "

5. The new ROK Representative, Mr. KIM Dong-Whie, made the following response:

"General Smith, I wish to thank you for your warm welcome on the occasion of my first attendance at a ROK-US Joint Committee meeting. I should also like to take this opportunity to pay my high tribute to you for your friendship and cooperation rendered to former Representative KOO Choong Whay.

"I am happy to join in this meeting as the Republic of Korea Representative of the ROK-US Joint Committee. I am also delighted to have the opportunity to work with you and all other members of the Joint Committee on our common problems in implementing the Status of Forces Agreement, which will, in turn, result in promoting the mutual defense interests

2   70th JC
                                           28 Jan 72

These minutes are considered as official documents pertaining to both Governments and will ●●t be released without mutual a●●eement.

of our two Governments and peoples.

"In assuming my responsibilities as the Republic of Korea Representative, I wish to assure you of our continued cooperation, as we work together in a spirit of friendship and good-will which is a key factor in carrying out the common objective in our mutual defense.

"In conclusion, I look forward to maintaining the close working relationships with you, General Smith, not only through efficient execution of official business but also by the warmest personal relationship. "

6. The US Representative stated that he would like to introduce a new member of the US component of the Joint Committee, Colonel Carl G. Schneider, Vice Commander, US Air Forces, Korea, who is replacing Colonel Robert G. Eklund who has departed Korea. Colonel Schneider served a tour with the US Air Force in Korea during the Korean War, and in his most recent assignment, he served as Wing Commander, Moody Air Force Base, Georgia. On behalf of the United States component of the Joint Committee, the US Representative extended a warm welcome to Colonel Schneider to the Joint Committee.

7. The ROK Representative stated that on behalf of the Korean component, the ROK Representative would like to extend his warm welcome to Colonel Carl G. Schneider, who is replacing Colonel Robert G. Eklund on the Joint Committee.

8. The US Representative presented ten new tasks for assignment to the Facilities and Areas Subcommittee. These new tasks consist of two requests for the acquisition of real estate on a permanent use basis (Inclosures 3 and 4), one request for the acquisition of an easement (Inclosure 5), and seven requests for the release of parcels of real estate (Inclosure 6). He proposed that these ten new tasks be assigned to the Facilities and Areas Subcommittee, and the ROK Representative concurred.

9. The ROK Representative presented one task to the Transportation Subcommittee, already assigned on an exigent basis (Inclosure 7). He proposed that the Joint Committee approve the inclusion in the minutes of this meeting the prior assignment of the exigent task to that Subcommittee. The US Representative concurred.

3 .

70th JC
28 Jan 72

These minutes are considered as official documents pertaining to both Governments and will not be released without mutual agreement.

10. The US Representative presented eight recommendations of the Facilities and Areas Subcommittee. These comprised two recommendations for the acquisition of land for permanent use (Inclosures 8 and 9), two recommendations concerning the extension of Temporary Use Permits (Inclosure 10), three recommendations for release of parcels of real estate (Inclosures 11 and 12), and one recommendation for the withdrawal of a previously made request for the conversion of land under acquisition from a temporary use to a permanent use basis (Inclosure 13). He proposed that the Joint Committee approve these eight recommendations of the Facilities and Areas Subcommittee, and the ROK Representative concurred.

11. The US Representative stated that the Transportation Subcommittee reached agreement on a distinctive new license plate for privately-owned vehicles of United States Forces Korea personnel and invited contractors on 20 December 1971. In order to expedite the reregistration process and the issuing of the new license plates, the Joint Committee approved the recommendation of the Transportation Subcommittee by exigent action on 30 December 1971 (Inclosure 14) He stated that he was pleased to announce that the US Forces Korea began to reregister privately-owned vehicles and to issue the new license plates in the Seoul area on 25 January and hoped to complete this process throughout the ROK as quickly as possible.

12. The US Representative proposed to include in the minutes of this meeting the recommendation of the Transportation Subcommittee approved by exigent action of the Joint Committee on 30 December 1971. The ROK Representative concurred.

13. The ROK Representative presented the fifth report of the Ad Hoc Subcommittee on Civil-Military Relations, which incorporates five recommendations for the consideration and approval of the Joint Committee (Inclosure 15). These recommendations include two from the Panel on Health and Sanitation, two from the Panel on Narcotics and Drug Control, and one from the Panel on Race Relations and Equality of Treatment.

14. The ROK Representative proposed that the fifth report of the Ad Hoc Subcommittee together with its five recommendations be accepted and approved by the Joint Committee, and be transmitted to the authorities concerned of both Governments for their implementation.

15. In this connection, the ROK Representative reported to the Joint Committee that in the early part of this month, under Presidential direction, a new "Base Community Clean-Up Committee" was organized

4

70th JC
28 Jan 72

These minutes are considered as official documents pertaining to both Governments and will not be released without mutual agreement.

to exert concerted and concentrated efforts for the amelioration of environment and conditions of Korean communities adjacent to the major US military compounds. A detailed description of this new interministerial committee is recorded in the minutes of the sixth Ad Hoc Subcommittee meeting.

16. The US Representative stated that he was pleased to concur in approval of the fifth report of the Ad Hoc Subcommittee on Civil-Military Relations, including the five recommendations of three of its panels. He noted that this will bring to 19 the number of approved recommendations of the Ad Hoc Subcommittee, and that the seven Ad Hoc Subcommittee panels continue to work on many other recommendations. He stated that the continued progress of the Ad Hoc Subcommittee, coupled with the vigorous efforts of the ROK Government to deal with the problems of the camp communities through its own "Base Community Clean-Up Committee" greatly enhances the prospects for significant improvement in the situation in the Korean communities adjacent to US military installations. These developments should facilitate continuation of the traditional friendly relations between the US serviceman and the Korean people and should assist in maximizing the contribution of these servicemen in the mutual defense of the ROK. On behalf of his Government, he stated that he would like to take note of and to commend his colleagues in the Government of the ROK for their increasingly vigorous efforts to improve civil-military relations and thereby strengthen our mutual defense position.

17. The ROK Representative stated that he understood that the recent labor disputes had been satisfactorily settled on a mutually agreeable basis, and he invited the US Representative to present this agenda item.

18. The US Representative proposed that the Memorandum of Understanding of 24 December 1971 (Inclosure 16), which terminated two recent labor disputes between the USFK and the Foreign Organizations Employees Union (FOEU) be recorded in the minutes of this Joint Committee meeting. One of the disputes involved the wage schedules for USFK Korean employees, and the new schedules became effective 1 January 1972. The other dispute involved severance pay for a small number of short tenure USFK Korean employees and also became effective 1 January 1972. He stated that these two disputes had been referred for conciliation to the Office of Labor Affairs of the Government of the ROK in accordance with paragraph 4 of Article XVII of the SOFA. The Memorandum of Understanding was signed by officials of the FOEU and USFK, and was countersighed by Mr. HAN Chin Hui, Director, Labor Affairs Bureau of the Office of Labor Affairs.

5

70th JC

28 Jan 72

...ese minutes are considered as official documents pertaining to both Governments and will not be released without mutual agreement.

19. The US Representative expressed his sincere appreciation for the assistance of the officials of the Government of the ROK in the amicable settlement of these labor disputes, in accordance with the provisions of the Labor Article of the SOFA. He said that settlement of these two disputes under the provisions of the SOFA again demonstrated the effectiveness of the Labor Article of that Agreement in the maintenance of fair and friendly relations between the USFK and its Korean employees.

20. The ROK Representative stated that he was pleased to concur in recording the Memorandum of Understanding of 24 December 1971 in the minutes of this Joint Committee meeting.

21. The US Representative presented memoranda to the Joint Committee informing the Government of the ROK of the designation of six US invited contractors under Article XV of the SOFA (Inclosures 17-23). He stated that these designations were made after consultations between ROK and US Commerce Subcommittee personnel in accordance with Joint Committee procedures. The invited contractors so designated are Lyon Associates, Incorporated; Daniel, Mann, Johnson, and Mendenhall; Trans Asia Engineering Company; Associated American Engineers Overseas, Incorporated; Collins Radio Company; and National Cash Register. He stated that all of these companies have one contract except National Cash Register which had two, and that the contract of American Engineers Overseas, Incorporated was in joint venture with a Korean firm. He indicated that pertinent data concerning employees of these invited contractors will be provided to the Government of the ROK in accordance with mutually agreed procedures.

22. The ROK Representative stated that he was pleased to acknowledge the designation of these invited contractors and he noted that agreed procedures had been duly observed in these designations.

23. The US Representative noted for the record that the US SOFA Secretariat had furnished the following information to the ROK SOFA Secretariat in accordance with the provisions of the SOFA and Joint Committee decisions.

a. Five copies of reports on the US armed forces disposition of cases for the month of November 1971.

b. One copy of pertinent information on cargo consigned to US armed forces non-appropriated fund organizations in the ROK for the months of November and December 1971.

6

70th JC
28 Jan 72

These minutes are considered as official documents pertaining to both Governments and will not be released without mutual agreement.

c. Twenty copies of the report of US armed forces personnel, the civilian component, invited contractors, and the dependents of each, entering or departing the Republic of Korea during the months of November and December 1971.

d. Twenty copies of the quarterly listing of all US invited contractors and their contracts as of 31 December 1971.

24. The ROK Representative acknowledged the receipt of reports enumerated by the US Representative.

25. The ROK Representative proposed that a special press release commemorating the fifth anniversary of the entry into force of the SOFA on 9 February 1972 be issued by the Joint Committee on that date. He also proposed that the press release be developed by both the ROK and US SOFA Secretaries and approved by both the ROK and US Representatives prior to its release.

26. The US Representative stated that he was glad to concur in the ROK Representative's proposal that a joint press release be issued in commemoration of the fifth anniversary of the entry into force of the Republic of Korea-United States Status of Forces Agreement on 9 February 1972. He also agreed that the respective Secretaries in cooperation with other appropriate Korean and American officials should develop such a proposed press release for the review and approval of the two Representatives.

27. The US Representative proposed that the ROK and US Representatives also participate in a joint television program on the American Forces Korean Network. This program, in connection with the fifth anniversary of the SOFA, would be designed primarily to inform the American serviceman about the SOFA and some of the significant activities of the Joint Committee relating to them.

28. The ROK Representative concurred in the US Representative's proposal for the joint television program, in connection with the fifth anniversary of the entry into force of the SOFA.

29. The ROK Representative asked the US Representative if he would like to propose the date, time, and place for the next Joint Committee meeting. The US Representative responded by proposing that the seventy-first meeting of the Joint Committee be held in the US SOFA Conference Room on Thursday, 24 February 1972, at 1400 hours. The ROK Representative agreed.

7

70th JC
28 Jan 72

These minutes are considered as official documents pertaining to both Governments and will not be released without mutual agreement.

30. The ROK Representative proposed approval of the joint press release as drafted by the two SOFA Secretaries and as distributed in advance (Inclosure 24). The US Representative stated that he was happy to approve the joint press release for the seventieth Joint Committee meeting as distributed in advance.

31. The meeting was adjourned at 1630 hours.

24 Incl

KIM DONG-WHIE
Republic of Korea
Representative

ROBERT N. SMITH
Lieutenant General
United States Air Force
United States Representative

8

70th JC
28 Jan 72

125

These minutes are considered as official documents pertaining to both Governments and will not be released without mutual agreement.

AGENDA FOR THE SEVENTIETH MEETING
OF THE ROK-US JOINT COMMITTEE
1530 HOURS, 28 JANUARY 1972, ROK CAPITOL BUILDING

I.   Presentation of Credentials by the ROK Representative.

II.   Assignment of Tasks to Facilities and Areas Subcommittee - US Presentation.

III.   Assignment of Task to Transportation Subcommittee - ROK Presentation.

IV.   Recommendations of Facilities and Areas Subcommittee - US Presentation.

V.   Recommendation of Transportation Subcommittee - US Presentation.

VI.   Consideration of Fifth Report and Recommendations of Ad Hoc Subcommittee on Civil-Military Relations - ROK and US Presentations.

VII.   Memorandum of Understanding of 24 December 1971, which Resolve Two Labor Disputes in Accordance with the Procedures of SOFA Article XVII - US Presentation.

VIII.   Memoranda on the Designation of US Invited Contractors - US Presentation.

IX.   Memoranda Presented to the ROK Government by the US in the Implementation of the SOFA - US Presentation.

X.   Publicity Relating to Fifth Anniversary of SOFA - ROK and US Presentations.

XI.   Proposed Time of Next Meeting - 1400 Hours, Thursday, 24 February 1972, in the US SOFA Conference Room.

XII.   Agreement on Joint Press Release.

XIII.   Adjourn.

9   70th JC (Incl 1)
28 Jan 72

| MINISTRY OF FOREIGN AFFAIRS |
| REPUBLIC OF KOREA |

C O P Y

OMY-6

     The Ministry of Foreign Affairs presents its
compliments to the Embassy of the United States of
America and has the honor to inform the Embassy of
the appointment of the new Republic of Korea Representative to the Joint Committee established under
the provisions of Article XXVIII of the Agreement
under Article IV of the Mutual Defense Treaty between
the Republic of Korea and the United States of
America, Regarding Facilities and Areas and the
Status of United States Armed Forces in the Republic
of Korea.

     Effective 4th January 1972, the new Representa-
tive of the Republic of Korea will be Mr. Kim, Dong
Whie, Director, Bureau of European and American
Affairs, Ministry of Foreign Affairs, who will replace Mr. Koo Choong Whay.

     The Ministry of Foreign Affairs avails itself
of this opportunity to renew to the Embassy of the
United States of America the assurances of its highest consideration.

Seoul, 4th January 1972 10

Embassy of the United States of America

Seoul

70th JC (Incl 2)
28 Jan 72

These minutes are considered as official documents pertaining to both Governments and will not be released without mutual agreement.

**JOINT COMMITTEE
UNDER
THE REPUBLIC OF KOREA AND THE UNITED STATES
STATUS OF FORCES AGREEMENT**

27 January 1972

MEMORANDUM FOR: Chairmen, Facilities and Areas Subcommittee

SUBJECT: Request for Acquisition of Real Estate

1. SOFA provides in Article II, paragraph 2, that the Governments of the Republic of Korea and the United States may agree that facilities and areas or portions thereof shall be returned to the Republic of Korea or that additional facilities and areas may be provided.

2. Pursuant to paragraph 1 above, it is requested that a recommendation be presented to the Joint Committee concerning a request for the acquisition of a total of 30.33 acres of land located in Yangju-gun, Kyonggi-do. Of this acreage, 30 acres located in two noncontiguous areas are required on a permanent use basis, and the remaining 0.33 acre is required on a perpetual restrictive easement basis. This land is required as a source of crushed road products and for an access road to the crushing site.

KIM DONG-WHIE
Republic of Korea
Representative

ROBERT N. SMITH
Lieutenant General
United States Air Force
United States Representative

11

70th JC (Incl 3)
28 Jan 72

These minutes are considered as official documents pertaining to both Governments and will not be released without mutual agreement.

**JOINT COMMITTEE
UNDER
THE REPUBLIC OF KOREA AND THE UNITED STATES
STATUS OF FORCES AGREEMENT**

28 January 1972

MEMORANDUM FOR: Chairmen, Facilities and Areas Subcommittee

SUBJECT: Request for Acquisition of Real Estate

1. SOFA provides in Article II, paragraph 2, that the Governments of the Republic of Korea and the United States may agree that facilities and areas or portions thereof, shall be returned to the Republic of Korea or that additional facilities and areas may be provided.

2. Pursuant to paragraph 1 above, it is requested that a recommendation be presented to the Joint Committee concerning a request for the acquisition of a total of 114 square feet of building space on a permanent use basis, located in Chinhae City, Kyongsangnam-do. This real estate is required to expand a bunker operation at that location, which is currently held under Acquisition No. PAC-185.

KIM DONG-WHIE
Republic of Korea
Representative

ROBERT N. SMITH
Lieutenant General
United States Air Force
United States Representative

12

70th JC (Incl 4)
28 Jan 72

These minutes are considered as official documents pertaining to both Governments and will not be released without mutual agreement.

**JOINT COMMITTEE
UNDER
THE REPUBLIC OF KOREA AND THE UNITED STATES
STATUS OF FORCES AGREEMENT**

28 January 1972

MEMORANDUM FOR: Chairmen, Facilities and Areas Subcommittee

SUBJECT: Request for Acquisition of Easement

1. SOFA provides in Article II, paragraph 2, that the Governments of the Republic of Korea and the United States may agree that facilities and areas or portions thereof, shall be returned to the Republic of Korea or that additional facilities and areas may be provided.

2. Pursuant to paragraph 1 above, it is requested that a recommendation be presented to the Joint Committee concerning a request for the acquisition, on a perpetual restrictive easement basis, of 4.17 acres of land located in Kwangju-gun, Kyonggi-do, for the installation of underground communication cables.

KIM DONG-WHIE
Republic of Korea
Representative

ROBERT N. SMITH
Lieutenant General
United States Air Force
United States Representative

13

70th JC (Incl 5)
28 Jan 72

These minutes are considered as official documents pertaining to both
Governments and wil█ot be released without mutual █reement.

27 January 1972

MEMORANDUM FOR: Chairmen, Facilities and Areas Subcommittee

SUBJECT: Requests for Release of Real Estate

1. SOFA provides in Article II, paragraph 2, that the Governments of
the Republic of Korea and the United States may agree that facilities
and areas or portions thereof shall be returned to the Republic of Korea
or that additional facilities and areas may be provided.

2. Pursuant to paragraph 1 above, it is requested that recommendations be presented to the Joint Committee concerning requests for the
following actions:

a. Release of 505.517 acres of land, constituting the Hyongga-Ri
Tank Range, currently held under Acquisition No. 7X-5, located in
Yonchon-gun, Kyonggi-do, subject to the conditions specified below.
This request for release includes a total of four buildings and facilities located on the installation. The conditions attached to this request for release are that: (1) The I Corps (ROK/US) Group retain
scheduling control over the range area activities; (2) The Republic of
Korea Ministry of National Defense insure that this range will be made
available only for the use and occupancy of the VI ROK Army Corps
element solely for training range purposes; and (3) The VI ROK Army
Corps element be solely responsible for the security and operational
maintenance of all of the real property located at the Hyonggi-Ri Tank
Range.

b. Release of 21.039 acres of land, constituting a portion of Camp
Richmond installation held under Acquisition Nos. ACS-300 and AAC-
391, and located in Buchon-gun, Kyonggi-do. This request for release
includes a total of 83 buildings and facilities, of which 55 are USFK-
constructed and 28 are Korean-constructed. Excluded from this request for release are an overhead electric power line, three 25-KVA
transformers, a water pipeline, and one water storage tank, with unrestricted right of entry/exit thereto, as well as 0.604 acre of easement land and 0.36 acre of land held on an exclusive use basis, as
shown on maps in the possession of the Republic of Korea Ministry of
National Defense and the Engineer, USFK.

70th JC (Incl 6)
14   28 Jan 72

These minutes are considered as official documents pertaining to both Governments and will not be released without mutual agreement.

c. Release of 12.07 acres of land, constituting Tracy Installation held under Acquisition No. SAC-673, and located in Seoul City. This request for release includes 80 USFK-constructed buildings and facilities and two Korean-constructed facilities. This real estate has become excess to USFK requirements.

d. Release of 2.58 acres of land, constituting a portion of Yuma Installation held under Acquisition No. AAC-397, and located in Inchon City, Kyonggi-do. This request for release includes 5,559 linear feet of 8-inch underground POL pipeline and one 570 square foot pump house. This real estate has become excess to USFK requirements.

e. Release of 6.635 acres of land, constituting a portion of Alamo Installation held under Acquisition Nos. 7X-13 and 7X-174, and located in Yonchon-gun, Kyonggi-do. This request for release includes a total of 29 USFK-constructed buildings and facilities located on the Installation. This real estate has become excess to USFK requirements.

f. Release of 15.72 acres of land, constituting a portion of Camp Mercer Installation held under Acquisition No. ASCOM-378, and located in Kimpo-gun, Kyonggi-do. This request for release includes a total of 17 USFK-constructed buildings and facilities located on the Installation. This real estate has become excess to USFK requirements.

g. Release of 45.757 acres of land, constituting a portion of ASP #46 Installation held under Acquisition No. SAC-715, and located in Seoul City. This request for release includes a total of 84 USFK-constructed buildings and facilities, and a total of 10 Korean-constructed buildings and facilities. This request for release is contingent upon the provision by the Republic of Korea Ministry of National Defense, without cost to the US Government, of the following activities: (1) Construction of approximately 460 linear feet of barbed wire security fencing at a specified location; (2) Construction of approximately 1,585 linear feet of barbed wire security fencing with one vehicle gate, at another location; (3) The relocation of Bldg. No. T-181 to the USFK-retained communication area; and (4) The installation of water and electric meters. The locations involved in activities (1) through (3) above are indicated on a map in possession of the Republic of Korea Ministry of National Defense and the USFK Engineer.

KIM DONG-WHIE
Republic of Korea
Representative

ROBERT N. SMITH
Lieutenant General
United States Air Force
United States Representative

15

70th JC (Incl 6)
28 Jan 72

These minutes are considered as official documents pertaining to both
Governments and will not be released without mutual agreement.

JOINT COMMITTEE
UNDER
THE REPUBLIC OF KOREA AND THE UNITED STATES
STATUS OF FORCES AGREEMENT

13 January 1972

MEMORANDUM FOR: Chairmen, Transportation Subcommittee

SUBJECT: Applicability of Certain Provisions of Ministry of Transportation Instruction #335 to USFK Personnel Departing the Republic of Korea in a Leave Status

1. Mutual consultations are requested concerning whether paragraph 4,
Item 5, of Article 12 of the Ministry of Transportation Instruction #335,
of 8 July 1969, relating to avionics facility management, pertains to
those persons who are subject to the Republic of Korea-United States
Status of Forces Agreement and who depart the Republic of Korea via
commercial aircraft utilizing a commercial airport terminal facility,
and whose travel is in a leave status.

2. It is further requested that upon completion of such consultations a
recommendation on this subject be transmitted to the Joint Committee.

KIM DONG WHIE
Republic of Korea
Representative

7M Romanick Cpt usn
for
ROBERT N. SMITH
Lieutenant General
United States Air Force
United States Representative

16

70th JC (Incl 7)
28 Jan 72

133

These minutes are considered as official documents pertaining to both Governments and will not be released without mutual agreement.

REPUBLIC OF KOREA - UNITED STATES
FACILITIES AND AREAS SUBCOMMITTEE

14 January 1971

MEMORANDUM FOR: THE JOINT COMMITTEE

1. Subcommittee Members:

United States	Republic of Korea
BG Philip T. Boerger, Chairman	BG PAK Woo Bum, Chairman
COL Leonard Edelstein, Alt. Chairman	Mr. MIN Won Sik, Secty
LTC Edward W. Lingel, USAF	Mr. KANG Hong Suk, Asst Secty
MAJ William S. Littlefield, J4, USFK	LTC SHIN Sang Pil
MAJ Allen D. Adams, USAFCS, K	Mr. KIM Hyung Kun
CPT James H. Smith, USAF	Mr. PAK Bung Hun
Mr. Francis K. Cook, J5, USFK	Mr. NOE Won Tae
Mr. S. F. O'Hop, ENJ-RE, Secty	Mr. PARK Byong Yong
Mr. E. H. Brummett, ENJ-RE,	Mr. DO Tae Ku
Alt. Secty	Mr. SUH Chin Hwan
	Mr. LEE Soung Woo
	Mr. PARK Dahl Young
	Mr. BAE Jeung Sun

2. Subject of Recommendation: Request for Acquisition of Real Estate, Joint Committee memorandum dated 24 November 1971.

3. Recommendation: Task 1115 The request for the acquisition, on a permanent use basis, of a total of 0.09 acre of land, comprising 3,938 square feet, located at the Tong-Taegu Railroad Station in Taegu City, Kyongsangbuk-do, has been approved by the Ministry of National Defense. Of this area, 2,871 square feet are required for office space and the remaining 1,067 square feet are required as a vehicle parking area. This real estate is in lieu of the existing Taegu RTO, which will be requested for release upon completion of the acquisition of the above-referenced 0.09 acre. The Ministry of National Defense and the USFK Engineer will prepare the necessary documents. It is recommended that the Joint Committee, SOFA, approve this acquisition request.

17
70th JC (Incl 8)
28 Jan 72

134

These minutes are considered as official documents pertaining to both Governments and will not be released without mutual agreement.

Task 1115

4. Security Classification: Unclassified.

_____
Brigadier General PAK Woo Bum
Chairman, ROK Component
Facilities and Areas Subcommittee

_____
Brigadier General Philip T. Boerger
Chairman, US Component
Facilities and Areas Subcommittee

APPROVED BY THE JOINT COMMITTEE ON
28 JANUARY 1972 AT SEVENTIETH MEETING

_____
KIM DONG-WHIE
Republic of Korea
Representative

_____
ROBERT N. SMITH
Lieutenant General
United States Air Force
United States Representative

135

18   70th JC (Incl 8)
            28 Jan 72

REPUBLIC OF KOREA - UNITED STATES
FACILITIES AND AREAS SUBCOMMITTEE

19 January 1972

MEMORANDUM FOR: THE JOINT COMMITTEE

1. Subcommittee Members:

United States	Republic of Korea
BG Philip T. Boerger, Chairman	BG PAK Woo Bum, Chairman
COL Leonard Edelstein, Alt. Chairman	Mr. MIN Won Sik, Secty
COL Eugene T. Blanton, USAF	Mr. KANG Hong Suk, Asst Secty
MAJ William S. Littlefield, J4, USFK	LTC SHIN Sang Pil
MAJ Allen D. Adams, USAFCS, K	Mr. KIM Young Sup
CPT James H. Smith, USAF	Mr. PAK Bung Hun
Mr. Francis K. Cook, J5, USFK	Mr. RHO Won Tae
Mr. S. F. O'Hop, ENJ-RE, Secty	Mr. SOUNG Baek Jon
Mr. E. H. Brummett, EMJ-RE,	Mr. DO Tae Ku
Alt. Secty	Mr. SUH Chin Hwan
	Mr. LEE Soung Woo
	Mr. PARK Dahl Young
	Mr. BAE Jeung Sun

2. Subject of Recommendation: Requests for Acquisition of Real Estate, Joint Committee memorandum dated 24 November 1971.

3. Recommendation: <u>Task 1116</u> The request for acquisition of a total of 0.212 acre of land located in the Han River bed, Seoul City (0.014 acre, consisting of six non-contiguous areas required on a permanent use basis for the erection of six power poles, and the remaining 0.198 acre required on a perpetual restrictive easement basis for the installation of overhead power and communication lines),

19

70th JC (Incl 9)₂₅

28 Jan 72

These minutes are considered as official documents pertaining to both Governments ●nd will not be released without ●utual agreement.

Task 1116

has been accepted by the Ministry of National Defense. The Ministry of National Defense and the USFK Engineer will prepare the necessary documents. It is recommended that the Joint Committee, SOFA, approve the attached proposed agreement.

4. Security Classification: Unclassified.

Brigadier General PAK Woo Bum
Chairman, ROK Component
Facilities and Areas Subcommittee

Brigadier General Philip T. Boerger
Chairman, US Component
Facilities and Areas Subcommittee

APPROVED BY THE JOINT COMMITTEE ON
28 JANUARY 1972 AT SEVENTIETH MEETING

KIM DONG-WHIE
Republic of Korea
Representative

ROBERT N. SMITH
Lieutenant General
United States Air Force
United States Representative

20   70th JC (Incl 9)
          28 Jan 72

These minutes are considered as official documents pertaining to both Governments and will not be released without mutual agreement.

REPUBLIC OF KOREA - UNITED STATES
FACILITIES AND AREAS SUBCOMMITTEE

19 January 1972

MEMORANDUM FOR: THE JOINT COMMITTEE

1. Subcommittee Members:

United States	Republic of Korea
BG Philip T. Boerger, Chairman	BG PAK Woo Bum, Chairman
COL Leonard Edelstein, Alt. Chairman	Mr. MIN Won Sik, Secty
COL Eugene T. Blanton, USAF	Mr. KANG Hong Suk, Asst Secty
MAJ William S. Littlefield, J4, USFK.	LTC SHIN Sang Pil
MAJ Allen D. Adams, USAFCS, K	Mr. KIM Young Sup
CPT James H. Smith, USAF	Mr. PAK Bung Hun
Mr. Francis K. Cook, J5, USFK	Mr. RHO Won Tae
Mr. S. F. O'Hop, ENJ-RE, Secty	Mr. SOUNG Baek Jon
Mr. E. H. Brummett, ENJ-RE,	Mr. DO Tae Ku
Alt. Secty	Mr. SUH Chin Hwan
	Mr. LEE Soung Woo
	Mr. PARK Dahl Young
	Mr. BAE Jeung Sun

2. Subject of Recommendation: Request for Extension of Temporary Use Permit, Joint Committee memorandum dated 24 November 1971.

3. Recommendation: Tasks 1125-1126 The following requests for Extension of Temporary Use Permits were accepted by the Ministry of National Defense.

a. Task 1125 Extension of Temporary Use Permit K-F-T-58, involving 31.0 acres of land located in Pyongtaek-gun, Kyonggi-do, from 1 December 1971 through 31 May 1972. Continued use of this land is required as a source of obtaining select material in troop housing construction at Camp Humphreys Installation.

21   70th JC (Incl 10)
                                            28 Jan 72

These minutes are considered as official documents pertaining to both Governments and will not be released without mutual agreement.

Tasks 1125 - 1126

b. <u>Task 1126</u> Extension of Temporary Use Permit K-G-T-15, involving 8.25 acres of riverbed located in Chilkok-gun, Kyongsangbuk-do, from 1 December through 30 November 1972. This land has been utilized as a source area for filling operations at Camp Carroll and there is a continuing need for its use for that purpose.

The Ministry of National Defense and the USFK Engineer will prepare the necessary documents. It is recommended that these two requests for extension of temporary use permits be approved by the Joint Committee, SOFA.

4. Security Classification: Unclassified.

Brigadier General PAK Woo Bum
Chairman, ROK Component
Facilities and Areas Subcommittee

Brigadier General Philip T. Boerger
Chairman, US Component
Facilities and Areas Subcommittee

APPROVED BY THE JOINT COMMITTEE ON
28 JANUARY 1972 AT SEVENTIETH MEETING

KIM DONG-WHIE
Republic of Korea
Representative

ROBERT N. SMITH
Lieutenant General
United States Air Force
United States Representative

22

70th JC (Incl 10)
28 Jan 72

REPUBLIC OF KOREA - UNITED STATES
FACILITIES AND AREAS SUBCOMMITTEE

19 January 1972

MEMORANDUM FOR: THE JOINT COMMITTEE

1. Subcommittee Members:

United States	Republic of Korea
BG Philip T. Boerger, Chairman	BG PAK Woo Bum, Chairman
COL Leonard Edelstein, Alt. Chairman	Mr. MIN Won Sik, Secty
LTC Edward W. Lingel, USAF	Mr. KANG Hong Suk, Asst Secty
MAJ William S. Littlefield, J4, USFK	LTC SHIN Sang Pil
MAJ Allen D. Adams, USAFCS, K	Mr. KIM Young Sup
CPT James H. Smith, USAF	Mr. PAK Bung Hun
Mr. Francis K. Cook, J5, USFK	Mr. NOE Won Tae
Mr. S. F. O'Hop, ENJ-RE, Secty	Mr. PARK Byong Yong
Mr. E. H. Brummett, ENJ-RE,	Mr. DO Tae Ku
Alt. Secty	Mr. SUH Chin Hwan
	Mr. LEE Soung Woo
	Mr. PARK Dahl Young
	Mr. BAE Jeung Sun

2. Subject of Recommendation: Request for Release of Real Estate, Joint Committee memorandum dated 16 December 1971.

3. Recommendation: <u>Task 1127</u> The request for release of 10.48 acres of land, constituting Thor Echo Installation currently held under Acq. No. IC-148, and located in Uijongbu-si, Kyonggi-do, has been approved by the Ministry of National Defense. This real estate contains a total of 48 buildings and facilities which will be released upon the release of the land. The Ministry of National Defense and the USFK Engineer will prepare the necessary documents. It is recommended that the Joint Committee, SOFA, approve this release request.

23

70th JC (Incl 11)
28 Jan 72

These minutes are considered as official documents pertaining to both Governments and will not be released without mutual agreement.

Task 1127

4. Security Classification: Unclassified.

Brigadier General PAK Woo Bum
Chairman, ROK Component
Facilities and Areas Subcommittee

Brigadier General Philip T. Boerger
Chairman, US Component
Facilities and Areas Subcommittee

APPROVED BY THE JOINT COMMITTEE ON
28 JANUARY 1972 AT SEVENTIETH MEETING

KIM DONG-WHIE
Republic of Korea
Representative

ROBERT N. SMITH
Lieutenant General
United States Air Force
United States Representative

24

70th JC (Incl 11)
28 Jan 72

REPUBLIC OF KOREA - UNITED STATES
FACILITIES AND AREAS SUBCOMMITTEE

19 January 1972

MEMORANDUM FOR: THE JOINT COMMITTEE

1. Subcommittee Members:

United States	Republic of Korea
BG Philip T. Boerger, Chairman	BG PAK Woo Bum, Chairman
COL Leonard Edelstein, Alt. Chairman	Mr. MIN Won Sik, Secty
LTC Edward W. Lingel, USAF	Mr. KANG Hong Suk, Asst Secty
MAJ William S. Littlefield, J4, USFK	LTC SHIN Sang Pil
MAJ Allen D. Adams, USAFCS, K	Mr. KIM Young Sup
CPT James H. Smith, USAF	Mr. PAK Bung Hun
Mr. Francis K. Cook, J5, USFK	Mr. NOE Won Tae
Mr. S. F. O'Hop, ENJ-RE, Secty	Mr. PARK Byong Yong
Mr. E. H. Brummett, ENJ-RE,	Mr. DO Tae Ku
Alt. Secty	Mr. SUH Chin Hwan
	Mr. LEE Soung Woo
	Mr. PARK Dahl Young
	Mr. BAE Jeung Sun

2. Subject of Recommendation: Requests for Release of Real Estate

3. Recommendation: <u>Tasks 1128-1129</u> The following requests for release
of real estate have been accepted by the Ministry of National Defense and
the United States Forces, Korea.

   a. <u>Task 1128</u> Release of 0.12 acre of land, currently held as a portion
of the area held under Acq. No. IC-207, and located in Uijongbu-si, Kyonggi-
do. This real estate has become excess to USFK requirements.

   b. <u>Task 1129</u> Release of 0.11 acre of land, currently held as a portion
of the area held under Acq. No. IC-168, and located in Uijongbu-si, Kyonggi-
do. This real estate has become excess to USFK requirements.

25

70th JC (Incl 12)
28 Jan 72

142

These minutes are considered as official documents pertaining to both Governments and will not be released without mutual agreement.

Tasks 1128-1129

The Ministry of National Defense and the USFK Engineer will prepare the necessary documents. It is recommended that the Joint Committee, SOFA, approve these two release requests.

4. Security Classification: Unclassified.

_____   _____
Brigadier General PAK Woo Bum   Brigadier General Philip T. Boerger
Chairman, ROK Component   Chairman, US Component
Facilities and Areas Subcommittee   Facilities and Areas Subcommittee

**APPROVED BY THE JOINT COMMITTEE ON
28 JANUARY 1972 AT SEVENTIETH MEETING**

_____   _____
KIM DONG-WHIE   ROBERT N. SMITH
Republic of Korea   Lieutenant General
Representative   United States Air Force
                                       United States Representative

26   70th JC (Incl 12)
            28 Jan 72

143

REPUBLIC OF KOREA - UNITED STATES
FACILITIES AND AREAS SUBCOMMITTEE

19 January 1972

MEMORANDUM FOR: THE JOINT COMMITTEE

1. Subcommittee Members:

United States	Republic of Korea
BG Philip T. Boerger, Chairman	BG PAK Woo Bum, Chairman
COL Leonard Edelstein, Alt. Chairman	Mr. MIN Won Sik, Secty
COL Eugene T. Blanton, USAF	Mr. KANG Hong Suk, Asst Secty
MAJ William S. Littlefield, J4, USFK	LTC SHIN Sang Pil
MAJ Allen D. Adams, USAFCS, K	Mr. KIM Young Sup
CPT James H. Smith, USAF	Mr. PAK Bung Hun
Mr. Francis K. Cook, J5, USFK	Mr. RHO Won Tae
Mr. S. F. O'Hop, ENJ-RE, Secty	Mr. SOUNG Baek Jon
Mr. E. H. Brummett, ENJ-RE,	Mr. DO Tae Ku
Alt. Secty	Mr. SUH Chin Hwan
	Mr. LEE Soung Woo
	Mr. PARK Dahl Young
	Mr. BAE Jeung Sun

2. Subject of Recommendation: Request for Conversion of Real Estate, Joint Committee memorandum dated 22 April 1971.

3. Recommendation: Task 976 The request for the conversion from the temporary use to permanent use land of 4,446 acres of land out of the 120,571.20 acres of land currently held under Acq. No. CAV-T-16, located in Changdan-gun, Kyonggi-do, to provide an adequate and unobstructed maneuver area and firing range for the US 2d Infantry Division, has been withdrawn by the US requesting agency upon the assurance of the Ministry of National Defense that the Republic

27

70th JC (Incl 13)
28 Jan 72

These minutes are considered as official documents pertaining to both Governments ● and will not be released without ● mutual agreement.

Task 976

of Korea Government will prohibit any construction, farming, or encroachments on this land, per letter RE: 947.01-2670, dated 9 September 1971, Ministry of National Defense. It is recommended therefore that no further action be taken on this task.

4. Security Classification: Unclassified.

_____
Brigadier General PAK Woo Bum
Chairman, ROK Component
Facilities and Areas Subcommittee

_____
Brigadier General Philip T. Boerger
Chairman, US Component
Facilities and Areas Subcommittee

APPROVED BY THE JOINT COMMITTEE ON
28 JANUARY 1972 AT SEVENTIETH MEETING

_____
KIM DONG-WHIE
Republic of Korea
Representative

_____
ROBERT N. SMITH
Lieutenant General
United States Air Force
United States Representative

28

70th JC (Incl 13)
28 Jan 72

These minutes are considered as official documents pertaining to both Governments and will ⬤ be released without mutual ag⬤ement.

US-ROK Transportation Subcommittee
Under the
US-ROK Joint Committee
Established by Article XXVIII of the
Status of Forces Agreement (SOFA)

20 December 1971

MEMORANDUM FOR: The Joint Committee

1. **Subcommittee Members:**

COL Maurice A. Gainey, Jr., Chairman	Mr. SUH In Soo, Chairman
LTC William W. Raitt, USAF	Mr. KIM Doo Bang
LTC Alan B. Cayo, USA	Mr. PARK Byung Sun
LTC Richard D. Le Doux, USAF	Mr. SHIN Young Kook
LTC Robert A. Neff, USAF	Mr. HWANG Sun Ku
LTC Robert B. Claypool, USAF	Mr. KIM Mun Sun
LTC Ralph E. Fisher, USAF	Mr. KIM Byung Yoon
LTC Charles W. Johns, USAF	Mr. LEE Yong Hoi
LTC Donald E. Lockstrom, USAF	Mr. LIM Uoo Soon
LCDR Robert E. Spydell, USN	Mr. BAK Yong Chun
MAJ Hames J. Hallihan, USA	Mr. PARK Hyung Hee
MAJ Dick J. Petersen, USAF	COL YOO Choong Hyeun
Mr. Sam Pollack, USFK	Mr. NOH Sung Ho
	LTC SUH Sang Ho

2. **Subject of Recommendation:** Distinctive License Plates for Privately-Owned Vehicles of USFK Personnel and Invited Contractors.

3. **Recommendation:** The first sentence of paragraph two of the Agreed Procedures for licensing and registration of privately-owned vehicles of United States Forces, Korea personnel and United States armed forces invited contractors approved by the Joint Committee at its twenty-eighth and thirty-second meetings on 3 July 1968 and 7 November 1968 respectively, be deleted and replaced with the following sentences:

29

70th JC (Incl 14)
28 Jan 72

These minutes are considered as official documents pertaining to both Governments and will ●t be released without mutual a●eement.

> "The Government of the Republic of Korea will produce a requisite number of license plates and seals of a distinctive design and specification after consultations between the vehicle registration authorities of the United States Forces, Korea and the Republic of Korea.
>
> "Revalidation of registration and issuance of license plates will be accomplished on an annual basis."

4. Security Classification: Unclassified.

SUH IN SOO
Chairman, ROK Component
Transportation Subcommittee

MAURICE A. GAINEY, JR, COL, USA
Chairman, US Component
Transportation Subcommittee

APPROVED BY THE JOINT COMMITTEE ON
30 DECEMBER 1971

KOO CHOONG WHAY
Republic of Korea
Representative

ROBERT N. SMITH
Lieutenant General
United States Air Force
United States Representative

30   70th JC (Incl 14)
                       28 Jan 72

공   란

공 란

공   란

공　　　란

공 란

공 란

공   란

공 란

공   란

공   란

공　　　란

These minutes are considered as official documents pertaining to both Governments and will be released without mutual agreement.

MEMORANDUM OF UNDERSTANDING

1971. 12. 2 4

1. The Foreign Organizations Employees Union (FOEU) accepts recently approved wage schedules (Inclosure 1) by USARPAC to be effective 1 January 1972. These schedules are applicable to all USFK Korean employees, including Korean Service Corps personnel. (Korean contractor and personal hire employees are not USFK employees.)

2. USFK agrees to reassess the Mess Attendant grade level during the course of CY 72 locality wage survey to determine pay comparability with prevailing wages.

3. USFK severance pay plan is adjusted (Inclosure 2) in part for short tenure employees to meet requirements of the Korean Labor Standards Law, and will be effective 1 January 1972.

4. The official labor disputes filed by FOEU on 26 November 1971 and 11 August 1970 with the Office of Labor Affairs (OLA) are terminated.

5. The FOEU and USFK agree that joint efforts will be made to improve long range planning for specialized training and outplacement actions under Korean Nationals Outplacement Program (KNOP).

FOR UNITED STATES FORCES, KOREA:

FREDRIC NEWMAN
Chairman
Joint Labor Affairs Committee

CARL J. BENDER, JR.
Executive Secretary
Joint Labor Affairs Committee

FOR FOREIGN ORGANIZATIONS EMPLOYEES UNION:

KANG CHU WON
President

CHANG SU TOK
Secretary General

HAN CHIN HUI
Director
Labor Affairs Bureau
Office of Labor Affairs

70th JC (Incl 16)
28 Jan 72

159

42

These minutes are considered as official documents pertaining to both Governments ● d wil ●● e released without ● tual a ●● ● ment

US FORCES WAGE SCHEDULE

KOREA
MANUAL (KWB) WAGE SCHEDULE
LOCALLY HIRED, NON-US CITIZEN EMPLOYEES

HOURLY STEP RATES (KOREAN WON)

KWB GRADE	STEP A	STEP B	STEP C	STEP D	STEP E	STEP F	STEP G	STEP H	STEP I	STEP J
1	93	98	102	107	111	115	120	124	129	133
2	116	121	127	132	138	144	149	155	160	166
3	139	145	152	158	165	172	178	185	191	198
4	160	168	176	183	191	199	206	214	222	229
5	183	192	201	209	218	227	235	244	253	262
6	206	216	225	235	245	255	265	274	284	294
7	228	238	249	260	271	282	293	304	314	325
8	250	262	274	286	298	310	322	334	346	358
9	272	285	298	311	324	337	350	363	376	389
10	295	309	323	337	351	365	379	393	407	421
11	360	378	395	412	429	446	463	480	498	515
12	423	444	464	484	504	524	544	564	585	605
13	486	510	533	556	579	602	625	648	672	695

Effective date: No earlier than 1 January 1972

BEN B BEESON
Asst DCSPER (Civ Per)
US Army, Pacific

JOHN E. TAYLOR
Director Civilian Personnel
US Pacific Air Forces

WILLIAM M. MEAUT
Fleet Civilian Personnel
Director
US Pacific Fleet

160

43

70th JC (Incl 1 to Incl 16)
28 Jan 72

These minutes are considered as official documents pertaining to both Governments and will not be released without mutual agreement.

US FORCES WAGE SCHEDULE

KOREA
NON-MANUAL (KGS) WAGE SCHEDULE
LOCALLY HIRED, NON-US CITIZEN EMPLOYEES

HOURLY STEP RATES (KOREAN WON)

KGS GRADE	STEP A	STEP B	STEP C	STEP D	STEP E	STEP F	STEP G	STEP H	STEP I	STEP J
1	100	105	109	114	119	124	129	133	138	143
2	133	139	145	152	158	164	171	177	183	190
3	165	172	180	188	196	204	212	220	227	235
4	197	206	215	225	234	243	253	262	271	281
5	228	239	250	261	272	283	294	305	316	326
6	260	273	285	298	310	322	335	347	360	372
7	292	306	320	334	348	362	376	390	404	418
8	324	340	355	371	386	401	417	432	448	463
9	375	392	410	428	446	464	482	500	517	535
10	425	445	466	486	506	526	546	567	587	607
11	475	498	521	543	566	589	611	634	657	679
12	553	579	605	632	658	684	711	737	763	790
13	630	660	690	720	750	780	810	840	870	900

Effective date: No earlier than 1 January 1972

BEN B BEESON
Asst DCSPER (Civ Per)
US Army, Pacific

JOHN E. TAYLOR
Director Civilian Personnel
US Pacific Air Forces

WILLIAM M. MEAUT
Fleet Civilian Personnel
Director
Pacific Fleet

161

44

70th JC (Incl 1 to Incl 16)
28 Jan 72

These minutes are considered as official documents pertaining to both Governments ██d will ██ be released without ██tual ██ ██ment.

US FORCES WAGE SCHEDULE

KOREA
MARINE (KM) WAGE SCHEDULE
LOCALLY HIRED, NON-US CITIZEN EMPLOYEES

HOURLY STEP RATES (KOREAN WON)

KM GRADE	STEP A	STEP B	STEP C	STEP D	STEP E	STEP F	STEP G	STEP H	STEP I	STEP J
1	139	146	153	159	166	173	179	186	193	199
2	155	162	169	177	184	191	199	206	213	221
3	173	181	190	198	206	214	222	231	239	247
4	189	198	207	216	225	234	243	252	261	270
5	221	231	242	252	263	274	284	295	305	316
6	249	261	273	285	297	309	321	333	345	356
7	296	310	324	338	352	366	380	394	408	422
8	343	359	375	392	408	424	441	457	473	490
9	449	470	491	513	534	555	577	598	619	641
10	512	537	561	586	610	634	659	683	708	732

Effective date: No earlier than 1 January 1972

BEN B BEESON
Asst DCSPER (Civ Pers)
US Army, Pacific

JOHN E. TAYLOR
Director Civilian Personnel
US Pacific Air Forces

WILLIAM M. MEAUT
Fleet Civilian Personnel
Director
US Pacific Fleet

70th JC (Incl 1 to Incl 16)
28 Jan 72

45

162

These minutes are considered as official documents pertaining to both Governments ● d will ●● be released without ● tual a● ●ment.

<u>Revised Provisions to Bring Lower Tenure Service to ROK Legal Minimum</u>

EA CPR 690-1, Extract

"60. c. Computation. Payment will be either the amount computed in (1) or (2) below whichever is the greater.

(1) Divide by three (3) the employee's total normal wages for (a) the 3-month period immediately preceding the date of separation or (b) any three (3) consecutive full month period which represents the highest wages earned; multiply the result of (a) or (b) whichever provides the greater base by the number of credit-months applicable to the type of separation and amount of creditable services as provided in Appendix E.

(2) Divide by three (3) the employee's total wages (including premium pay, allowances and prorated bonus) for the 3-month period immediately preceding the date of separation; multiply the result by the number of <u>full years</u> of continuous service.

(3) The following guidance pertains: The 3-month period immediately prior to effective date of separation is three (3) calendar months (e.g., from 15 July thru 14 October, if separation is effective 15 October) and any three (3) consecutive full months are in terms of full months (e.g., from 1 January thru 31 March or 1 February thru 30 April). Normal wage includes extended workweek, but is exclusive of all overtime, holiday pay, night differential, allowances and bonuses; non-pay status during the 3-month period is included as if the employee had received his normal basic pay for the period of non-pay status. Total wages include overtime pay, night differential, holiday pay, remote area allowance, subsistence allowance and the prorated bonuses received by the employee during 3-month period. Remote area allowance will be calculated based on number of full weeks (7 days) during the period multiplied by 600 won. Subsistence allowance of 230 won daily will be credited for each work day to those employees who were provided meals during the 3-month period. Prorated bonuses will be 25% of the normal wages earned during the period. Thus the format for deriving monthly base for severance pay computation is as follows:

<u>Normal Wage + OT Pay + ND + HW Pay + Remote Area All + Sub All + Bonus (Nor Wx25%)</u>"

3

These minutes are considered as official documents pertaining to both Governments ██ will ███ be released without ██tual ███ment.

**JOINT COMMITTEE
UNDER
THE REPUBLIC OF KOREA AND THE UNITED STATES
STATUS OF FORCES AGREEMENT**

MEMORANDUM FOR: THE JOINT COMMITTEE   80 DEC 1971

SUBJECT: Designation of US Invited Contractor under Article XV, Status of Forces Agreement

1. References:

   a. Paragraph 2, Article XV, Status of Forces Agreement.

   b. US Chairman, Commerce Subcommittee letter, dated 19 August 1971, subject as above (Incl 1).

   c. ROK Chairman, Commerce Subcommittee letter, dated 23 August 1971, subuect as above (Incl 2).

2. The United States, after consultation with the ROK Commerce Sub-committee and having duly considered their views, has designated Lyon Associates as a US invited contractor for execution of contract DACA 79-72-C-0040 for design of Phase II, Army Security Agency (ASA) Project Adventure, various locations, Korea.

3. Pertinent data concerning US or third country national employees will be provided to the Joint Secretariat by established reporting procedures.

2 Incl
as

ROBERT N. SMITH
Lieutenant General, USAF
United States Representative
Joint Committee

47

70th JC (Incl 17)
28 Jan 72

These minutes are considered as official documents pertaining to both
Governments and will not be released without mutual agreement.

REPUBLIC OF KOREA - UNITED STATES
COMMERCE SUBCOMMITTEE

19 August 1971

SUBJECT: Designation of US Invited Contractor Under Article XV,
Status of Forces Agreement

Republic of Korea Chairman, Commerce Subcommittee

1. Reference: Paragraph 2, Article XV of the Status of Forces Agreement.

2. The Government of the Republic of Korea is informed through this
written consultative process that the United States Forces Korea proposes
to extend invited contractor status to the qualified US firm on the contract for the design of Phase II, Army Security Agency (ASA) Project
Adventure, various locations throughout Korea.

3. The following data are provided:

a. Company name:

(1) Lyon Associates

(2) Adrian Wilson Associates

(3) Daniel, Mann, Johnson and Mendenhall

b. Local address: APO 96301

c. Identification of US citizen employees: To be provided later.

d. Number of US and ROK employees: To be provided later.

e. Reasons for designation as an invited contractor: Contracting
officer is bound by US law to select architect-engineer firms for professional services contracts in strict accordance with the procedures set
forth in paragraph 18-402 of the Armed Services Procurement Regulation
(ASPR). Such selection is not based upon competitive bidding procedures,
but rather upon the professional qualifications necessary for the satisfactory performance of the services required, subject to additional

48

70th JC (Incl 1 to Incl 17)
28 Jan 72

These minutes are considered as official documents pertaining to both Government ●●d will ●ot be released witho●● ●utual agreement.

19 August 1971

SUBJECT: Designation of US Invited Contractor Under Article XV, Status of Forces Agreement

considerations such as required specialized experience, demonstrated performance, and security qualifications. The contracting officer is prohibited from selecting from among other than those firms who have properly filed GSA Standard Form 251, "U.S. Government Architect-Engineer Questionnaire," and have been declared qualified to perform such services for the US Government under procedures prescribed in the ASPR. All firms listed in paragraph 2a, above, have properly filed qualification data in accordance with the procedures described above; have been declared fully qualified to perform such services and, there-fore, are eligible to be selected by contracting officer for professional services contracts. None other than US firms have thus far filed qualification data and met the prerequisites for selection. Accordingly, designation of US Invited Contractor is required for the performance of this work under the applicable terms of SOFA.

    f. Location of contract: Various locations throughout Korea.

    g. Type of contract: Firm, fixed price, A&E Services, type B.

    h. Length of contract: To be provided.

    i. Sponsoring component commander: US Army Engineer District, Far East.

RICHARD Z. CANN
Colonel, US Army
United States Chairman
Commerce Subcommittee

49

70th JC (Incl 1 to Incl 17)
28 Jan 72

These minutes are considered as official documents pertaining to both Governments and will not be released without mutual agreement.

MINISTRY OF COMMERCE AND INDUSTRY
REPUBLIC OF KOREA
SEOUL, KOREA

23 August 1971

Subject: Designation of US Invited Contractor under Article XV, Status of Forces Agreement

US Chairman, Commerce Subcommittee

1. Reference:

   a. Paragraph 2, Article XV, Status of Forces Agreement

   b. US Commerce Subcommittee Memorandum of Consultation, dated 19 August 1971 subject as above, pertaining to contract for the desugn of Phase II, Army Security Agency (ASA) Project Adventure, Various locations throughout Korea.

2. The US memorandum, reference 1b above, has been reviewed and the government of the Republic of Korea understands the requirement for an invited contractor in this instance.

Chung Jin Kil
Chairman
Commerce Subcommittee, ROK

70th JC (Incl 2 to Incl 17)
50   28 Jan 72

These minutes are considered as official documents pertaining to both Governments and will ⬛ t be released without mutual a⬛ ee ment.

**JOINT COMMITTEE
UNDER
THE REPUBLIC OF KOREA AND THE UNITED STATES
STATUS OF FORCES AGREEMENT**

MEMORANDUM FOR: THE JOINT COMMITTEE   6 JAN 1972

SUBJECT: Designation of US Invited Contractor under Article XV, Status of Forces Agreement

1. References:

    a. Paragraph 2, Article XV, Status of Forces Agreement.

    b. US Chairman, Commerce Subcommittee letter, dated 29 Sep 1971, subject as above (Incl 1).

    c. ROK Chairman, Commerce Subcommittee letter, dated 4 Oct 1971, subject as above (Incl 2).

2. The United States, after consultation with the ROK Commerce Subcommittee and having duly considered their views, has designated Daniel, Mann, Johnson and Mendenhall as a US invited contractor for execution of contract DACA 79-72-C-0042 for design of Autodin Switching Center, Camp Walker, Taegu.

3. Pertinent data concerning US or third country national employees will be provided to the Joint Secretariat by established reporting procedures.

2 Incl
as

ROBERT N. SMITH
Lieutenant General, USAF
United States Representative
Joint Committee

51

70th JC (Incl 18)
28 Jan 72

These minutes are considered as official documents pertaining to both Governments and will ▇t be released without mutual a▇eement.

REPUBLIC OF KOREA - UNITED STATES
COMMERCE SUBCOMMITTEE

29 September 1971

SUBJECT: Designation of US Invited Contractor Under Article XV, Status of Forces Agreement

ROK Chairman, Commerce Subcommittee

1. Reference paragraph 2, Article XV of the Status of Forces Agreement.

2. The Government of the Republic of Korea is informed through this written consultative process that the United States Forces, Korea, proposes to extend invited contractor status to the qualified US firms awarded the contract for design of Autodin Switching Center, Camp Walker, Korea.

3. The following data are provided:

   a. Company Name:

     (1) Adrian Wilson Associates
     (2) Associated American Engineers, Inc.
     (3) Daniel, Mann, Johnson & Mendenhall
     (4) Lyon Associates, Inc.
     (5) Pacific Architects & Engineers, Inc.

   b. Local Address:

     (1) Adrian Wilson Associates, APO 96301
     (2) Associated American Engineers, Inc., APO 96301
     (3) Daniel, Mann, Johnson & Mendenhall (None)
     (4) Lyon Associates, Inc., APO 96301
     (5) Pacific Architects & Engineers, Inc. (None)

   c. Identification of US Citizen Employees: To be provided after contract award.

   d. Number of US and ROK Employees: To be provided after contract award.

   e. Reasons for Designation of an Invited Contractor: Contracting Officer is bound by US law to select architect-engineer firms for professional services contracts in strict accordance with the procedures set

52

70th JC (Incl 1 to Incl 18)
28 Jan 72

These minutes are considered as official documents pertaining to both Governments ●●d will not be released without ●●tual agreement.

SUBJECT: Designation of US Invited Contractor Under Article XV, Status of Forces Agreement

forth in paragraph 18-402 of the Armed Services Procurement Regulation (ASPR). Such selection is not based upon competitive bidding procedures, but rather upon the professional qualifications necessary for the satisfactory performance of the services required, subject to additional considerations such as required specialized experience, demonstrated performance, and security qualifications. The Contracting Officer is prohibited from selecting from among other than those firms who have properly filed GSA Standard Form 251, "U. S. Government Architect-Engineer Questionnaire", and have been declared qualified to perform such services for the US Government under procedures prescribed in the ASPR. All firms listed in paragraph 3a above have properly filed qualification data in accordance with the procedures described above; have been declared fully qualified to perform such services, and, therefore, are eligible to be selected by Contracting Officer for professional services contracts. None other than U.S. firms have thus far filed qualification data and met the prerequisites for selection. Accordingly, designation of US Invited Contractor is required for the performance of this work under the applicable terms of SOFA.

f. Location of Contract: Taegu, Korea.

g. Type of Contract: Fixed Price, Type B contract for architect-engineer services to design an Autodin Switching Center, for relocation to Camp Walker. The Autodin Switching Center includes a pre-engineered building with extensive air conditioning and environmental control for communications equipment. The work will include the design of drainage structures, access road, standby power, heating, air conditioning, utilities and related aspects to provide a complete facility ready for installation of communication equipment.

h. Length of Contract: To be provided after contract award.

i. USFK Sponsor: District Engineer.

RICHARD T. CANN
Colonel, US Army
United States Chairman
Commerce Subcommittee

7.

70th JC (Incl 1 to Incl 18)
28 Jan 72

53

(70

These minutes are considered as official documents pertaining to both Governments and will not be released without mutual agreement.

MINISTRY OF COMMERCE AND INDUSTRY
REPUBLIC OF KOREA
SEOUL, KOREA

4 October 1971

Subject: Designation of US Invited Contractor under Article XV,
Status of Forces Agreement

US Chairman, Commerce Subcommittee

1. Reference:

    a. Paragraph 2, Article XV, Status of Forces Agreement

    b. US Commerce Subcommittee Memorandum of Consultation, dated 29 September 1971 subject as above, pertaining to contract for design of Autodin Switching Center, Camp Walker, Korea.

2. The US memorandum, reference 1b above, has been reviewed and the government of the Republic of Korea understands the requirement for an invited contractor in this instance.

Chung Min Kil
Chairman
Commerce Subcommittee, ROK

54   70th JC (Incl 2 toIncl 18)
28 Jan 72

These minutes are considered as official documents pertaining to both
Governments and will ● t JOINT COMMITTEE be released ● hout mutual agreement.
UNDER
THE REPUBLIC OF KOREA AND THE UNITED STATES
STATUS OF FORCES AGREEMENT

21 DEC 1971

MEMORANDUM FOR: THE JOINT COMMITTEE

SUBJECT: Designation of US Invited Contractor under Article XV,
Status of Forces Agreement

1.   References:

   a.   Paragraph 2, Article XV, Status of Forces Agreement.

   b.   US Chairman, Commerce Subcommittee letter, dated 10 Sep
1971, subject as above (Incl 1).

   c.   ROK Chairman, Commerce Subcommittee letter, dated 15 Sep
1971, subject as above (Incl 2).

2.   The United States, after consultation with the ROK Commerce
Subcommittee and having duly considered their views, has designated
Trans Asia Engineering Company as a US invited contractor for
execution of contract DACA79-72-C-0038 for design of POL systems,
Osan, Suwon, Taegu, Kwangju and Kunsan.

3.   Pertinent data concerning US or third country national employees
will be provided to the Joint Secretariat by established reporting
procedures.

2 Incl   ROBERT N. SMITH
as   Lieutenant General, USAF
                                        United States Representative
                                        Joint Committee

55   70th JC (Incl 19)
      28 Jan 72

REPUBLIC OF KOREA - UNITED STATES
COMMERCE SUBCOMMITTEE   10 September 1971

SUBJECT: Designation of US Invited Contractor Under Article XV, Status of Forces Agreement

ROK Chairman, Commerce Subcommittee

1. Reference paragraph 2, Article XV of the Status of Forces Agreement.

2. The Government of the Republic of Korea is informed through this written consultative process that the United States Forces, Korea, proposes to extend invited contractor status to the qualified US firm awarded the contract for design of POL systems, Osan, Suwon, Taegu, Kwangju and Kunsan Air Bases.

3. The following data are provided:

   a. Company Name:

      (1) Trans Asia Engineering Associates, APO 96301
      (2) The Hinchman Company, Detroit, Michigan
      (3) Harco Corporation, Cleveland, Ohio

   b. Local Address of each firm:

      (1) Trans Asia Engineering Associates: APO 96301
      (2) The Hinchman Company: None
      (3) Harco Corporation: None

   c. Identification of US Citizen Employees: To be provided after contract award.

   d. Number of US and ROK Employees: To be provided after contract award.

   e. Reasons for Designation of an Invited Contractor:

      (1) Contracting Officer is bound by US law to select architect-engineer firms for professional services contracts in strict accordance with the procedures set forth in paragraph 18-402 of the Armed Services Procurement Regulation (ASPR). Such selection is not based upon competitive bidding

56   70th JC (Incl 1 to Incl 19)
                                          28 Jan 72

These minutes are considered as official documents pertaining to both Governments and will not be released without mutual agreement.

procedures, but rather upon the professional qualifications necessary for the satisfactory performance of the services required, subject to additional considerations such as required specialized experience, demonstrated performance, and security qualifications. The Contracting Officer is prohibited from selecting from among other than those firms who have properly filed GSA Standard Form 251, "U.S. Government Architect-Engineer Questionnaire", and have been declared qualified to perform such services for the US Government under procedures prescribed in the ASPR. All firms listed in paragraph 2a, above, have properly filed qualification data in accordance with the procedures described above; have been declared fully qualified to perform such services, and therefore, are eligible to be selected by Contracting Officer for professional services contracts. None other than U.S. Firms have thus far filed qualification data and met the prerequisities for selection. Accordingly, designation of US Invited Contractor is required for the performance of this work under the applicable terms of SOFA.

     (2) "A recognized expert in the field of Cathodic Protection is required, the design per usual American Practices is needed to facilitate later maintenance.

    f. Location of Contract: Osan, Suwon, Taegu, Kwangju and Kunsan

    g. Type of Contract: Fixed Price, Type B

    h. Length of Contract: To be provided after contract award.

    i. USFK Sponsor: Far East District, Corps of Engineers

RICHARD T. CANN
Colonel, U.S. Army
United States Chairman
Commerce Subcommittee

MINISTRY OF COMMERCE AND INDUSTRY
REPUBLIC OF KOREA
SEOUL, KOREA

15 September 1971

Subject: Designation of US Invited Contractor under Article XV, Status of Forces Agreement

US Chairman, Commerce Subcommittee

1. Reference:

    a. Paragraph 2, Article XV, Status of Forces Agreement

    b. US Commerce Subcommittee Memorandum of Consultation, dated 10 September 1971 subject as above, pertaining to contract for design of POL systems, Osan, Suwon, Taegu, Kwangju and Kunsan Air Bases, Korea.

2. The US memorandum, reference 1b above, has been reviewed and the government of the Republic of Korea understands the requirement for an invited contractor in this instance.

Chung Min Kil
Chairman
Commerce Subcommittee, ROK

58

70th JC (Incl 2 to Incl 19)
28 Jan 72

These minutes are considered as official documents pertaining to both Governments and will ██ be released without mutual a██eement.

**JOINT COMMITTEE
UNDER
THE REPUBLIC OF KOREA AND THE UNITED STATES
STATUS OF FORCES AGREEMENT**

11 JAN 1972

MEMORANDUM FOR: THE JOINT COMMITTEE

SUBJECT: Designation of US Invited Contractor under Article XV, Status of Forces Agreement

1. References:

    a. Paragraph 2, Article XV, Status of Forces Agreement.

    b. US Chairman, Commerce Subcommittee letter, dated 25 Feb 1971, subject as above (Incl 1).

    c. ROK Chairman, Commerce Subcommittee letter, dated 5 Mar 1971, subject as above (Incl 2).

2. The United States, after consultation with the ROK Commerce Subcommittee and having duly considered their views, has designated Associated American Engineers Overseas, Inc., as a US invited contractor, in joint venture with a Korean firm, for execution of contract F62087-72-C-0054 for operation and maintenance services for Air Force installations, Korea.

3. Pertinent data concerning US or third country national employees will be provided to the Joint Secretariat by established reporting procedures.

2 Incl
as

ROBERT N. SMITH
Lieutenant General, USAF
United States Representative
Joint Committee

59

70th JC (Incl 20)
28 Jan 72

These minutes are considered as official documents pertaining to both
Governments and will █ be released without mutual a█████ement.

REPUBLIC OF KOREA - UNITED STATES
COMMERCE SUBCOMMITTEE

25 February 1971

SUBJECT: Designation of US Invited Contractor Under Article XV,
Status of Forces Agreement

ROK Chairman, Commerce Subcommittee

1. Reference Paragraph 2, Article XV of the Status of Forces Agreement.

2. The Government of the Republic of Korea is informed through this
written consultative process that the United States Forces, Korea,
proposes to extend invited contractor status to the US member of the
successful negotiated bidder among qualified joint venture firms for
the forthcoming Facilities Engineering Services Contract for the
US Air Force Bases and sites in Korea. This new contract will
replace contract DAJB03-67-C-0592.

3. The following data are provided:

   a. Company Name: The list of contractors being considered is
attached as inclosure 1.

   b. Local Address: To be supplied upon designation.

   c. Identification of US Citizen Employees: To be supplied upon
designation.

   d. Number of US and ROK Employees: It is estimated that 14 US
citizens and 466 Koreans will be employed under the contract.

   e. Reason for Designation of a Joint Venture Contractor: Open
competitive bidding is not practicable due to the following:

   (1) A contract utilizing ROK contractor only would not be feasible
due to the extensive security requirements demanded by the US Air Force.
The contractor will be involved in the operations and maintenance of
critical support facilities which directly affect the mission capabilities of the US Air Force. He will be involved with programming
actions which may be classified and contain information not releasable
to foreign nationals.

70th JC (Incl 1 to Incl 20)
60
28 Jan 72

These minutes are considered as official documents pertaining to both Governments and will not be released without mutual agreement.

25 February 1971

SUBJECT: Designation of US Invited Contractor Under Article XV, Status of Forces Agreement

(2) Fully qualified and trained managers and supervisors are essential to meet civil engineering requirements. The management of government resources placed in the hands of the contractor such as supplies, equipment, tools, and vehicles require that the contractor be responsible for and responsive to USAF policies and requirements. Fire Department operations require personnel familiar with aircraft fire protection and crash rescue procedures and equipment.

(3) The contractor is required to comply with various Air Force manuals and regulations and other applicable publications which are technical in nature. The facilities and technical equipment are US design and manufacture and must be maintained to USAF standards which in most cases is above that of local standards and beyond the capability of local national personnel without US supervision.

f. Location of Contract: US Air Force Korea.

g. Type of Contracts: Award of a single contract for the management, operation, maintenance and repair of real property facilities, to include fire protection and crash rescue service is contemplated.

h. Length of Contract: 1 July 1971 through 30 June 1972 with an option to extend the contract up to two additional years. The contract will also provide for a 30-day transition period at the end of the contract to assist a successor contractor. Total duration of the contract, including options and period of transition, will not exceed thirty-seven (37) months.

i. Sponsoring Component Commander: Commander, Air Forces, Korea.

1 Incl
as

RICHARD T. CANN
Colonel, U.S. Army
ACofS, J4

61

70th JC (Incl 1 to Incl 20)
28 Jan 72

These minutes are considered as official documents pertaining to both Governments and will ●t be released without mutual a●eement.

MINISTRY OF COMMERCE AND INDUSTRY
REPUBLIC OF KOREA
SEOUL, KOREA

5 March 1971

Subject: Designation of US Invited Contractor under Article XV
Status of Forces Agreement

US Chairman, Commerce Subcommittee

1. Reference:

a. Paragraph 2, Article XV, Status of Forces Agreement

b. US Commerce Subcommittee Memorandum of Consultation, dated 25 February 1971, subject as above, pertaining to joint venture contract for Facilities Engineering Services for the US Air Base, Korea.

2. The US memorandum reference 1b above, has been reviewed and the Government of the Republic of Korea understands the requirement for invited contractor status to the US member of ROK/US joint venture contract firm in this instance.

3. The list of qualified Korean contractors to be considered for joint venture with US firms for the above contract is attached herewith.

Chung Min Kil
Chairman
Commerce Subcommittee, ROK

These minutes are considered as official documents pertaining to both Governments and will ● be released without mutual a●●eement.

JOINT COMMITTEE
UNDER
THE REPUBLIC OF KOREA AND THE UNITED STATES
STATUS OF FORCES AGREEMENT

MEMORANDUM FOR: The Joint Committee   19 January 1972

SUBJECT: Designation of US Invited Contractor Under Article XV, Status
of Forces Agreement

1. References:

    a. Paragraph 2, Article XV, Status of Forces Agreement.

    b. US Chairman, Commerce Subcommittee letter, dated 22 June 1971,
subject as above (Inclosure 1).

    c. ROK Chairman, Commerce Subcommittee letter, dated 24 August 1971,
subject as above (Inclosure 2).

2. The United States, after consultation with the ROK Commerce Subcommittee, and having duly considered their views, has designated Collins
Radio Company as a US invited contractor for execution of Contract DAAB 07-
72-C-0010 for a new 60 channel add-on to the existing ROKA Backbone
Microwave System.

3. Pertinent data concerning US citizen employees will be provided to the
Joint Secretariat in the established format.

2 Incl
as
                              ROBERT N. SMITH
                              Lieutenant General, USAF
                              United States Representative
                              Joint Committee

These minutes are considered as official documents pertaining to both Governments and will ● be released without mutual a●eement.

REPUBLIC OF KOREA - UNITED STATES
COMMERCE SUBCOMMITTEE

22 June 1971

SUBJECT: Designation of US Invited Contractor Under Article XV, Status of Forces Agreement

ROK Chairman, Commerce Subcommittee

1. Reference: Paragraph 2, Article XV, of the Status of Forces Agreement.

2. The Government of the Republic of Korea is informed through this written consultative process that the United States Forces, Korea, proposes to extend invited contractor status to the Collins Radio Company to develop an engineering plan, provide and install associated radio and multiplex equipment, and perform all system tests and alignments for a new 60 channel add-on to the existing ROKA Backbone Microwave System.

3. The following data are provided:

   a. Company Name: Collins Radio Company

   b. Local Address: Office #1113, Ko-Ryo Building, 24, 1-Ka, Shin Moon-Ro, Chongro-ku, Seoul, Korea

   c. Identification of US Citizen Employees: To be supplied upon award of contract.

   d. Number of US and ROK Employees: The number of US citizens and Korean employees is not known at this time and will be supplied upon conclusion of negotiations.

   e. Reasons for Designation of an Invited Contractor: Open competitive bidding is not practicable due to the exclusive type US Manufactured equipments to be installed on a now-existing system. This equipment must be manufactured by the Collins Radio Company, as specified in Article VII of the Memorandum of Agreement, SUBJECT: Utilization of the Republic of Korea Army (ROKA) Microwave (M/W) System

64

70th JC (Incl 21)
28 Jan 72

These minutes are considered as official documents pertaining to both Governments ⬤d will not be released without ⬤tual agreement.

SUBJECT: Designation of US Invited Contractor Under Article XV, Status of Forces Agreement

by the United Nations Command/United States Forces, Korea, dated 5 June 1970. This Memorandum of Agreement was agreed to and authorized in accordance with Article III, paragraph 2(8), of the United States of America and the Republic of Korea Status of Forces Agreement, third edition dated July 1969.

(1) Invited Contractor Status is considered necessary to insure that the US equipment provided will be installed, tested, and placed in operation so as to meet all specifications as stated in the Memorandum of Agreement. This is addressed in paragraph g, Article VII of the Memorandum of Agreement which states: "g. ROKA will authorize access to ROKA microwave sites of US personnel as required to conduct joint surveys, path profiles, installation and maintenance necessary to engineer and install the expanded R/F path and 60-channel supergroup on the ROKA microwave system. If Korean technicians, in US employ, are required, their clearance will be subject to approval by ROK security agency." This clearly identifies that the award will be to a US Contractor who gains the option to use Korean Technicians, if required.

(2) End to end telecommunications utilizing media from two countries, as stated in the Memorandum of Agreement, is required. To meet operational standards it is essential that only one firm be held responsible to insure that they are met over the entire system. To achieve this, the procurement, installation, and testing cannot be subdivided or piece-mealed out.

f. Location of Contract: Contract installation work will be performed at the following ROKA microwave sites:

(1) Seoul

(2) Mangyung-dae

(3) Paegunsan

(4) Yongwhabong

(5) Hakkasan

(6) Palgongsan

(7) Taegu

(8) Pulmosan

(9) Changsan

70th JC (Incl 2 to Incl 21)
28 Jan 72

These minutes are considered as official documents pertaining to both Governments and will not be released without mutual agreement.

22 June 1971

SUBJECT: Designation of US Invited Contractor Under Article XV, Status of Forces Agreement

g. Type of Contract: The contactor will provide system engineering, equipment installation and testing for a 60-channel add-on to the ROKA Backbone Microwave System.

h. Length of Contract: Approximately 10 months.

·i. Sponsoring Component Command: Commanding General, Eighth United States Army.

Norman W. Hammes, COL

RICHARD T. CANN
Colonel, US Army
United States Chairman
Commerce Subcommittee

66

70th JC (Incl 1 to Incl 21)
28 Jan 72

These minutes are considered as official documents pertaining to both Governments and will ▮t be released without mutual a▮eement.

MINISTRY OF COMMERCE AND INDUSTRY
REPUBLIC OF KOREA
SEOUL, KOREA

24 August 1971

Subject: Designation of US Invited Contractor under Article XV, Status of Forces Agreement

US Chairman, Commerce Subcommittee

1. Reference:

a. Paragrph 2, Article XV, Status of Forces Agreement

b. U੭ Commerce Subcommittee Memorandum of Consultation, dated 22 June 1971 subject as above, pertaining to contract for a new 60 channel add-on to the existing ROKA Backbone Microwave System, Korea.

2. The US memorandum, reference 1b above, has been reviewed and the government of the Republic of Korea understands the requirement for an invited contractor in this instance.

Chung Min Kil
Chairman
Commerce Subcommittee, ROK

67

70th JC (Incl 2 to Incl 21)
28 Jan 72

184

These minutes are considered as official documents pertaining to both.
Governments and will not be released without mutual agreement.

JOINT COMMITTEE
UNDER
THE REPUBLIC OF KOREA AND THE UNITED STATES
STATUS OF FORCES AGREEMENT

2 1 DEC 1971

MEMORANDUM FOR: THE JOINT COMMITTEE

SUBJECT: Designation of US Invited Contractor under Article XV, Status
of Forces Agreement

1. References:

a. Paragraph 2, Article XV, Status of Forces Agreement.

b. US Chairman, Commerce Subcommittee letter, dated 1 Sep 1971,
subject as above (Incl 1).

c. ROK Chairman, Commerce Subcommittee letter, dated 8 Sep 1971,
subject as above (Incl 2).

2. The United States, after consultation with the ROK Commerce Subcommittee and having duly considered their views, has designated the
National Cash Register Company as a US invited contractor for execution
of contract BK-71-0104 for maintenance of NCR machines for the Korea
Regional Exchange.

3. Pertinent data concerning US or third country national employees will
be provided to the Joint Secretariat by established reporting procedures.

ROBERT N. SMITH
Lieutenant General, USAF
United States Representative
Joint Committee

2 Incl
as

70th JC (Incl 22)
28 Jan 72

68

185

**REPUBLIC OF KOREA - UNITED STATES
COMMERCE SUBCOMMITTEE**

1 September 1971

SUBJECT: Designation of US Invited Contractor under Article XV, Status of Forces Agreement

ROK Chairman, Commerce Subcommittee

1. Reference: Para 2, Article XV, Status of Forces Agreement.

2. The Government of the Republic of Korea is informed through this written consultative process that the United States Forces, Korea, proposes to extend invited contractor status to the National Cash Register Company, Korea Branch, for maintenance and repair of NCR machines for the Korea Regional Exchange.

2. The following data are provided:

   a. Company Name: National Cash Register Company, Korea Branch.

   b. Local Address: #24-738, Hanam-dong, Yongsan-ku, Seoul, Korea.

   c. Identification of US Citizen Employee: Mr. Edmond A. Potter.

   d. Number of US and ROK Employees: It is anticipated that one (1) US and thirty (30) Korean personnel will be employed under this contract.

   e. Reason for Designation of US Invited Contractor: Open competitive bidding is not practical due to local unavailability of materials or services required by US standards as explained below:

   (1) NCR factory-made spare parts are available only from bonafide NCR Company operation. No other US or Korean firm can furnish NCR parts.

   (2) NCR provides guarantee and warranty services. NCR guarantees that all equipment delivered in Korea shall be in good operating condition and it shall replace free of charge during the first year any defective parts and it will make any other repairs and adjustments required during the one (1) year guarantee period free of charge.

   (3) The NCR warranty is automatically voided if the equipment is serviced by other than a certified NCR employee.

186

69

70th JC (Incl 1 to Incl 22)
28 Jan 72

These minutes are considered as official documents pertaining to both Government and will not be released without mutual agreement.

1 September 1971

SUBJECT: Designation of US Invited Contractor under Article XV Status of Forces Agreement

    (4) NCR furnished for the initial training period, supervised equipment operator training and instruction of USFK employees.

    f. Location of Contract: Korea Regional Exchange installations throughout the Republic of Korea.

    g. Type of Contract: Fixed price contract for maintenance and repair of NCR machines.

    h. Length of Contract: Two years with three (3) one year renewal options.

    i. Sponsoring Component Command: PACEX Procurement Office - Korea.

RICHARD T. CANN
Colonel, U.S. Army
United States Chairman
Commerce Subcommittee

- These minutes are considered as official documents pertaining to both Governments and will ▉ be released without mutual a▉eement.

MINISTRY OF COMMERCE AND INDUSTRY
REPUBLIC OF KOREA
SEOUL, KOREA

8 September 1971

Subject: Designation of US Invited Contractor under Article XV, Status of Forces Agreement

US Chairman, Commerce Subcommittee

1. Reference:

    a. Paragraph 2, Article XV, Status of Forces Agreement

    b. US Commerce Subcommittee Memorandum of Consultation, dated 1 September 1971 subject as above, pertaining to contract for maintenance and repair of NCR machines for the Korea Regional Exchange-PACEX.

2. The US memorandum, reference 1b above, has been reviewed and the government of the Republic of Korea understands the requirement for an invited contractor in this instance.

for Chung Min Kil
Chairman
Commerce Subcommittee, ROK

These minutes are considered as official documents pertaining to both
Governments and will ⬤t be released without mutual agreement.

**JOINT COMMITTEE
UNDER
THE REPUBLIC OF KOREA AND THE UNITED STATES
STATUS OF FORCES AGREEMENT**

21 DEC 1971

MEMORANDUM FOR: THE JOINT COMMITTEE

SUBJECT: Designation of US Invited Contractor under Article XV, Status
of Forces Agreement

1. References:

    a. Paragraph 2, Article XV, Status of Forces Agreement.

    b. US Chairman, Commerce Subcommittee letter, dated 1 Sep 1971,
subject as above (Incl 1).

    c. ROK Chairman, Commerce Subcommittee letter, dated 8 Sep 1971,
subject as above (Incl 2).

2. The United States, after consultation with the ROK Commerce Subcommittee and having duly considered their views, has designated the
National Cash Register Company as a US invited contractor for execution
of contract DAJB03-72-C-3033 for maintenance of National Cash Register
and Multilith machines.

3. Pertinent data concerning US or third country national employees
will be provided to the Joint Secretariat by established reporting procedures.

ROBERT N. SMITH
Lieutenant General, USAF
United States Representative
Joint Committee

2 Incl
as

72

70th JC (Incl 23)
28 Jan 72

REPUBLIC OF KOREA – UNITED STATES
COMMERCE SUBCOMMITTEE

1 September 1971

SUBJECT: Designation of US Invited Contractor under Article XV Status of Forces Agreement

ROK Chairman, Commerce Subcommittee

1. Reference: Para 2, Article XV, Status of Forces Agreement.

2. The Government of the Republic of Korea is informed through this written consultative process that the United States Forces, Korea, proposes to extend invited contractor status to the National Cash Register Company, Korea Branch, for maintenance and repair of NCR machines and multilith duplicating machines at various Eighth Army activities.

3. The following data are provided:

   a. Company Name: National Cash Register Company, Korea Branch.

   b. Local Address: APO 96301.

   c. Identification of US Citizen Employee: Mr. E. A. Potter.

   d. Number of US and ROK Employees: It is anticipated that one (1) US and thirty (30) Korean personnel will be employed.

   e. Reasons for Designation of a US Invited Contractor: Open competitive bidding is not practicable due to local unavailability of materials or services required by US standards as explained below:

   (1) NCR factory-made spare parts are available only from bonafide NCR Company operation. No other US or Korean firm can furnish NCR parts.

   (2) NCR provides guarantee and warranty services. NCR guarantees that all equipment delivered in Korea shall be in good operating condition and it shall replace free of charge during the first year any defective parts and it will make any other repairs and adjustments required during the one year guarantee period free of charge.

   (3) The NCR warranty is automatically voided if the equipment is serviced by other than a certified NCR employee.

73

70th JC (Incl 1 to Incl 23)
28 Jan 72

SUBJECT: Designation of US Invited Contractor under Article XV Status of Forces Agreement

(4) NCR furnishes for the initial training period, supervised equipment operator training and instruction of USFK employees.

f. <u>Location of Contract</u>: Eighth US Army installations throughout the Republic of Korea.

g. <u>Type of Contract</u>: Fixed Price contract for maintenance and repair of NCR machines and duplicating machines.

h. <u>Length of Contract</u>: 12 months.

i. <u>Sponsoring Component Commander</u>: US Army Korea Procurement Agency.

RICHARD X. CANN
Colonel, U.S. Army
United States Chairman
Commerce Subcommittee

74

70th JC (Incl 1 to Incl 23)
28 Jan 72

These minutes are considered as official documents pertaining to both Governments and will ▮ be released without mutual ag▮eement.

MINISTRY OF COMMERCE AND INDUSTRY
REPUBLIC OF KOREA
SEOUL, KOREA

8 September 1971

Subject: Designation of US Invited Contractor under Article XV,
Status of Forces Agreement

US Chairman, Commerce Subcommittee

1. Reference:

    a. Paragraph 2, Article XV, Status of Forces Agreement

    b. US Commerce Subcommittee Memorandum of Consultation, dated 1 September 1971 subject as above, pertaining to contract for maintenance and repair of NCR machines and duplicating machines at various Eighth Army activities.

2. The US memorandum, reference 1b above, has been reviewed and the government of the Republic of Korea understands the requirement for an invited contractor in this instance.

for *Changsuk Chu*
Chung Min Kil
Chairman
Commerce Subcommittee, ROK

192

75

70th JC (Incl 2 to Incl 23)
28 Jan 72

These minutes are considered as official documents pertaining to both
Governments and will ● be released without mutual agreement.

JOINT ROK-US PRESS RELEASE
SEVENTIETH ROK-US JOINT COMMITTEE MEETING
28 JANUARY 1972

The ROK-US Joint Committee completed its first five years of

work in implementation of the Status of Forces Agreement with the

holding of the seventieth meeting at the Foreign Ministry Conference

Room in the ROK Capitol Building on 28 January. The new ROK

Government Representative, Mr. KIM Dong Whie, who recently was

named Director of the Europe and America Bureau of the Foreign

Ministry, presided at the meeting which included fourteen agenda items.

The Joint Committee approved the fifth report of its Ad Hoc Sub-

committee on Civil-Military Relations, including a total of five recom-

mendations from its Panels on Health and Sanitation, Narcotics and

Drug Control, and Race Relations and Equality of Treatment. This

brings to nineteen the number of recommendations of the Ad Hoc Sub-

committee on Civil-Military Relations which have been approved by the

Joint Committee and reflects the increasing emphasis of both Govern-

ments in improving civil-military relations in the Korean communities

adjacent to US military installations in the ROK.

The Joint Committee also approved ten recommendations of its

Facilities and Areas Subcommittee and noted for the record the earlier

exigent approval of a recommendation of its Transportation Subcommittee

which has enabled the re-registration and licensing of the privately

76

70th JC (Incl 24)
28 Jan 72

These minutes are considered as official documents pertaining to both Governments and will ██ be released ██without mutual a██eement.

owned vehicles of United States Forces Korea personnel to begin this week.

Among the other actions of the Joint Committee at its seventieth meeting were the assignment of ten additional tasks to its Facilities and Areas Subcommittee, one task to its Transportation Subcommittee, designation of six new US invited contractors, and the noting for the record of the recent resolution of two labor disputes in accordance with the procedures of the SOFA Labor Article.

The Joint Committee also approved plans for observation of the fifth anniversary of the entering into force of the SOFA which comes on 9 February 1972. The next meeting of the Joint Committee is scheduled for 24 February in the US SOFA Conference Room.

77

70th JC (Incl 24)
28 Jan 72

대한민국 외무부
공보관실
전화 74-3576

보 도 자 료

이 기사는 제공처인 외무부를
밝히고 보도할수 있음

외무보도   호

제 70차 한.미 합동위원회
공 동 발 표 문

72. 1. 28.

한.미 합동위원회는 1월 28일 중앙청 외무부 회의실에서 제 70차 회의를 가졌으며 이로써 한.미 행정협정 시행의 첫 5 개년사업을 완료하였다. 최근에 외무부 구미국장으로 임명된바 있는 신임 김동휘 한국측 대표는 14개 항목의 의제를 다룬 이번회의를 사회하였다.

합동위원회는 군.민관기 임시분과위원회 제 5차 보고서를 채택하였는 바, 동 보고서에는 건강위생조사반, 마약관리조사반, 인종관기조사반이 상정한 5 개항의 건의가 포함되어있다. 이로써 합동위원회가 승인한 군.민관기 임시분과위원회의 건의는 19 개항에 달하였으며 이것은 양국정부가 미군주둔지역 까지에 있어서의 군.민관기 개선에 더욱 치중하고 있음을 반영하는 것이다.

합동위원회는 또한 시설구역 분과위원회의 10 개항 건의를 승인하였으며 금주부터 주한미군 자가용 차량의 재등록을 실시하도록 한 교통분과위원회의 기왕의 긴급건의 채택을 회의록에 남기도록 하였다.

70차 합동위원회가 취한 이밖의 조치는 시설구역 분과위원회에 대한 10 개과제, 교통분과위원회에 대한 1 개과제의 부여와 6명의 신규 미국인 초청계약자의 지정, ~~손정~~ ~~계약자 1명의 과정참파등~~ 이며 행정협정 노무조항에따라최근에 해결된바있는 두건의 노동쟁의를 회의록 기록에 남기기로 하였다.

합동위원회는 2월 9일의 행정협정 발효 5주년기념 행사계획을 승인하고 다음 회의는 2월 24일 미군 행정협정 회의실에서 개최하기로 하였다.

2. 제기차, 1972. 2. 24

196

기 안 용 지

분류기호 문서번호	미이 723 -	(전화번호　　　　)	전 결 규 정　조　항 **국 장**　전 결 사 항	
처 리 기 간				
시 행 일 자				
보 존 년 한		국　　　　장		
보 조 기 관	북미2과장　*(서명)*		협	
기 안 책 임 자	김성실　북미2과 (72. 2. 17)		조	
경 유 수 신 참 조	수신처 참조	*(발송 도장)* No. 4947 1972. 2. 18 외무부		
제 　 목	한.미 합동위원회 회의개최 통지			

　오는 1972년 2월 24일 (목요일) 14:00 미측 SOFA 회의실에서

한.미 합동위원회 제 71차 회의가 개최될 예정이오니 각 위원께서는

회의에 필히 참석하여 주시기 바라며, 의제및 회의자료는 추후 통보

위계입니다. 끝.

수신처 :　법무부장관 (법무실장, 검찰국장, 출입국관리국장),		정서
국방부장관 (기획국장, 시설국장),　재무부장관 (관세국장),		
상공부장관 (상역국장), 교통부장관 (종합수송 담당관),		관인
노동청장 (노정국장)		
		발송

공동서식1-2(갑)
1967. 4. 4. 승인

190mm×268mm(1 급인쇄용지70g ㎡)
조달청　(500,000매 인쇄)

(1. FOR YOUR INFORMATION: The ROK Representative has no new tasks for assignment to the Facilities and Areas Subcommittee. He does, however, have two tasks which were assigned to that Subcommittee on an exigent basis in the interval since the last Joint Committee meeting, which he should be invited to present for notation in the minutes of this meeting. These two prior assigned tasks consist of one request for the limited use by Korean farmers of certain areas adjacent to Kunsan Air Base, and one request for the release of certain areas adjacent to the USFK military port in Chinhae for the construction of a public beach.)

2. I understand that the Republic of Korea Representative has two tasks which were assigned on an exigent basis to the Facilities and Areas Subcommittee, which he wishes to present now for recording in the official minutes of this meeting.

(3. FOR YOUR INFORMATION: The ROK Representative will then present these two tasks.)

4. The United States Representative is pleased to concur in the recording in the minutes of this meeting of the prior assignment of the specified two tasks to the Facilities and Areas Subcommittee.

AGENDA ITEM I   2. US Presentation

1. The United States Representative would like to present eight
new tasks for assignment to the Facilities and Areas Subcommittee.
These consist of one request for the acquisition of an easement, one
request for the acquisition of a Temporary Use Permit, two requests
for the extension of existing Temporary Use Permits, and four requests
for the release of parcels of real estate. All details concerning these
eight tasks are contained in memoranda which have been distributed to
both sides.

2. It is proposed that these eight new tasks be assigned to the
Facilities and Areas Subcommittee.

(3. FOR YOUR INFORMATION: The ROK SOFA Secretary has
indicated that the ROK Representative will concur in this proposal.)

(1. FOR YOUR INFORMATION: The ROK Representative has no recommendations of the Facilities and Areas Subcommittee to present at this meeting. Therefore, the US Representative should proceed to present nine recommendations of that Subcommittee.)

2. The United States Representative would like to present nine recommendations received from the Facilities and Areas Subcommittee. These comprise one recommendation concerning the acquisition of an easement, one recommendation involving the acquisition of a Temporary Use Permit, and seven recommendations for the release of parcels of real estate. All details concerning these recommendations will be found in memoranda which have been distributed to both sides.

3. It is proposed that the Joint Committee approve these nine recommendations of the Facilities and Areas Subcommittee.

(4. FOR YOUR INFORMATION: The ROK SOFA Secretary has indicated that the ROK Representative will concur in this proposal.)

200

(1. FOR YOUR INFORMATION: The ROK Representative will

present the sixth report of the Ad Hoc Subcommittee on Civil-Military

Relations (attached herewith) and request Joint Committee approval

for the report and the seven recommendations included therein. These

recommendations include three from the Panel on Narcotics and Drug

Control, two from the Panel on Larceny and Black Marketing, and two

from the Panel on People-to-People Projects.)

2. The United States Representative is pleased to concur in

approval of the sixth report of the Ad Hoc Subcommittee on Civil-Military

Relations, including seven additional recommendations of three of its

panels. I am glad to note the continued progress of the Ad Hoc Subcom-

mittee, as well as the vigorous efforts of the ROK Government to deal

with the problems of the camp communities through its own "Base

Community Clean-Up Committee." These Korean and joint Republic of

Korea-United States programs should result in significant improvements

in civil-military relations, thereby further strengthening our mutual

defense.

1. The United States Representative wishes to present memoranda to the Joint Committee informing the Government of the Republic of Korea of the designation of five United States invited contractors under Article XV of the Status of Forces Agreement. These designations were made after consultations between Republic of Korea and United States Commerce Subcommittee personnel in accordance with Joint Committee procedures. The invited contractors so designated are International Electronics Corporation; Air America, Incorporated; Southern Air Transport, Incorporated; Minnesota (3M) Services Supply Limited; and Universal American Enterprises, Incorporated. Each of these companies has one contract. The contract of Universal American Enterprises, Incorporated is in joint venture with a Korean firm.

2. Pertinent data concerning employees of these invited contractors will be provided to the Government of the Republic of Korea in accordance with mutually agreed procedures.

(3. FOR YOUR INFORMATION: The ROK SOFA Secretary has indicated that the ROK Representative will acknowledge the designation of these invited contractors.)

1. The United States Representative wishes to present a memorandum to the Joint Committee informing the Government of the Republic of Korea that Morrison-Knudsen International Company, Incorporated, has completed all contracts with the United States which require work in the Republic of Korea and consequently their designation as an invited contractor is withdrawn.

(2. FOR YOUR INFORMATION: The ROK SOFA Secretary has indicated the ROK Representative will acknowledge this withdrawal of designation of this invited contractor.)

US Presentation

1. The United States Representative wishes to note for the record that the United States Status of Forces Agreement Secretariat has furnished the following information to the Republic of Korea Status of Forces Agreement Secretariat in accordance with the provisions of the Status of Forces Agreement and Joint Committee decisions.

a. Five copies of reports on the United States armed forces dis-position of cases for the month of December 1971.

b. Twenty copies of the report of United States armed forces personnel, the civilian component, invited contractors, and the dependents of each, entering or departing the Republic of Korea during the month of January 1972.

c. Twenty copies of the USFK quarterly listing of all United States invited contractor employees and dependents as of 31 December 1971.

(2. FOR YOUR INFORMATION: The ROK SOFA Secretary has indicated that the ROK Representative will acknowledge receipt of these documents.)

(1. FOR YOUR INFORMATION: The ROK Representative will propose that the special press release, attached herewith, commemorating the fifth anniversary of the entry into force of the SOFA on 9 February 1972, which was issued by the Joint Committee on 8 February 1972, be included (for the record) in the minutes of this Joint Committee meeting.)

2. The United States Representative is glad to concur with the Republic of Korea Representative's proposal that the joint Republic of Korea-United States press release, which was issued in connection with the fifth anniversary of the entry into force of the Republic of Korea-United States Status of Forces Agreement on 9 February 1972, be included in the minutes of this meeting. I was glad to note that this special Joint Committee press release received good coverage in both the Korean and English language news media.

(1.   FOR YOUR INFORMATION: In accordance with the procedures for selecting the date for the next Joint Committee meeting, the US Representative, as the presiding chairman, will ask the ROK Representative if he would like to propose the date, time, and place for the next meeting.)

2.   Mr. Kim, when and where would you like to hold the next Joint Committee meeting?

(3.   FOR YOUR INFORMATION: The ROK SOFA Secretary has indicated that the ROK Representative will propose that the seventy-second Joint Committee meeting be held at 1530, Thursday, 23 March 1972, in the ROK Capitol Budilding.)

4.   The United States Representative is happy to concur in the proposed date, time, and place for the next Joint Committee meeting.

1. The United States Representative would like to propose approval of the press release for the seventy-first Joint Committee meeting, as prepared by our respective Secretaries and distributed in advance to both components of the Committee.

(2. FOR YOUR INFORMATION: The ROK SOFA Secretary has indicated that the ROK Representative will approve the proposed joint press release.)

1. Do you have any further items to present at this meeting, Mr. Kim?

(2. FOR YOUR INFORMATION: The ROK Secretary has indi- cated that the ROK Representative will reply in the negative.)

3. If there is no other business to come before the Joint Committee, I declare the seventy-first meeting of the Joint Committee adjourned.

MINUTES OF THE SEVENTY-FIRST MEETING

24 February 1972
Headquarters
US Forces, Korea
Seoul, Korea

1. The meeting was convened at 1400 hours by Lieutenant General Robert N. Smith, the US Representative, who presided at the meeting. A copy of the agenda is attached as Inclosure 1.

2. The following were in attendance:

ROK	US
Mr. KIM Dong-Whie	LTG Robert N. Smith, USAF
Mr. LEE Chong Won	Captain Frank M. Romanick, USN
MG CHO Jae Joon	COL David P. Heekin, USA
BG PAK Woo Bum	COL Carl G. Schneider, USAF
Mr. JUNG Ik Won	COL Bruce T. Coggins, USA
Mr. KIM Young Sup	Mr. Richard W. Finch, US Embassy
Mr. KIM Kee Joe	Mr. Robert A. Kinney, USFK
Mr. CHUNG Tai Ik	MAJ Dick J. Petersen, USAF
Mr. KWON Chan	Mr. Francis K. Cook, USFK

3. The ROK Representative stated that he had two tasks which were already assigned to the Facilities and Areas Subcommittee on an exigent basis in the interval since the last Joint Committee meeting. He said that these two prior assigned tasks consist of one request for the limited use by Korean farmers of certain areas adjacent to Kunsan Air Base/and one request for the release of certain areas adjacent to the (Inclosure 2) USFK military port in Chinhae for the construction of a public beach/ (Inclosure 3 He proposed that the prior assignment of these two tasks to the Facilities and Areas Subcommittee be noted in the minutes of this meeting. The US Representative concurred.

4. The US Representative presented eight new tasks for assignment to the Facilities and Areas Subcommittee. These consisted of
one request for the acquisition of an easement (Inclosure 4), one
request for the acquisition of a Temporary Use Permit (Inclosure 5),
two requests for the extension of existing Temporary Use Permits
(Inclosure 6), and four requests for the release of parcels of real estate (Inclosure 7). He stated that details concerning these eight tasks
were contained in memoranda which have been distributed to both sides.
He proposed that these eight new tasks be assigned to the Facilities
and Areas Subcommittee, and the ROK Representative concurred.

5. The US Representative presented nine recommendations received from the Facilities and Areas Subcommittee, including one
recommendation concerning the acquisition of an easement (Inclosure 8),
one recommendation involving the acquisition of a Temporary Use Permit (Inclosure 9), and seven recommendations for the release of parcels of real estate (Inclosure 10). He stated that details concerning
these recommendations were include* in memoranda which had been
distributed to both sides. He proposed that the Joint Committee approve these nine recommendations of the Facilities and Areas Subcommittee and the ROK Representative concurred.

6. The ROK Representative stated that he was happy to note that
the Ad Hoc Subcommittee on Civil-Military Relations had made

2

significant progress thus far in solving many difficult problems in the military base communities. He proposed that the sixth report of the Ad Hoc Subcommittee together with seven recommendations from three of its panels be approved and recorded in the minutes of this Joint Committee meeting (Inclosure 11).

7. The US Representative concurred in approval of the sixth report of the Ad Hoc Subcommittee on Civil-Military Relations, including seven additional recommendations of three of its panels. He stated that he was glad to note the continued progress of the Ad Hoc Subcommittee, as well as the vigorous efforts of the ROK Government to deal with the problems of the camp communities through its own "Base Community Clean-Up Committee." He said that these Korean and joint ROK-US programs should result in significant improvements in civil-military relations, thereby further strengthening our mutual defense.

8. The US Representative presented memoranda to the Joint Committee informing the Government of the ROK of the designation of five US invited contractors under Article XV of the SOFA. These designations were made after consultations between ROK and US Commerce Subcommittee personnel in accordance with Joint Committee procedures. He stated that the invited contractors so designated were International Electronics Corporation (Inclosure 12); Air America, Incorporated (Inclosure 13); Southern Air Transport, Incorporated

3

(Inclosure 14); Minnesota (3M) Services Supply Limited (Inclosure 15); and Universal American Enterprises, Incorporated (Inclosure 16). He said that each of these companies had one contract and that the contract of Universal American Enterprises, Incorporated was in joint venture with a Korean firm. He stated that pertinent data concerning employees of these invited contractors would be provided to the Government of the ROK in accordance with mutually agreed procedures.

9. The ROK Representative acknowledged the designation of five invited contractors and he noted that agreed procedures had been duly observed in these designations.

10. The US Representative presented a memorandum to the Joint Committee informing the Government of the ROK that Morrison-Knudsen International Company, Incorporated, had completed all contracts with the US which require work in the ROK and consequently their designation as an invited contractor is withdrawn (Inclosure 17). The ROK Representative acknowledged the withdrawal of the designation of this US invited contractor.

11. The US Representative noted for the record that the US SOFA Secretariat had furnished the following information to the ROK SOFA Secretariat in accordance with the provisions of the SOFA and Joint Committee decisions:

a. Five copies of reports on the US armed forces disposition of

4

cases for the month of December 1971.

b. One copy of pertinent information on cargo consigned to US armed forces non-appropriated fund organizations in the ROK for the month of January 1972.

c. Twenty copies of the report of US armed forces personnel, the civilian component, invited contractors, and the dependents of each, entering or departing the ROK during the month of January 1972.

d. Twenty copies of the USFK quarterly listing of all US invited contractor employees and dependents as of 31 December 1971.

12. The ROK Representative acknowledged the receipt of these reports as enumerated by the US Representative.

13. The ROK Representative proposed that the special press release commemorating the fifth anniversary of the entry into force of the SOFA on 9 February 1972, which was issued by the Joint Committee on 8 February 1972, be included in the minutes of this Joint Committee meeting (Inclosure 18).

14. The US Representative concurred in the ROK Representative's proposal that the joint ROK-US press release, which was issued in connection with the fifth anniversary of the entry into force of the ROK-US SOFA on 9 February 1972, be included in the minutes of this meeting. He noted that this special Joint Committee press release received good coverage in both the Korean and English language news media.

5

15. The ROK Representative presented a new task to the Finance (Personnel Affairs) Subcommittee (Inclosure 19). He stated that since the inception of SOFA, no customs declaration and certification forms had been designed specifically to apply to the imports under paragraph 3 of SOFA Article IX. For convenience, the forms for the purpose of various USFK imports under paragraph 2 of same Article had been utilized also for the importation of goods consigned to and for the personal use of SOFA personnel until the end of last year. He said that the ROK customs authorities recently have initiated an EDPS program to improve the formalities of overall customs clearance. Accordingly, they would like to develop a better formula applicable to both the purposes mentioned above. With this idea in mind, the ROK Representative proposed a task to the Finance (Personnel Affairs) Subcommittee to review the current customs clearance forms and to submit appropriate recommendations to the Joint Committee.

16. The US Representative concurred in the assignment of the specified task to the Finance (Personnel Affairs) Subcommittee.

17. The ROK Representative proposed that the next meeting of the Joint Committee be held at 1530, Thursday, 23 March 1972, in the ROK Capitol Building. The US Representative concurred.

18. The US Representative proposed that the press release for the seventy-first Joint Committee meeting, as prepared by our respective Secretaries and distributed in advance to both components of the

Committee be approved (Inclosure 20). The ROK Representative concurred.

19. The meeting was adjourned at 1425 hours.

20 Incl.

_____   _____

7

AGENDA FOR THE SEVENTY-FIRST MEETING
OF THE ROK-US JOINT COMMITTEE
1400 HOURS, 24 FEBRUARY 1972, US SOFA CONFERENCE ROOM

I.   Assignment of Tasks to Facilities and Areas Subcommittee.

       1. Two Tasks - ROK Presentation.

       2. Eight Tasks - US Presentation.

II.   Recommendations of Facilities and Areas Subcommittee - US Presentation.

III.   Consideration of Sixth Report and Recommendations of Ad Hoc Subcommittee on Civil-Military Relations - ROK and US Presentations.

IV.   Memoranda on the Designation of US Invited Contractors - US Presentation.

V.   Memorandum on the Withdrawal of Designation of US Invited Contractor - US Presentation.

VI.   Memoranda Presented to the ROK Government by the US in the Implementation of the SOFA - US Presentation.

VII. Press Release Relating to Fifth Anniversary of SOFA - ROK Presentation.

VIII. Assignment of Task to Finance (Personnel Affairs) Subcommittee - ROK Presentation.

IX.   Proposed Time of Next Meeting - 1530 Hours, Thursday, 23 March 1972, in the ROK Capitol Building.

X.   Agreement on Joint Press Release.

XI.   Adjourn

10 February 1972

MEMORANDUM FOR: Chairmen, Facilities and Areas Subcommittee

SUBJECT: Request for Use of Idle Land

1. SOFA provides in Article II, paragraph 2, that the Governments of the Republic of Korea and the United States may agree that facilities and areas or portions thereof shall be returned to the Republic of Korea or that additional facilities and areas may be provided.

2. Pursuant to paragraph 1 above it is requested that a recommendation be presented to the Joint Committee concerning a request for the use, by farmers for cultivation during the period of the farming season, of certain areas under US acquisition adjacent to Kunsan Air Base, Cholla-pukto.

KIM DONG-WHIE
Republic of Korea
Representative

ROBERT N. SMITH
Lieutenant General
United States Air Force
United States Representative

10 February 1972

MEMORANDUM FOR: Chairmen, Facilities and Areas Subcommittee

SUBJECT: Request for Release of Portion of Military Port for Construction of Public Beach

1. SOFA provides in Article II, paragraph 2, that the Governments of the Republic of Korea and the United States may agree that facilities and areas or portions thereof shall be returned to the Republic of Korea or that additional facilities and areas may be provided.

2. Pursuant to paragraph 1 above, it is requested that a recommendation be presented to the Joint Committee concerning a request for the release of certain areas adjacent to the USFK military port, located at Haeng-am-san, Chinhae, Kyungsang Nam-do, required for construction of a public beach.

KIM DONG-WHE
Republic of Korea
Representative

ROBERT N. SMITH
Lieutenant General
United States Air Force
United States Representative

24 February 1972

MEMORANDUM FOR: Chairmen, Facilities and Areas Subcommittee

SUBJECT: Requests of Release of Real Estate

1. SOFA provides in Article II, paragraph 2, that the Governments of the Republic of Korea and the United States may agree that facilities and areas or portions thereof shall be returned to the Republic of Korea or that additional facilities and areas may be provided.

2. Pursuant to paragraph 1 above, it is requested that recommendations be presented to the Joint Committee concerning requests for the following actions:

   a. Release of 11.467 acres of land, constituting a portion of Kanghwa-do Installation, currently held under Acquisition Nos. Inchon-268, ASCOM-379, and K-E-401, and located in Kanghwa-gun, Kyonggi-do. This request for release includes a total of 56 USFK-constructed buildings and facilities located on that Installation. This real estate has become excess to USFK requirements.

   b. Release of 37.89 acres of land, constituting the A-102 Airfield which is a portion of Market Installation held under Acquisition No. AAC-396, and located in Inchon City, Kyonggi-do. This request for release includes two Korean-constructed buildings and a total of 68 USFK-constructed buildings and facilities. This real estate has become excess to USFK requirements.

   c. Release of one Korean-constructed building (No. S-230), constituting a portion of the acquisition held under Acquisition No. PAC-Taegu-113, and located on Camp Henry Installation, Taegu City, Kyongsangbuk-do. This building has deteriorated beyong economical repair and maintenance.

219

d. Release of 13.36 acres of land, constituting Stonestown Installation, currently held under Acquisition No. SAC-PAC-135, and located
in Taejon City, Chungchongnam-do. This request for release includes
a total of 20 Korean-constructed buildings and facilities and a total of
70 USFK-constructed buildings and facilities which are located on the
Installation. This real estate has become excess to USFK requirements.

KIM DONG-WHIE
Republic of Korea
Representative

ROBERT N. SMITH
Lieutenant General
United States Air Force
United States Representative

24 February 1972

MEMORANDUM FOR: Chairmen, Facilities and Areas Subcommittee

SUBJECT: Requests for Extension of Temporary Use Permits

1. SOFA provides in Article II, paragraph 2, that the Governments of the Republic of Korea and the United States may agree that facilities and areas or portions thereof shall be returned to the Republic of Korea or that additional facilities and areas may be provided.

2. Pursuant to paragraph 1 above, it is requested that recommendations be presented to the Joint Committee concerning requests for the following actions:

   a. Extension of Temporary Use Permit K-G-T-14, involving 25 acres of river bed area located in Chilgok-gun, Kyongsangbuk-do, from 25 February 1972 through 24 February 1973. This land has been utilized since 1971, and there is a continuing need for its use as a source of gravel and sand materials for use in construction.

   b. Extension of Temporary Use Permit IC-T-15, involving 207.40 acres of land located in Yangju-gun, Kyonggi-do, from 1 April 1972 through 30 September 1972. This land has been utilized since 1962 as an ammunition demolition area, and there is a continuing need for its use for that purpose.

KIM DONG-WHIE
Republic of Korea
Representative

ROBERT N. SMITH
Lieutenant General
United States Air Force
United States Representative

**JOINT COMMITTEE
UNDER
THE REPUBLIC OF KOREA AND THE UNITED STATES
STATUS OF FORCES AGREEMENT**

24 February 1972

MEMORANDUM FOR: Chairmen, Facilities and Areas Subcommittee

SUBJECT: Request for Acquisition of an Easement

1. SOFA provides in Article II, paragraph 2, that the Governments of the Republic of Korea and the United States may agree that facilities and areas or portions thereof shall be returned to the Republic of Korea or that additional facilities and areas may be provided.

2. Pursuant to paragraph 1 above, it is requested that a recommendation be presented to the Joint Committee concerning a request for the acquisition, on a perpetual restrictive easement basis, of 0.66 acre (4,121 feet in length and 6 feet in width), located in Sihung-gun, Kyonggi-do. This real estate is required for the installation of underground communication cables.

KIM DONG-WHIE
Republic of Korea
Representative

ROBERT N. SMITH
Lieutenant General
United States Air Force
United States Representative

24 February 1972

MEMORANDUM FOR: Chairmen, Facilities and Areas Subcommittee

SUBJECT: Request for Acquisition of a Temporary Use Permit

1. SOFA provides in Article II, paragraph 2, that the Governments of the Republic of Korea and the United States may agree that facilities and areas or portions thereof shall be returned to the Republic of Korea or that additional facilities and areas may be acquired.

2. Pursuant to paragraph 1 above, it is requested that a recommendation be presented to the Joint Committee concerning a request for the acquisition of a Temporary Use Permit, involving 0.681 acre of land located in Suwon City, Kyonggi-do, for the period 1 June 1972 through 28 February 1973. This real estate is required to conduct exploratory water well drilling.

KIM DONG-WHIE
Republic of Korea
Representative

ROBERT N. SMITH
Lieutenant General
United States Air Force
United States Representative

REPUBLIC OF KOREA - UNITED STATES
FACILITIES AND AREAS SUBCOMMITTEE

17 February 1972

MEMORANDUM FOR: THE JOINT COMMITTEE

1. Subcommittee Members:

United States	Republic of Korea
BG Philip T. Boerger, Chairman	BG PAK Woo Bum, Chairman
COL Leonard Edelstein, Alt. Chairman	Mr. MIN Won Sik, Secty
LTC Edward W. Lingel, USAF	Mr. KANG Hong Suk, Asst Secty
MAJ William S. Littlefield, J4, USFK	LTC Shin Sang Pil
MAJ Allen D. Adams, USAFCS, K	Mr. KIM Hyung Kun
CPT James H. Smith, USAF	Mr. PAK Bung Hun
Mr. Francis K. Cook, J5, USFK	Mr. NOE Won Tae
Mr. S. F. O'Hop, ENJ-RE, Secty	Mr. PARK Byong Yong
Mr. E. H. Brummett, ENJ-RE,	Mr. DO Tae Ku
Alt. Secty	Mr. SUH Chin Hwan
	Mr. LEE Soung Woo
	Mr. PARK Daho Young
	Mr. BAE Jeung Sun

2. Subject of Recommendation: Request for Acquisition of Easement,
Joint Committee memorandum dated 22 April 1971.

3. Recommendation: <u>Task 980</u> The request for acquisition, on a perpetual
restrictive easement basis, of 8.22 acres of land (35,802 linear feet by
10 feet in width) at various locations throughout the area of responsibility
of I Corps (Group) Rear Area, has been approved by the Ministry of National
Defense. This real estate is required to insure uninterrupted telephonic
communications within the I Corps (Group) Rear Area. The Ministry of
National Defense and the USFK Engineer will prepare the necessary documents. It is recommended that the Joint Committee, SOFA, approve this
recommendation.

.24

<u>Task 980</u>

4. Security Classification: Unclassified.

Brigadier General PAK Woo Bum
Chairman, ROK Component
Facilities and Areas Subcommittee

Brigadier General Philip T. Boerger
Chairman, US Component
Facilities and Areas Subcommittee

2

REPUBLIC OF KOREA - UNITED STATES
FACILITIES AND AREAS SUBCOMMITTEE

17 February 1972

MEMORANDUM FOR: THE JOINT COMMITTEE

1. Subcommittee Members

United States   Republic of Korea

BG Philip T. Boerger, Chairman   BG PAK Woo Bum, Chairman
COL Leonard Edelstein, Alt. Chairman   Mr. MIN Won Sik, Secty
COL Eugene T. Blanton, USAF   Mr. KANG Hong Suk, Asst Secty
MAJ William S. Littlefield, J4, USFK   LTC SHIN Sang Pil
MAJ Allen D. Adams, USAFCS, K   Mr. KIM Young Sup
CPT James H. Smith, USAF   Mr. SONG Jae Kun
Mr. Francis K. Cook, J5, USFK   Mr. RHO Won Tae
Mr. S. F. O'Hop, ENJ-RE, Secty   Mr. SOUNG Baek Jon
Mr. E. H. Brummett, ENJ-RE,   Mr. DO Tae Ku
    Alt. Secty   Mr. SUH Chin Hwan
                                        Mr. LEE Soung Woo
                                        Mr. PARK Dahl Young
                                        Mr. BAE Jeung Sun

2. Subject of Recommendation: Request for the Acquisition of Temporary
Use Permit, Joint Committee memorandum dated 24 November 1971.

3. Recommendation: Task 1123   The request for acquisition, on a temporary
use basis, of 18.72 acres of river bed area located in Paju-gun, Kyonggi-do
(15.80 acres to provide river bed aggregates in support of a rock crushing plant
located thereon and 2.92 acres to provide an access road from the plant to the
borrow area), from 1 November 1971 through 31 October 1972 has been

<u>Task 1123</u>

accepted by the Ministry of National Defense with the stipulation that no
excessive digging or damage be done to the adjacent farm land or dikes.
This acquisition is in support of the 802d Engineer Battalion's roadway
improvement and maintenance requirements in the Paju area. The Ministry
of National Defense and the USFK Engineer will prepare the necessary
documents. It is recommended that the Joint Committee, SOFA, approve
this acquisition request.

4. Security Classification: Unclassified.

Brigadier General PAK Woo Bum
Chairman, ROK Component
Facilities and Areas Subcommittee

Brigadier General Philip T. Boerger
Chairman, US Component
Facilities and Areas Subcommittee

2

REPUBLIC OF KOREA - UNITED STATES
FACILITIES AND AREAS SUBCOMMITTEE

17 February 1972

MEMORANDUM FOR: THE JOINT COMMITTEE

1. Subcommittee Members:

United States	Republic of Korea
BG Philip T. Boerger, Chairman	BG PAK Woo Bum, Chairman
COL Leonard Edelstein, Alt. Chairman	Mr. MIN Won Sik, Secty
COL Eugene T. Blanton, USAF	Mr. KANG Hong Suk, Asst Secty
MAJ William S. Littlefield, J4, USFK	LTC SHIN Sang Pil
MAJ Allen D. Adams, USAFCS, K	Mr. KIM Young Sup
CPT James H. Smith, USAF	Mr. SONG Jae Kun
Mr. Francis K. Cook, J5, USFK	Mr. RHO Won Tae
Mr. S. F. O'Hop, ENJ-RE, Secty	Mr. SOUNG Baek Jon
Mr. E. H. Brummett, ENJ-RE,	Mr. DO Tae Ku
Alt. Secty	Mr. SUH Chin Hwan
	Mr. LEE Soung Woo
	Mr. PARK Dahl Young
	Mr. BAE Jeung Sun

2. Subject of Recommendation: Requests for Release of Real Estate, Joint Committee memorandum dated 27 January 1972.

3. Recommendation: <u>Tasks 1130-1136</u> The following requests for release of real estate have been accepted by the Ministry of National Defense.

a. <u>Task 1130</u> Release of 505.517 acres of land, constituting the Hyongga-ri Tank Range, currently held under Acq. No. 7X-5, located in Yonchon-gun, Kyonggi-do, subject to the conditions specified below. This request for release includes a total of four buildings and facilities located on the installation. The conditions attached to this request for release are that: (1) The I Corps (ROK/US) Group retain scheduling control over the range area activities; (2) The Republic of Korea Ministry of National Defense insure that this range will be made available only for the use and occupancy of the VI ROK Army Corps element solely for training range purposes; and (3) The VI ROK Army Corps element be solely responsible for the security and operational maintenance of all of the real property located at the Hyonggi-ri Tank Range.

b. **Task 1131** Release of 21.039 acres of land, constituting a portion of Camp Richmond installation held under Acq. Nos. ACS-300 and AAC-391, and located in Buchon-gun, Kyonggi-do. This request for release includes a total of 83 buildings and facilities, of which 55 are USFK-constructed and 28 are Korean-constructed. Excluded from this request for release are an overhead electric power line, three 25-KVA transformers, a water pipeline, and one water storage tank, with unrestricted right of entry/exit thereto, as well as 0.604 acre of easement land and 0.36 acre of land held on an exclusive use basis, as shown on maps in the possession of the Republic of Korea Ministry of National Defense and the Engineer, USFK.

c. **Task 1132** Release of 12.07 acres of land, constituting Tracy Installation held under Acq. No. SAC-673, and located in Seoul City. This request for release includes 80 USFK-constructed buildings and facilities and two Korean-constructed facilities. This real estate has become excess to USFK requirements.

d. **Task 1133** Release of 2.58 acres of land, constituting a portion of Yuma Installation held under Acq. No. AAC-397, and located in Inchon City, Kyonggi-do. This request for release includes 5,559 linear feet of 8-inch underground POL pipeline and one 570 square foot pump house. This real estate has become excess to USFK requirements.

e. **Task 1134** Release of 6.635 acres of land, constituting a portion of Alamo Installation held under Acq. Nos. 7X-13 and 7X-174, and located in Yonchon-gun, Kyonggi-do. This request for release includes a total of 29 USFK-constructed buildings and facilities located on the Installation. This real estate has become excess to USFK requirements.

f. **Task 1135** Release of 15.72 acres of land, constituting a portion of Camp Mercer Installation held under Acq. No. ASCOM-378, and located in Kimpo-gun, Kyonggi-do. This request for release includes a total of 17 USFK-constructed buildings and facilities located on the Installation. This real estate has become excess to USFK requirements.

2

g. **Task 1136** Release of 45.757 acres of land, constituting a portion of ASP #46 Installation held under Acq. No. SAC-715, and located in Seoul City. This request for release includes a total of 84 USFK-constructed buildings and facilities, and a total of 10 Korean-constructed buildings and facilities. This request for release is contigent upon the provision by the Republic of Korea Ministry of National Defense, without cost to the US Government, of the following activities: (1) Construction of approximately 460 linear feet of barbed wire security fencing at a specified location; (2) Construction of approximately 1,585 linear feet of barbed wire security fencing with one vehicle gate, at another location; (3) The relocation of Bldg. No. T-181 to the USFK-retained communication area; and (4) The installation of water and electric meters. The locations involved in activities (1) through (3) above are indicated on a map in possession of the Republic of Korea Ministry of National Defense and the USFK Engineer.

The Ministry of National Defense and the USFK Engineer will prepare the necessary documents. It is recommended that the Joint Committee, SOFA, approve these seven requests.

4. Security Classification: Unclassified.

Brigadier General PAK Woo Bum
Chairman, ROK Component
Facilities and Areas Subcommittee

Brigadier General Philip T. Boerger
Chairman, US Component
Facilities and Areas Subcommittee

230

3

MEMORANDUM FOR: The Joint Committee

SUBJECT: Designation of US Invited Contractor Under Article XV,
Stauts of Forces Agreement

1. References:

a. Paragraph 2, Article XV, Status of Forces Agreement.

b. US Chairman, Commerce Subcommittee letter, dated 19 Oct
71, subject as above (Incl 1).

c. ROK Chairman, Commerce Subcommittee letter, dated 1 Nov
71, subject as above (Incl 2).

2. The United States, after consultation with the ROK Commerce
Subcommittee and having duly considered its views, has designated
Minnesota (3M) Services Supply Limited as a US invited contractor
for execution of contract DAJB03-72-C-3034 for service and supply
of 3M office copying machines, US Army installations.

3. Pertinent data concerning US or third country national employees
will be provided to the Joint Secretariat by established reporting
procedures.

2 Incl
as

ROBERT N. SMITH
Lieutenant General, USAF
United States Representative
Joint Committee

REPUBLIC OF KOREA - UNITED STATES
COMMERCE SUBCOMMITTEE

19 October 1971

SUBJECT: Designation of US Invited Contractor Under Article XV, Status
of Forces Agreement

ROK Chairman, Commerce Subcommittee

1. Reference paragraph 2, Article XV of the Status of Forces Agreement.

2. The Government of the Republic of Korea is informed through this
written consultative process that the United States Forces, Korea, proposes to extend invited contractor status to the Minnesota (3M) Services
Supply Limited for contract for service and supply of 3M office copying
machines, US Army installations.

3. The following data are provided:

a. Company Name: Minnesota (3M) Services Supply Limited.

b. Local Address: APO 96301.

c. Identification of US Citizen Employees: To be provided after
award.

d. Number of US and ROK Employees: It is estimated that 2 US and
7 Koreans will be employed.

e. Reasons for Designation of an Invited Contractor:

(1) Limitation of US Procurement Law. Under Title 10 United States
Code 2202 promulgated by the Armed Services Procurement Regulations (ASPR),
procurement of supplies outside the US is subject to certain restrictions
because of the Balance of Payments Program. Reference is made to paragraph 6-805, Part 8, Section VI of the Armed Services Procurement Regulations. This particular law places certain limitations on the procurement
of supplies outside the US, but certain exceptions are provided in some
cases so that local indigenous sources may be used. The interpretation
in this particular case, of supplies for office equipment, is that no
direct exception is provided and that procurement must be made from US
firms.

SUBJECT: Designation of US Invited Contractor Under Article XV, Status
     of Forces Agreement

(2) Unavailability of materials and services by US standards. The
office machines and equipment are of US design and manufacture. It is
highly essential that the maintenance service and parts and supply sources
function in accordance with US standards of high reliability of operation,
minimum number of equipment failures and minimum down time for lack of
service, parts and supplies. By US standards the contractors are expected
to provide satisfactory performance to ordering activities with minimal
administrative aid. In this case, US standards of service are best
assured if the contract is US managed and supervised.

f. Location of Contract: US Army installations, Korea.

g. Type of Contract: Fixed Price Contract for Maintenance and Repair
of 3M office copying machines.

h. Length of Contract: Initially for 7 months, with option to extend
for 12 months.

i. USFK Sponsor: US Army Korea Procurement Agency.

RICHARD T. CANN
Colonel, US Army
United States Chairman
Commerce Subcommittee

2

MINISTRY OF COMMERCE AND INDUSTRY
REPUBLIC OF KOREA
SEOUL, KOREA

1 November 1971

Subject: Designation of US Invited Contractor under Article XV,
Status of Forces Agreement

US Chairman, Commerce Subcommittee

1. Reference:

a. Paragraph 2, Article XV, Status of Forces Agreement

b. US Commerce Subcommittee Memorandum of Consultation,
dated 19 October 1971 subject as above, pertaining to contract
for service and supply of 3M office copying machines, US Army
installations.

2. The US memorandum, reference 1b above, has been reviewed
and the government of the Republic of Korea understands the
requirement for an invited contractor in this instance.

Chung Min Kil
Chairman
Commerce Subcommittee, ROK

234

5 FEB 1972

MEMORANDUM FOR: The Joint Committee

SUBJECT: Designation of US Invited Contractor Under Article XV,
Status of Forces Agreement

1. References:

    a. Paragraph 2, Article XV, Status of Forces Agreement.

    b. US Chairman, Commerce Subcommittee letter, dated 22 Oct
1971, subject as above (Incl 1).

    c. ROK Chairman, Commerce Subcommittee letter, dated 1 Nov
1971, subject as above (Incl 2).

2. The United States, after consultation with the ROK Commerce
Subcommittee and having duly considered its views, has designated
Southern Air Transport, Incorporated as a US invited contractor
for execution of contract F11626-71-C-0042 for international air
transportation services for the Military Airlift Command in Korea.

3. Pertinent data concerning US or third country national employees
will be provided to the Joint Secretariat by established reporting
procedures.

2 Incl
as

ROBERT N. SMITH
Lieutenant General, USAF
United States Representative
Joint Committee

REPUBLIC OF KOREA - UNITED STATES
COMMERCE SUBCOMMITTEE

21 October 1971

SUBJECT: Designation of US Invited Contractor Under Article XV, Status
of Forces Agreement

ROK Chairman, Commerce Subcommittee

1. Reference paragraph 2, Article XV of the Status of Forces Agreement.

2. The Government of the Republic of Korea is informed through this
written consultative process that the United States Forces, Korea
proposes to extend invited contractor status to the Southern Air Transport, Inc., for international air transportation services for the
Military Airlift Command, United States Air Force.

3. The following data are provided:

a. Company Name: Southern Air Transport, Inc.

b. Local Address: Osan Air Base, Korea

c. Identification of US Citizen Employees: To be provided by
periodic reports.

d. Number of US and ROK Employees: One US, twenty-three Koreans
and one third-country national will be employed under this contract.

e. Reasons for Designation of an Invited Contractor:

(1) Security considerations. The contractor is required to transport classified cargo, registered mail and other regular mail for which
only US registered carriers are authorized to transport.

(2) Local unavailability of material and services required by US
standards. Contract specifies that the contractor will provide B-727
aircraft with guaranteed allowable cabin load of 16.5 ton cargo or 105
passengers and properly trained manpower for this type aircraft.

(3) Limitations of US Law. All equipment and operations must
comply with the Federal Aviation Regulations of the US Government.

236

INCL 1

SUBJECT: Designation of US Invited Contractor Under Article XV, Status
          of Forces Agreement

    f. <u>Location of Contract</u>: Air Force bases, Korea

    g. <u>Type of Contract</u>: Contract for air transportation services for
US military and other authorized personnel and cargo.

    h. <u>Length of Contract</u>: One year with option to extend three months.

    i. <u>USFK Sponsor</u>: US Air Forces Korea.

                        RICHARD T. CANN
                        Colonel, US Army
                        United States Chairman
                        Commerce Subcommittee

2

MINISTRY OF COMMERCE AND INDUSTRY
REPUBLIC OF KOREA
SEOUL, KOREA

1 November 1971

Subject: Designation of US Invited Contractor under Article XV,
           Status of Forces Agreement

US Chairman, Commerce Subcommittee

1. Reference:

    a. Paragraph 2, Article XV, Status of Forces Agreement

    b. US Commerce Subcommittee Memorandum of Consultation, dated
21 October 1971 subject as above, pertaining to contract for
international air transportation services for the Military Airlift
Command, United States Air Force, Korea

2. The US memorandum, reference 1b above, has been reviewed and
the government of the Republic of Korea understands the requirement
for an invited contractor in this instance.

                                Chung Mi Kil
                                Chairman
                                Commerce Subcommittee, ROK

5 FEB 1972

MEMORANDUM FOR: THE JOINT COMMITTEE

SUBJECT: Designation of US Invited Contractor under Article XV, Status of Forces Agreement

1. References:

   a. Paragraph 2, Article XV, Status of Forces Agreement.

   b. US Chairman, Commerce Subcommittee letter, dated 6 Oct 1971, subject as above (Incl 1).

   c. ROK Chairman, Commerce Subcommittee letter, dated 1 Nov 1971, subject as above (Incl 2).

2. The United States, after consultation with the ROK Commerce Subcommittee and having duly considered its views, has designated International Electronics Corporation as a US invited contractor for execution of contract GS-00S-07831 for repair and maintenance of non-tactical radio equipment.

3. Pertinent data concerning US or third country national employees will be provided to the Joint Secretariat by established reporting procedures.

2 Incl
as

ROBERT N. SMITH
Lieutenant General, USAF
United States Representative
Joint Committee

REPUBLIC OF KOREA – UNITED STATES
COMMERCE SUBCOMMITTEE

6 October 1971

SUBJECT: Designation of US Invited Contractor Under Article XV,
Status of Forces Agreement

ROK Chairman, Commerce Subcommittee

1. Reference paragraph 2, Article XV of the Status of Forces Agreement.

2. The Government of the Republic of Korea is informed through this
written consultative process that the United States Forces, Korea, proposes to extend invited contractor status to the International Electronics
Corporation for repair and maintenance of non-tactical radio equipment.

3. The following data are provided:

   a. Company Name: International Electronics Corporation

   b. Local Address: APO 96301

   c. Identification of US Citizen Employees: To be reported monthly.

   d. Number of US and ROK Employees: It is estimated that four (4) US
and fourteen (14) Korean personnel will be employed under this contract.

   e. Reasons for Designation of an Invited Contractor:

   (1) Security requirements of the US Air Force. The contractor will
be involved in the operation and maintenance of radio nets which directly
affect the mission capabilities of the US Air Force. The increasing Air
Force mission in Korea frequently requires revision of one or more nets
and the contractor's assistance is required in system layout and planning,
equipment selection and technical operation which may be classified and
contain information not releasable to foreign nationals.

   (2) Unavailability of materials or services required by US standards:

   (a) Fully qualified, trained and experienced supervisors and technical personnel are essential to insure that all equipment is installed,
tested and placed into operation to meet all specifications. The management of US equipment and supplies placed in the hands of the contractor
requires that the contractor be responsible for and responsive to USAF
policies and requirements.

SUBJECT: Designation of US Invited Contractor Under Article XV,
            Status of Forces Agreement

(b) The contractor is required to comply with various Air Force manuals, regulations and other applicable publications which are technical in nature. All equipment is US design and manufactured and must be maintained to standards which can best be met by using US supervisory personnel.

(c) It is the policy of the manufacturer to provide price lists, operating and repair manuals and associated data only to their authorized representatives to warrant all equipment. This warranty is void if the equipment is serviced by other than an authorized representative.

(d) Replacement parts are available only from the manufacture's representative.

f. Location of Contract: US Air Forces bases in Korea

g. Type of Contract: Fixed Price requirements contract for maintenance and repair of non-tactical radio equipment.

h. Length of Contract: One year with option to extend for periods of one year.

i. USFK Sponsor: US Air Force, Korea

RICHARD T. CANN
Colonel, US Army
United States Chairman
Commerce Subcommittee

2

MINISTRY OF COMMERCE AND INDUSTRY
REPUBLIC OF KOREA
SEOUL, KOREA

1 November 1971

Subject : Designation of US Invited Contractor under Article XV,
Status of Foreces Agreement

US Chairman, Commerce Subcommittee

1. Reference:

    a. Paragraph 2, Article XV, Status of Forces Agreement

    b. US Commerce Subcommittee Memorandum of Consultation,
dated 6 October 1971 subject as above, pertaining to contract
for repair and maintenance of non-tactical reoio equipment,
US Air Force, Korea.

2. The US memorandum, reference 1b above, has been reviewed
and the government of the Republic of Korea understands the
requirement for an invited contractor in this instance.

                    Chung Jin Hil
                    Chairmen
                    Commerce Subcommittee, ROK

242

5 FEB 1972

MEMORANDUM FOR: The Joint Committee

SUBJECT: Designation of US Invited Contractor Under Article XV, Status of Forces Agreement

1. References:

    a. Paragraph 2, Article XV, Status of Forces Agreement.

    b. US Chairman, Commerce Subcommittee letter, dated 29 July 1971, subject as above (Incl 1).

    c. ROK Chairman, Commerce Subcommittee letter, dated 11 August 1971, subject as above (Incl 2).

2. The United States, after consultation with the ROK Commerce Subcommittee and having duly considered its views, has designated Universal American Ent. Inc., the US member firm of the ROK - US joint venture, as a US invited contractor for execution of contract DAJB03-72-C-6049 for facilities engineering (Pyongtaek and Sihung-ni).

3. Pertinent data concerning US or third country national employees will be provided to the Joint Secretariat by established reporting procedures.

2 Incl
as

ROBERT N. SMITH
Lieutenant General, USAF
United States Representative
Joint Committee

REPUBLIC OF KOREA - UNITED STATES
COMMERCE SUBCOMMITTEE

29 July 1971

SUBJECT: Designation of US Invited Contractor Under
Article XV, Status of Forces Agreement

ROK Chairman, Commerce Subcommittee

1. Reference: Paragraph 2, Article XV, of the Status of
Forces Agreement.

2. The Government of the Republic of Korea is informed
through this written consultative process that the United
States Forces, Korea, proposes to extend invited contractor
status to the US member of the successful negotiated bidder
among qualified joint venture firms for the forthcoming
Facilities Engineering contract for the Pyongtaek/Sihungni
Area, Korea.

3. The following data are provided:

a. <u>Company Name:</u> Names of the US firms to be considered
are inclosed.

b. <u>Local Address:</u> To be submitted upon designation.

c. <u>Identification of US Citizen Employees:</u> To be submitted
upon designation.

d. <u>Number of US and ROK Employees:</u> It is estimated that
14 US and 466 Korean personnel will be employed.

e. <u>Reasons for Designation of a Joint Venture Contractor:</u>
Open competitive bidding is not practical because:

(1) Security considerations for handling the classified
portions of the project require US personnel.

(2) Special management and technical skills are required.

(3) Management experience in this type of operation is
required.

244

INCL 1

SUBJECT: Designation of US Invited Contractor   29 July 1971
         Under Article XV, Status of Forces Agreement

    f. Location of Contract: Pyongtaek/Sihungni Area, Korea.

    g. Type of Contract: A Cost-Plus-Fixed Fee contract
for the management, operation, maintenance and repair of
real property facilities.

    h. Length of Contract: 1 January 1972 through 30 June
1972. The contract will have a 30 day transition period
at the end of the contract.

    i. Sponsoring Component Commander: Commanding General,
Eighth United States Army.

                              RICHARD T. CANN
                              Colonel, US Army
                              United States Chairman
                              Commerce Subcommittee

MINISTRY OF COMMERCE AND INDUSTRY
REPUBLIC OF KOREA
SEOUL, KOREA

11 August 1971

Subject: Designation of US Invited Contractor under Article XV,
          Status of Forces Agreement

US Chairman, Commerce Subcommittee

1. Reference:

    a. Paragraph 2, Article XV, Status of Forces Agreement

    b. US Commerce Subcommittee Memorandum of Consultation, dated
29 July 1971, subject as above, pertaining to contract for Facilities
Engineering contract for the Pyongtaek/Sihungni Area, Korea.

2. The US memorandum reference 1b above, has been reviewed and the
Government of the Republic of Korea understands the requirement for
an invited contractor status to the US member firm of the ROK-US
joint venture contract in this instance.

                              Chung Min Kil
                              Chairman
                              Commerce Subcommittee, ROK

246.

Incl :

5 FEB 1972

MEMORANDUM FOR: The Joint Committee

SUBJECT: Designation of US Invited Contractor Under Article XV, Status of Forces Agreement

1. References:

    a. Paragraph 2, Article XV, Status of Forces Agreement.

    b. US Chairman, Commerce Subcommittee letter, dated 20 Oct 1971, subject as above (Incl 1).

    c. ROK Chairman, Commerce Subcommittee letter, dated 1 Nov 1971, subject as above (Incl 2).

2. The United States, after consultation with the ROK Commerce Subcommittee and having duly considered its views, has designated Air America, Incorporated as a US invited contractor for execution of contract DOT-FA72PC-907 for maintenance of FAA T-39 aircraft, Korea.

3. Pertinent data concerning US or third country national employees will be provided to the Joint Secretariat by established reporting procedures.

2 Incl
as

ROBERT N. SMITH
Lieutenant General, USAF
United States Representative
Joint Committee

247

REPUBLIC OF KOREA - UNITED STATES
COMMERCE SUBCOMMITTEE

20 October 1971

SUBJECT: Designation of US Invited Contractor Under Article XV, Status
of Forces Agreement

ROK Chairman, Commerce Subcommittee

1. Reference paragraph 2, Article XV of the Status of Forces Agreement.

2. The Government of the Republic of Korea is informed through this
written consultative process that the United States Forces, Korea
proposes to extend invited contractor status to Air America, Inc. for
maintenance of T-39 aircraft.

3. The following data are provided:

a. Company Name: Air America

b. Local Address: Osan Air Base, Korea

c. Identification of US Citizen Employees: To be provided by
periodic reports.

d. Number of US and ROK Employees: One US and nine Koreans.

e. Reasons for Designation of an Invited Contractor:

(1) Local unavailability of material and services required by US
standards. Contract specifies that the contractor must possess required
technical skills and supplies for maintenance and repair services of the
T-39 aircraft in accordance with FAA regulations. Mechanics are trained
by FAA in accordance with FAA regulations.

(2) Limitations of US Law. All maintenance services must comply
with the Federal Aviation Regulations of the US Government.

f. Location of Contract: Air Force bases, Korea

g. Type of Contract: T-39 aircraft maintenance

249 INCL 1

SUBJECT: Designation of US Invited Contractor Under Article XV, Status
of Forces Agreement

h. Length of Contract: One year with option to extend for additional
periods of one year.

i. USFK Sponsor: US Air Forces Korea

RICHARD/T. CANN
Colonel, US Army
United States Chairman
Commerce Subcommittee

2

MINISTRY OF COMMERCE AND INDUSTRY
REPUBLIC OF KOREA
SEOUL, KOREA

1 November 1971

Subject : Designation of US Invited Contractor under Article XV,
Status of Forces Agreement

US Chairman, Commerce Subcommittee

1. Reference:

   a. Paragraph 2, Article XV, Status of Forces Agreement

   b. US Commerce Subcommittee Memorandum of Consultation,
dated 20 October 1971 subject as above, pertaining to contract
for maintenance of T-39 aircraft, Korea.

2. The US memorandum, reference 1b above, has been reviewed and
the government of the Republic of Korea understands the requirement
for an invited contractor in this instance.

Chung Min Kil
Chairman
Commerce Subcommittee, ROK

250.

INCL 2

MEMORANDUM FOR: The Joint Committee

SUBJECT: Withdrawal of US Invited Contractor Status Under Article
XV, SOFA

1. Reference: Paragraph 2(a), Article XV, Status of Forces Agreement.

2. Morrison-Knudsen International Company, Incorporated has completed all contracts with the United States which require work in the Republic of Korea and in accordance with the above reference, their designation as an invited contractor is withdrawn.

7M Romanich Capt USN

for ROBERT N. SMITH
Lieutenant General, USAF
United States Representative
Joint Committee

DISPOSITION FORM

For use of this form, see AR 340-15; the proponent agency is The Adjutant General's Office.

REFERENCE OR OFFICE SYMBOL	SUBJECT
USFK-AJ	Entry/Exit Report (ROK/US SOFA)

TO	FROM	DATE	CMT 1
ACofS, J5	ACofS, J1	16 Feb 72 SSG Smith/3181	

1. Reference: USFK PD 7-20, subject: USFK Personnel Entering and Departing the Republic of Korea.

2. In accordance with the above reference, the following subject report for Jan 1972 is submitted.

Airport of Entry/Exit	US Armed Forces		Civilian Components		Invited Contractors		Dependents (Combined Total)	
	ARR	DPT	ARR	DPT	ARR	DPT	ARR	DPT
Osan	5,149	6,671	110	113	207	82	112	176
Kwang Ju	258	234	8	9	0	0	0	0
Kunsan	167	318	0	0	0	0	0	0
Pusan	10	18	3	6	0	0	26	66
Taegu	221	318	17	13	0	0	7	21
Total	5,805	7,559	138	141	207	82	145	263

DANA F. McFALL, JR
Colonel, USAF
ACofS, J1

252

DA FORM 2496 REPLACES DD FORM 96, EXISTING SUPPLIES OF WHICH WILL BE
1 FEB

ROK-US Joint Committee Press Release
Fifth Anniversary of Entry into Force of SOFA
9 February 1972

The fifth anniversary of the entry into force of the ROK-US Status of Forces Agreement (SOFA) is being observed on 9 February 1972. The ROK-US SOFA is a comprehensive agreement containing 31 articles covering almost all facets of the relations between the ROK and US Governments relating to the presence of US military forces in Korea. The SOFA provides that this agreement will remain in force while the 1954 ROK-US Defense Treaty remains in force unless terminated earlier by agreement between the two Governments.

The successful implementation of the SOFA during its first five years has been the work of the ROK-US Joint Committee which was established in accordance with SOFA provisions to implement this Agreement and to deal with all problems except those concerning telecommunications. This Government-to-Government body, which includes a ROK Representative who is the Director of the Bureau of European and American Affairs and a US Representative who is the Chief of Staff, United States Forces, Korea, has held seventy formal meetings and innumerable other conferences in the last five years, and has taken up hundreds of topics relating to the implementation of the ROK-US SOFA. The current ROK Representative, Mr. KIM Dong-Whie, Director of the European and American Bureau of the Foreign Ministry, is assisted on the Joint Committee by eight senior Bureau directors from six major Ministries as well as by a SOFA Secretariat which is headed by the Chief of the North America Second Section of the MOFA, Mr. KIM Young Sup. The US Representative who, for the past 34 months, has been Lieutenant General Robert N. Smith, Chief of Staff, USFK, is supported on the US component of the Joint Committee, by representatives of all the major components of USFK as well as by the USFK Staff Judge Advocate, an Embassy SOFA Political Advisor, and a US SOFA Secretariat which is headed by the senior American civilian officer in USFK, Mr. Robert A. Kinney.

Since the Joint Committee deals with all problems relating to the presence of US forces in the ROK, it has organized 12 joint ROK-US Subcommittees for the purpose of giving advice and making recommendations to the Joint Committee. During the first five years of operations, the Joint Committee has assigned a total of 1212 tasks to these Subcommittees. The Subcommittees have submitted mutually agreed recommendations on 1176 of these tasks, which, in turn, have been approved by the ROK-US Joint Committee. Many of the 36 tasks outstanding at this time were recently assigned to the respective Subcommittees for deliberation and recommendation. The SOFA provides that in the event the Joint Committee cannot resolve a problem, the problem shall be referred to the respective Governments. Thus far, in its

2

first five years of operations, the Joint Committee has not referred any problems to higher levels of their Governments for it has either resolved them on a mutually satisfactory basis, or is still working on them.

One of the busiest of the twelve Joint Committee Subcommittees is its Facilities and Areas Subcommittee, which deals with the acquisition and release of facilities and areas required by the United States military forces in the ROK. During the first five years of the SOFA, the Joint Committee has assigned 1139 tasks to this Subcommittee, and the Subcommittee, in turn, has submitted 1113 recommendations which have been accepted by the Joint Committee. Only 26 tasks are outstanding in this Subcommittee as of the end of the first five years of the SOFA, ten of which were assigned within the past two weeks.

The SOFA provides that the ROK Government may assume criminal jurisdiction over USFK personnel under certain circumstances, in accordance with the provisions of the SOFA Criminal Jurisdiction Article (XXII). From 1967 through 30 January 1972, the ROK Government had assumed jurisdiction over US personnel in 191 cases with 157 convictions and three acquittals thus far. Of the 157 personnel convicted, 114 were fined, 36 had confinement suspended, and seven were sent to the ROK prison at Suwon. At present, only one US citizen who is in Korea under the SOFA is serving his term in a ROK

3

255

prison. Many of the cases involving US personnel in Korea, over which the US military authorities have jurisdiction in accordance with SOFA provisions, have been tried by US military courts martial. The ROK Government, however, assumes jurisdiction over cases "of particular importance" to the Republic of Korea.

The SOFA Labor Article (XVII) has exerted a positive influence in developing stable and effective labor relations between the USFK and its more than 27,000 Korean direct-hire and US invited contractor employees. Provisions of Article XVII relating to mediation of disputes has provided an effective instrument for resolution of disputes between the Foreign Organizations Employees Union (FOEU) and the USFK. USFK wage levels for its Korean employees are established on the basis of periodic wage surveys in the ROK. The enlightened labor relations policies of the USFK, coupled with   close cooperation of the FOEU and the ROK Government have resulted in continuing improvement in the generally favorable labor relations between the Korean nationals working for USFK and the US command in Korea. In the first five years of the SOFA, all labor disputes have been settled in accordance with provisions of the SOFA.

The SOFA has assigned the responsibility for the settlement of most claims involving USFK personnel to the ROK Government, and through 31 January 1972, a total of 3664 claims have been processed

4

under Article XXIII of the SOFA. Of these claims, a total of 2268 have been paid on the agreed basis of 75 percent by the United States and 25 percent by the Republic of Korea. A total of 149 claims out of the 3664 submitted have been disallowed.

In its operation, the Joint Committee has met the changing situations confronting it and it has provided that in urgent situations, exigent action can be taken by the US and ROK Representatives without formally convening a Joint Committee meeting. A recent illustration of the dynamic operation of the Joint Committee is its establishment of an Ad Hoc Subcommittee on Civil-Military Relations in September 1971 in order to deal more effectively with problems in civil-military relations in the Korean communities adjacent to US military installations. This Subcommittee has made information gathering field trips to almost all the major US bases and adjacent Korean communities in Korea, and thus far has submitted a series of 19 recommendations, all of which were approved by the Joint Committee, to improve relations between US military personnel and the Korean people. The US-ROK Ad Hoc Subcommittee has supported the current program of the ROK Government to improve the conditions in these camp communities through the ROK inter-ministerial "Base Community Clean-Up Committee."

The Ad Hoc Subcommittee on Civil-Military Relations has seven panels which work on specific areas of civil-military relations, inclu-

5

257

ding local community and governmental relations, ROK police-US military police cooperation and coordination, health and sanitation, narcotics and drug control, larceny and black marketing, race relations and equality of treatment, and people-to-people projects. It is anticipated that the camp communities will be better and more comfortable for all concerned as a result of these activities.

Other Joint Committee subcommittees have been organized to function in various areas of SOFA responsibility, including Criminal Jurisdiction, Civil Jurisdiction, Finance, Commerce, Transportation, Entry and Exit, and Labor, respectively. Only the Joint Committee, however, can make decisions; the Subcommittees only give advice and make reccommendations.

During its first five years of operation, the ROK-US Joint Committee has demonstrated that the ROK-US SOFA is a living and vital agreement which has exerted a positive influence in the promotion of continued ROK-US friendship and strengthening our mutual defense against Communist aggression.

6

24 February 1972

MEMORANDUM FOR: Chairmen, Finance (Personnel Affairs)
Subcommittee

SUBJECT: Declaration and Certification on Imports Consigned to
Persons Subject to the ROK-US SOFA

1. Reference: Recommendation of the Finance (Personnel Affairs)
Subcommittee on the subject of determination of procedures relating
specifically to the forms and methods of presentation of the appropriate certification to be made on various USFK imports, approved by
the ROK-US Joint Committee on 11 April 1967, and contained as Inclosure 5 to the official minutes of the fifth meeting of the ROK-US Joint
Committee on 11 April 1967.

2. The declaration and certification process as described in reference
has to date been applied not only to imports by the agencies specified
in paragraph 2 of SOFA Article IX, but also to imports consigned to individuals who are subject to the ROK-US SOFA.

3. It is requested that mutual consultation be undertaken to determine
whether any revision is required in current procedures in effect for the
declaration and certification of imports consigned by name to persons
who are subject to the ROK-US SOFA. If it is determined that such revision is required, it is further requested that a recommendation be
transmitted to the Joint Committee on this subject.

KIM DONG-WHIE
Republic of Korea
Representative

ROBERT N. SMITH
Lieutenant General
United States Air Force
United States Representative

JOINT ROK-US PRESS RELEASE
SEVENTY-FIRST ROK-US JOINT COMMITTEE MEETING
24 FEBRUARY 1972

The ROK-US Joint Committee received the sixth report and seven additional recommendations of its Ad Hoc Subcommittee on Civil-Military Relations at its seventy-first meeting held in the US SOFA Conference Room on 24 February. The Joint Committee has thus far approved 26 recommendations of the Ad Hoc Subcommittee and its seven panels, which are designed to improve relations between American servicemen and the Korean people.

The Joint Committee also approved nine recommendations of its Facilities and Areas Subcommittee and assigned ten new tasks to that Subcommittee.

The US Representative, LTG Robert N. Smith, presided at this Joint Committee meeting and designated five US invited contractors, in accordance with Joint Committee procedures. The next meeting of the Committee is scheduled to be held on 23 March in the ROK Capitol Building with the ROK Representative, Mr. KIM Dong-Whie, presiding.

260

기 안 용 지

분류기호 문서번호	미이 720 -	(전 화 번 호　　　)	전결규정　조　항 국장　전 결 사 항
처 리 기 간			
시 행 일 자			국　　　장
보 존 년 한			

보 조 기 관	과 장	(서명)		협	

기 안 책 임 자	김성실	북미 2과 (72. 3. 1)

경 유	
수 신	수신처 참조
참 조	

제 목	한.미 합동위원회 회의록 송부

　　1.　한.미간 군대지위협정에 따른 한.미 합동위원회 제 71차회의가

72. 2. 24. 개최되었는 바, 동 회의 회의록을 별첨 송부하오니 합동위

결의사항중 귀 부 소관사항을 시행하시고 그 결과를 당부에 통보하여

주시기 바랍니다.

　　2.　본 회의록은 한.미 양측의 합의에 의하여서만 공개할수 있는

문서이오니 유념하시기 바랍니다.

첨부 : 합동위원회 제 71차 회의록.　끝.

수신처 : 법무부장관 (법무심장, 검찰국장, 출 입국 관미국장),

　　　　국방부장관 (기획국장, 시설국장),　재무부장관 (세관국장,

　　　　세제국장), 상공부장관 (상역국장),　노동청장 (노정국장),

　　　　교통부장관 (종합수송담당관),　내무부장관 (치안국장),

경제기획원장관 (물가정책관), 주미대사, 주일대사, 주중 대사,

주 비대사.

262

SOFA 한.미 합동위가 채택한 합의 사항 (미次 会議ᆞ)

1. 지방 행정관계 : 없음.

2. 한.미 군경 협조문제 : 없음.

3. 보건위생문제 (Panel on Health and Sanitation)

   1) 건의제목 : 면세 특권없는 한국인의 한국 관광협회소속 유흥
      업체 줄입

      내 용 : (1) 유흥업체 소유자 및 지배인은 유흥업체내에
              있는 한국남자가 동 유흥업체와 정당한 관련성을
              가지고 있느냐를 확인할것.

              (2) 유흥업체 소유자 및 지배인은 유흥업체를 무상
              줄입하는 위안부가 동 업체와 정당한 관계를
              갖고, 또한 필요한 현행 보건증을 소지하고
              있는지를 확인할것.

              (3) 국적을 불문하고 미성년자는 고용되거나 줄입
              못하도록 감독할것.

   2) 건의제목 : 유흥구역내의 한국 관광협회 소속이 아닌 음식점의
      위생문제

      내 용 : (1) 한국 관광협회소속 유흥업체 소재 구역내에있는
              음식점 (막걸리집 및 대포집 포함) 에 대한
              보건위생 검열을 강학하고 동 구역내에있는

263

음식 취급자들로 하여금 한국법령에 의한 기본적
위생요건을 준수토록 할것.

(2) 상기 검역구역을 확장하여 음식점 관계자가 거주
하거나, 대여하였거나, 또는 잠정적으로 타인이
이동케되는 주변 주택구역까지 포함케함.

(3) 상기 음식점 출입구에 위생검열 표식을 뚜렷하게
게시하게하고 이러한 검열표식을 게시하지않은
음식점 또는 구역에는 미군 출입 제한구역으로
선포 할것임.

4. 마약단속 문제 (Panel on Narcotics and Drug Control)

1) 건의제목 : 교육 계획과 운영방법을 통하여 한.미 군경 합동조사반의
친선 도모

내 용 : 친선도모 프로그램은 한.미 군경 합동조사반이 공동
으로 추진할것.

2) 건의제목 : 마약과 습관성 약품의 불법거래 및 매매행위에 대한
통제

내 용 : (1) 미군 우편시설을 통하여 마약 및 부정약품이
한국에 불법 반입되는 것을 방지하기 위하여 미군
당국은 우편경로를 통한 약품의 불법유입을 방지
토록 모든노력을 경주할것.

(2) 마약과 부정약품의 상습 복용자에 대하여 아래와
같은 통제를 강구할것 :

264

(가) 미군당국은 상습 복용자의 신원을 확인
하여 분리치료 및 이들을 후송시킬것.

(나) 한국당국은 마약을 상습 복용하는 위안부
들의 영업행위 금지토록할것.

(3) 마약 거래자와 마약 초기 복용자에 대하여
적절한 행정적 또는 형사적 조치를 취할것.

3) 건의제목 : 주한미군에 대한 약품판매 통제

내 용 : 1970. 11. 3. 공표한 대통령령 제5378호에 포함
되는 약품의 판매는 여하한 경우에도 의사의 처방
없이는 미군에게 판매하지말것.

5. 도난 및 암시장문제 (Panel on Larceny and Black Marketing)

1) 건의제목 : 도난 및 암거래문제 방지책

내 용 : 주한미군 당국은 미군장비를 훔쳐서 한국인에게
판매하는 미군인에 대한 처벌결과를 요약형식으로
한국정부에 통보할것.

2) 건의제목 : 도난 및 암거래문제 방지책

내 용 : 주한미군 당국은 한국관계 당국과 협조하여 P.X.
및 그 미써리 (Commissary)의 제한품목을
더욱 추가할것이며, 군인 사병이 필요한 적적량
이상의 물품이 흘러나오지 않도록 감시하는 방지책을
더욱 보강할것.

265

6. 인종차별문제 (Panel on Race Relations and Equality of Treatment)

   건의제목 : 기지촌 한국인의 바, 나이트클럽 및 기타 유흥시설의 명칭

   내   용 : 대한민국 관계 정부당국은 유흥시설의 명칭이 한국인에게 불쾌하거나 인종배척 또는 인종차별을 의미할때는 미군기지 사령관과 협조하여 동 클럽의 명칭을 검토할것. 따라서 관계 미군당국은 이러한 유흥시설 명칭의 변경이유와 필요성을 미군인에게 주지시키는 교육을 하도록 노력할것.

7. 대민관계문제 (Panel on People-to-People Projects)

   1) 건의제목 : 한국학생과 주한미군 과의 우호친선계획 및 예산지원

      내   용 : (1) 한.미 양 당국은 한국학생과 주한미군 과의 친선 도모를 장려하여 회합 및 여행등에 의한 교육 활동, 합동경기, 오락등 여러가지 프로그램을 시행할것.

                (2) 시설 사회단체 및 전문기관으로부터 지원을 최대로 얻기위하여 한국학생과 주한미군의 친선계획에 대한 적절한 홍보활동을 할것.

   2) 건의제목 : 국제친선협회 한국지부 및 한국내의 친선회의 승인과 지원

      내   용 : 한국정부와 주한미군 당국은 국제친선협회 (PTP)

246

한국지부의 설립과 한.미 친선관계를 도모함에 있어
서의 역할을 인정할것.   또한 한국 내의 제반 친선
협회 설립을 장려하고 지원할것.

247

These minutes are considered as official documents pertaining to both Governments and will not be released without mutual agreement.

MINUTES OF THE SEVENTY-FIRST MEETING

24 February 1972
Headquarters
US Forces, Korea
Seoul, Korea

1. The meeting was convened at 1400 hours by Lieutenant General Robert N. Smith, the US Representative, who presided at the meeting. A copy of the agenda is attached as Inclosure 1.

2. The following were in attendance:

ROK	US
Mr. KIM Dong-Whie	LTG Robert N. Smith, USAF
Mr. LEE Chong Won	Captain Frank M. Romanick, USN
MG CHO Jae Joon	COL David P. Heekin, USA
BG PAK Woo Dum	COL Carl G. Schneider, USAF
Mr. JUNG Ik Won	COL Bruce T. Coggins, USA
Mr. KIM Young Cup	Mr. Richard W. Finch, US Embassy
Mr. KIM Kee Joe	Mr. Robert A. Kinney, USFK
Mr. CHUNG Tai Ik	MAJ Dick J. Petersen, USAF
Mr. KWON Chan	Mr. Francis K. Cook, USFK

3. The ROK Representative stated that he had two tasks which were already assigned to the Facilities and Areas Subcommittee on an exigent basis in the interval since the last Joint Committee meeting. He said that these two prior assigned tasks consist of one request for the limited use by Korean farmers of certain areas adjacent to Kunsan Air Base (Inclosure 2) and one request for the release of certain areas adjacent to the USFK military port in Chinhae for the construction of a public beach (Inclosure 3). He proposed that the prior assignment of these two tasks to the Facilities and Areas Subcommittee be noted in the minutes of this meeting. The US Representative concurred.

4. The US Representative presented eight new tasks for assignment to the Facilities and Areas Subcommittee. These consisted of one request for the acquisition of an easement (Inclosure 4), one request for the acquisition of a Temporary Use Permit (Inclosure 5),

71st JC
24 Feb 72

These minutes are considered as official documents pertaining to both Governments and will not be released without mutual agreement.

two requests for the extension of existing Temporary Use Permits (Inclosure 6), and four requests for the release of parcels of real estate (Inclosure 7). He stated that details concerning these eight tasks were contained in memoranda which have been distributed to both sides. He proposed that these eight new tasks be assigned to the Facilities and Areas Subcommittee, and the ROK Representative concurred.

5. The US Representative presented nine recommendations received from the Facilities and Areas Subcommittee, including one recommendation concerning the acquisition of an easement (Inclosure 8), one recommendation involving the acquisition of a Temporary Use Permit (Inclosure 9), and seven recommendations for the release of parcels of real estate (Inclosure 10). He stated that details concerning these recommendations were included in memoranda which had been distributed to both sides. He proposed that the Joint Committee approve these nine recommendations of the Facilities and Areas Subcommittee and the ROK Representative concurred.

6. The ROK Representative stated that he was happy to note that the Ad Hoc Subcommittee on Civil-Military Relations had made significant progress thus far in solving many difficult problems in the military base communities. He proposed that the sixth report of the Ad Hoc Subcommittee together with seven recommendations from three of its panels be approved and recorded in the minutes of this Joint Committee meeting (Inclosure 11).

7. The US Representative concurred in approval of the sixth report of the Ad Hoc Subcommittee on Civil-Military Relations, including seven additional recommendations of three of its panels. He stated that he was glad to note the continued progress of the Ad Hoc Subcommittee, as well as the vigorous efforts of the ROK Government to deal with the problems of the camp communities through its own "Base Community Clean-Up Committee." He said that these Korean and joint ROK-US programs should result in significant improvements in civil-military relations, thereby further strengthening our mutual defense.

8. The US Representative presented memoranda to the Joint Committee informing the Government of the ROK of the designation of five US invited contractors under Article XV of the SOFA. These designations were made after consultations between ROK and US Commerce Subcommittee personnel in accordance with Joint Committee procedures. He stated that the invited contractors so designated were International Electronics Corporation (Inclosure 12); Air American, Incorporated

2

71st JC
24 Feb 72

These minutes are considered as official documents pertaining to both Governments and will not be released without mutual agreement.

(Inclosure 13); Southern Air Transport, Incorporated (Inclosure 14); Minnesota (3M) Services Supply Limited (Inclosure 15); and Universal American Enterprises, Incorporated (Inclosure 16). He said that each of these companies had one contract and that the contract of Universal American Enterprises, Incorporated was in joint venture with a Korean firm. He stated that pertinent data concerning employees of these invited contractors would be provided to the Government of the ROK in accordance with mutually agreed procedures.

9. The ROK Representative acknowledged the designation of five invited contractors and he noted that agreed procedures had been duly observed in these designations.

10. The US Representative presented a memorandum to the Joint Committee informing the Government of the ROK that Morrison-Knudsen International Company, Incorporated, had completed all contracts with the US which require work in the ROK and consequently their designation as an invited contractor is withdrawn (Inclosure 17). The ROK Representative acknowledged the withdrawal of the designation of this US invited contractor.

11. The US Representative noted for the record that the US SOFA Secretariat had furnished the following information to the ROK SOFA Secretariat in accordance with the provisions of the SOFA and Joint Committee decisions:

a. Five copies of reports on tne US armed forces disposition of cases for the month of December 1971.

b. One copy of pertinent information on cargo consigned to US armed forces non-appropriated funds organizations in the ROK for the month of January 1972.

c. Twenty copies of the report of US armed forces personnel, the civilian component, invited contractors, and the dependents of each, entering or departing the ROK during the month of January 1972.

d. Twenty copies of the USFK quarterly listing of all US invited contractor employees and dependents as of 31 December 1971.

12. The ROK Representative acknowledged the receipt of these reports as enumerated by the US Representative.

3

71st JC
24 Feb 72

These minutes are consi_ered as official documents pertaining to both Governments and will not be released without mutual agreement.

13. The ROK Representative proposed that the special press release commemorating the fifth anniversary of the entry into force of the SOFA on 9 February 1972, which was issued by the Joint Committee on 8 February 1972, be included in the minutes of this Joint Committee meeting (Inclosure 18).

14. The US Representative concurred in the ROK Representative's proposal that the joint ROK-US press release, which was issued in connection with the fifth anniversary of the entry into force of the ROK-US SOFA on 9 February 1972, be included in the minutes of this meeting. He noted that this special Joint Committee press release received good coverage in both the Korean and English language news media.

15. The ROK Representative presented a new task to the Finance (Personnel Affairs) Subcommittee (Inclosure 19). He stated that since the inception of SOFA, no customs declaration and certification forms had been designed specifically to apply to the imports under paragraph 3 of SOFA Article IX. For convenience, the forms for the purpose of various USFK imports under paragraph 2 of same Article had been utilized also for the importation of goods consigned to and for the personal use of SOFA personnel until the end of last year. He said that the ROK customs authorities recently have initiated an EDPS program to improve the formalities of overall customs clearance. Accordingly, they would like to develop a better formula applicable to both the purposes mentioned above. With this idea in mind, the ROK Representative proposed a task to the Finance (Personnel Affairs) Subcommittee to review the current customs clearance forms and to submit appropriate recommendations to the Joint Committee.

16. The US Representative concurred in the assignment of the specified task to the Finance (Personnel Affairs) Subcommittee.

17. The ROK Representative proposed that the next meeting of the Joint Committee be held at 1530, Thursday, 23 March 1972, in the ROK Capitol Building. The US Representative concurred.

18. The US Representative proposed that the press release for the seventy-first Joint Committee meeting, as prepared by our respective Secretaries and distributed in advance to both components of the Committee be approved (Inclosure 20). The ROK Representative concurred.

4

71st JC
24 Feb 72

271

These minutes are considered as official documents pertaining to both Governments and will not be released without mutual agreement.

19. The meeting was adjourned at 1425 hours.

20 Incl

_____
KIM DONG-WHIE
Republic of Korea
Representative

_____
ROBERT N. SMITH
Lieutenant General
United States Air Force
United States Representative

5

71st JC
24 Feb 72

AGENDA FOR THE SEVENTY-FIRST MEETING
OF THE ROK-US JOINT COMMITTEE
1400 HOURS, 24 FEBRUARY 1972, US SOFA CONFERENCE ROOM

I.   Assignment of Tasks to Facilities and Areas Subcommittee.

      1. Two Tasks - ROK Presentation.

      2. Eight Tasks - US Presentation.

II.   Recommendations of Facilities and Areas Subcommittee - US Presentation.

III.   Consideration of Sixth Report and Recommendations of Ad Hoc Subcommittee on Civil-Military Relations - ROK and US Presentations.

IV.   Memoranda on the Designation of US Invited Contractors - US Presentation.

V.   Memorandum on the Withdrawal of Designation of US Invited Contractor - US Presentation.

VI.   Memoranda Presented to the ROK Government by the US in the Implementation of the SOFA - US Presentation.

VII.   Press Release Relating to Fifth Anniversary of SOFA - ROK Presentation.

VIII. Assignment of Task to Finance (Personnel Affairs) Subcommittee - ROK Presentation.

IX.   Proposed Time of Next Meeting - 1530 Hours, Thursday, 23 March 1972, in the ROK Capitol Building.

X.   Agreement on Joint Press Release.

XI.   Adjourn

6   71st JC (Incl 1)
                 24 Feb 72

These minutes are considered as official documents pertaining to both Governments and will not be released without mutual agreement.

JOINT COMMITTEE
UNDER
THE REPUBLIC OF KOREA AND THE UNITED STATES
STATUS OF FORCES AGREEMENT

10 February 1972

MEMORANDUM FOR: Chairmen, Facilities and Areas Subcommittee

SUBJECT: Request for Use of Idle Land

1. SOFA provides in Article II, paragraph 2, that the Governments of the Republic of Korea and the United States may agree that facilities and areas or portions thereof shall be returned to the Republic of Korea or that additional facilities and areas may be provided.

2. Pursuant to paragraph 1 above it is requested that a recommendation be presented to the Joint Committee concerning a request for the use, by farmers for cultivation during the period of the farming season, of certain areas under US acquisition adjacent to Kunsan Air Base, Cholla-pukto.

KIM DONG-WHIE
Republic of Korea
Representative

ROBERT N. SMITH
Lieutenant General
United States Air Force
United States Representative

7

71st JC (Incl 2)
24 Feb 72

These minutes are considered as official documents pertaining to both Governments and will not be released without mutual agreement.

JOINT COMMITTEE
UNDER
THE REPUBLIC OF KOREA AND THE UNITED STATES
STATUS OF FORCES AGREEMENT

10 February 1972

MEMORANDUM FOR: Chairmen, Facilities and Areas Subcommittee

SUBJECT: Request for Release of Portion of Military Port for Construction of Public Beach

1. SOFA provides in Article II, paragraph 2, that the Governments of the Republic of Korea and the United States may agree that facilities and areas or portions thereof shall be returned to the Republic of Korea or that additional facilities and areas may be provided.

2. Pursuant to paragraph 1 above, it is requested that a recommendation be presented to the Joint Committee concerning a request for the release of certain areas adjacent to the USFK military port, located at Haeng-am-san, Chinhae, Kyungsang Nam-do, required for construction of a public beach.

KIM DONG-WHE
Republic of Korea
Representative

ROBERT N. SMITH
Lieutenant General
United States Air Force
United States Representative

8

71st JC (Incl 3)
24 Feb 72

These minutes are considered as official documents pertaining to both Governments and will not be released without mutual agreement.

**JOINT COMMITTEE
UNDER
THE REPUBLIC OF KOREA AND THE UNITED STATES
STATUS OF FORCES AGREEMENT**

24 February 1972

MEMORANDUM FOR: Chairmen, Facilities and Areas Subcommittee

SUBJECT: Request for Acquisition of an Easement

1. SOFA provides in Article II, paragraph 2, that the Governments of the Republic of Korea and the United States may agree that facilities and areas or portions thereof shall be returned to the Republic of Korea or that additional facilities and areas may be provided.

2. Pursuant to paragraph 1 above, it is requested that a recommendation be presented to the Joint Committee concerning a request for the acquisition, on a perpetual restrictive easement basis, of 0.66 acre (4,121 feet in length and 6 feet in width), located in Sihung-gun, Kyonggi-do. This real estate is required for the installation of underground communication cables.

KIM DONG-WHIE
Republic of Korea
Representative

ROBERT N. SMITH
Lieutenant General
United States Air Force
United States Representative

9

71st JC (Incl 4)
24 Feb 72

These minutes are considered as official documents pertaining to both
Governments and will not be released without mutual agreement.

**JOINT COMMITTEE
UNDER
THE REPUBLIC OF KOREA AND THE UNITED STATES
STATUS OF FORCES AGREEMENT**

24 February 1972

MEMORANDUM FOR: Chairmen, Facilities and Areas Subcommittee

SUBJECT: Request for Acquisition of a Temporary Use Permit

1. SOFA provides in Article II, paragraph 2, that the Governments of
the Republic of Korea and the United States may agree that facilities
and areas or portions thereof shall be returned to the Republic of Korea
or that additional facilities and areas may be acquired.

2. Pursuant to paragraph 1 above, it is requested that a recommendation be presented to the Joint Committee concerning a request for the
acquisition of a Temporary Use Permit, involving 0.681 acre of land
located in Suwon City, Kyonggi-do, for the period 1 June 1972 through
28 February 1973. This real estate is required to conduct exploratory
water well drilling.

KIM DONG-WHIE
Republic of Korea
Representative

ROBERT N. SMITH
Lieutenant General
United States Air Force
United States Representative

10

71st JC (Incl 5)
24 Feb 72

These minutes are considered as official documents pertaining to both
Governments and will not be released without mutual agreement.

**JOINT COMMITTEE
UNDER
THE REPUBLIC OF KOREA AND THE UNITED STATES
STATUS OF FORCES AGREEMENT**

24 February 1972

MEMORANDUM FOR: Chairmen, Facilities and Areas Subcommittee

SUBJECT: Requests for Extension of Temporary Use Permits

1. SOFA provides in Article II, paragraph 2, that the Governments of
the Republic of Korea and the United States may agree that facilities
and areas or portions thereof shall be returned to the Republic of Korea
or that additional facilities and areas may be provided.

2. Pursuant to paragraph 1 above, it is requested that recommendations
be presented to the Joint Committee concerning requests for the following
actions:

    a. Extension of Temporary Use Permit K-G-T-14, involving 25
acres of river bed area located in Chilgok-gun, Kyongsangbuk-do, from
25 February 1972 through 24 February 1973. This land has been utilized
since 1971, and there is a continuing need for its use as a source of gravel and sand materials for use in construction.

    b. Extension of Temporary Use Permit IC-T-15, involving 207.40
acres of land located in Yangju-gun, Kyonggi-do, from 1 April 1972
through 30 September 1972. This land has been utilized since 1962 as
an ammunition demolition area, and there is a continuing need for its
use for that purpose.

KIM DONG-WHIE
Republic of Korea
Representative

ROBERT N. SMITH
Lieutenant General
United States Air Force
United States Representative

11

71st JC (Incl 6)
24 Feb 72

JOINT COMMITTEE
UNDER
THE REPUBLIC OF KOREA AND THE UNITED STATES
STATUS OF FORCES AGREEMENT

24 February 1972

MEMORANDUM FOR: Chairmen, Facilities and Areas Subcommittee

SUBJECT: Requests of Release of Real Estate

1. SOFA provides in Article II, paragraph 2, that the Governments of the Republic of Korea and the United States may agree that facilities and areas or portions thereof shall be returned to the Republic of Korea or that additional facilities and areas may be provided.

2. Pursuant to paragraph 1 above, it is requested that recommendations be presented to the Joint Committee concerning requests for the following actions:

a. Release of 11.467 acres of land, constituting a portion of Kanghwa-do Installation, currently held under Acquisition Nos. Inchon-268, ASCOM-379, and K-11-401, and located in Kanghwa-gun, Kyonggi-do. This request for release includes a total of 56 USFK-constructed buildings and facilities located on that Installation. This real estate has become excess to USFK requirements.

b. Release of 37.89 acres of land, constituting the A-102 Airfield which is a portion of Market Installation held under Acquisition No. AAC-396, and located in Inchon City, Kyonggi-do. This request for release includes two Korean-constructed buildings and a total of 68 USFK-constructed buildings and facilities. This real estate has become excess to USFK requirements.

c. Release of one Korean-constructed building (No. S-230), constituting a portion of the acquisition held under Acquisition No. PAC-Taegu-113, and located on Camp Henry Installation, Taegu City, Kyongsangbuk-do. This building has deteriorated beyong economical repair and maintenance.

12

71st JC (Incl 7)
24 Feb 72

These minutes are considered as official documents pertaining to both Governments and will not be released without mutual agreement.

    d. Release of 13.36 acres of land, constituting Stonestown Install-ation, currently held under Acquisition No. SAC-PAC-135, and located in Taejon City, Chungchongnam-do. This request for release includes a total of 20 Korean-constructed buildings and facilities and a total of 70 USFK-constructed buildings and facilities which are located on the Installation. This real estate has become excess to USFK requirements.

KIM DONG-WHIE
Republic of Korea
Representative

ROBERT N. SMITH
Lieutenant General
United States Air Force
United States Representative

71st JC (Incl 7)
24 Feb 72

13

280

These minutes are considered as official documents pertaining to both Governments and will not be released without mutual agreement.

REPUBLIC OF KOREA - UNITED STATES
FACILITIES AND AREAS SUBCOMMITTEE

17 February 1972

MEMORANDUM FOR: THE JOINT COMMITTEE

1. Subcommittee Members

United States	Republic of Korea
BG Philip T. Boerger, Chairman	BG PAK Woo Bum, Chairman
COL Leonard Edelstein, Alt. Chairman	Mr. MIN Won Sik, Secty
COL Eugene T. Blanton, USAF	Mr. KANG Hong Suk, Asst Secty
MAJ William S. Littlefield, J4, USFK	LTC SHIN Sang Pil
MAJ Allen D. Adams, USAFCS, K	Mr. KIM Young Sup
CPT James H. Smith, USAF	Mr. SONG Jae Kun
Mr. Francis K. Cook, J5, USFK	Mr. RHO Won Tae
Mr. S. F. O'Hop, ENJ-RE, Secty	Mr. SOUNG Baek Jon
Mr. E. H. Brummett, ENJ-RE,	Mr. DO Tae Ku
Alt. Secty	Mr. SUH Chin Hwan
	Mr. LEE Soung Woo
	Mr. PARK Dahl Young
	Mr. BAE Jeung Sun

2. Subject of Recommendation: Request for the Acquisition of Temporary Use Permit, Joint Committee memorandum dated 24 November 1971.

3. Recommendation: <u>Task 1123</u> The request for acquisition, on a temporary use basis, of 18.72 acres of river bed area located in Paju-gun, Kyonggi-do (15.80 acres to provide river bed aggregates in support of a rock crushing plant located thereon and 2.92 acres to provide an access road from the plant to the borrow area), from 1 November 1971 through 31 October 1972 has been

14

71st JC (Incl 8)
24 Feb 72

281

These minutes are considered as official documents pertaining to both Governments and will not be released without mutual agreement.

Task 1123

accepted by the Ministry of National Defense with the stipulation that no excessive digging or damage be done to the adjacent farm land or dikes. This acquisition is in support of the 802d Engineer Battalion's roadway improvement and maintenance requirements in the Paju area. The Ministry of National Defense and the USFK Engineer will prepare the necessary documents. It is recommended that the Joint Committee, SOFA, approve this acquisition request.

4. Security Classification: Unclassified.

Brigadier General PAK Woo Bum
Chairman, ROK Component
Facilities and Areas Subcommittee

Brigadier General Philip T. Boerger
Chairman, US Component
Facilities and Areas Subcommittee

APPROVED BY THE JOINT COMMITTEE ON
24 FEBRUARY 1972 AT SEVENTY-FIRST MEETING

KIM DONG-WHIE
Republic of Korea
Representative

ROBERT N. SMITH
Lieutenant General
United States Air Force
United States Representative

15

71st JC (Incl 8)
24 Feb 72

REPUBLIC OF KOREA - UNITED STATES
FACILITIES AND AREAS SUBCOMMITTEE

17 February 1972

MEMORANDUM FOR: THE JOINT COMMITTEE

1. Subcommittee Members:

United States	Republic of Korea
BG Philip T. Boerger, Chairman	BG PAK Woo Bum, Chairman
COL Leonard Edelstein, Alt. Chairman	Mr. MIN Won Sik, Secty
LTC Edward W. Lingel, USAF	Mr. KANG Hong Suk, Asst Secty
MAJ William S. Littlefield, J4, USFK	LTC Shin Sang Pil
MAJ Allen D. Adams, USAFCS, K	Mr. KIM Hyung Kun
CPT James H. Smith, USAF	Mr. PAK Bung Hun
Mr. Francis K. Cook, J5, USFK	Mr. NOE Won Tae
Mr. S. F. O'Hop, ENJ-RE, Secty	Mr. PARK Byong Yong
Mr. E. H. Brummett, ENJ-RE,	Mr. DO Tae Ku
Alt. Secty	Mr. SUH Chin Hwan
	Mr. LEE Soung Woo
	Mr. PARK Daho Young
	Mr. BAE Jeung Sun

2. Subject of Recommendation: Request for Acquisition of Easement,
Joint Committee memorandum dated 22 April 1971.

3. Recommendation: Task 980 The request for acquisition, on a perpetual
restrictive easement basis, of 8.22 acres of land (35,802 linear feet by
10 feet in width) at various locations throughout the area of responsibility
of I Corps (Group) Rear Area, has been approved by the Ministry of National
Defense. This real estate is required to insure uninterrupted telephonic
communications within the I Corps (Group) Rear Area. The Ministry of
National Defense and the USFK Engineer will prepare the necessary documents. It is recommended that the Joint Committee, SOFA, approve this
recommendation.

16

71st JC (Incl 9)
24 Feb 72

282

These minutes are considered as official documents pertaining to both
Governments and will not be released without mutual agreement.

Task 980

4. Security Classification: Unclassified.

Brigadier General PAK Woo Bum
Chairman, ROK Component
Facilities and Areas Subcommittee

Brigadier General Philip T. Boerger
Chairman, US Component
Facilities and Areas Subcommittee

APPROVED BY THE JOINT COMMITTEE ON
24 FEBRUARY 1972 AT SEVENTY-FIRST MEETING

KIM DONG-WHIE
Republic of Korea
Representative

ROBERT N. SMITH
Lieutenant General
United States Air Force
United States Representative

17

71st JC (Incl 9)
24 Feb 72

These minutes are considered as official documents pertaining to both Governments and w██ not be released without mutua█ █gree ment.

REPUBLIC OF KOREA - UNITED STATES
FACILITIES AND AREAS SUBCOMMITTEE

17 February 1972

MEMORANDUM FOR: THE JOINT COMMITTEE

1. Subcommittee Members:

United States	Republic of Korea
BG Philip T. Boerger, Chairman	BG PAK Woo Bum, Chairman
COL Leonard Edelstein, Alt. Chairman	Mr. MIN Won Sik, Secty
COL Eugene T. Blanton, USAF	Mr. KANG Hong Suk, Asst Secty
MAJ William S. Littlefield, J4, USFK	LTC SHIN Sang Pil
MAJ Allen D. Adams, USAFCS, K	Mr. KIM Young Sup
CPT James H. Smith, USAF	Mr. SONG Jae Kun
Mr. Francis K. Cook, J5, USFK	Mr. RHO Won Tae
Mr. S. F. O'Hop, ENJ-RE, Secty	Mr. SOUNG Baek Jon
Mr. E. H. Brummett, ENJ-RE,	Mr. DO Tae Ku
Alt. Secty	Mr. SUH Chin Hwan
	Mr. LEE Soung Woo
	Mr. PARK Dahl Young
	Mr. BAE Jeung Sun

2. Subject of Recommendation: Requests for Release of Real Estate, Joint Committee memorandum dated 27 January 1972.

3. Recommendation: Tasks 1130-1136 The following requests for release of real estate have been accepted by the Ministry of National Defense.

    a. Task 1130 Release of 505.517 acres of land, constituting the Hyongga-ri Tank Range, currently held under Acq. No. 7X-5, located in Yonchon-gun, Kyonggi-do, subject to the conditions specified below. This request for release includes a total of four buildings and facilities located on the installation. The conditions attached to this request for release are that: (1) The I Corps (ROK/US) Group retain scheduling control over the

285

18   71st JC (Incl 10)
            24 Feb 72

These minutes are considered as official documents pertaining to both Governments and will not be released without mutual agreement.

Tasks 1130-1136

range area activities; (2) The Republic of Korea Ministry of National Defense insure that this range will be made available only for the use and occupancy of the VI ROK Army Corps element solely for training range purposes; and (3) The VI ROK Army Corps element be solely responsible for the security and operational maintenance of all of the real property located at the Hyonggi-ri Tank Range.

   b. **Task 1131** Release of 21.039 acres of land, constituting a portion of Camp Richmond Installation held under Acq. Nos. ACS-300 and AAC-391, and located in Buchon-gun, Kyonggi-do. This request for release includes a total of 83 buildings and facilities, of which 55 are USFK-constructed and 28 are Korean-constructed. Excluded from this request for release are an overhead electric power line, three 25-KVA transformers, a water pipeline, and one water storage tank, with unrestricted right of entry/exit thereto, as well as 0.604 acre of easement land and 0.36 acre of land held on an exclusive use basis, as shown on maps in the possession of the Republic of Korea Ministry of National Defense and the Engineer, USFK.

   c. **Task 1132** Release of 12.07 acres of land, constituting Tracy Installation held under Acq. No. SAC-673, and located in Seoul City. This request for release includes 80 USFK-constructed buildings and facilities and two Korean-constructed facilities. This real estate has become excess to USFK requirements.

   d. **Task 1133** Release of 2.58 acres of land, constituting a portion of Yuma Installation held under Acq. No. AAC-397, and located in Inchon City, Kyonggi-do. This request for release includes 5,559 linear feet of 8-inch underground POL pipeline and one 570 square foot pump house. This real estate has become excess to USFK requirements.

   e. **Task 1134** Release of 6.635 acres of land, constituting a portion of Alamo Installation held under Acq. Nos. 7X-13 and 7X-174, and located in Yonchon-gun, Kyonggi-do. This request for release includes a total of 29 USFK-constructed buildings and facilities located on the Installation. This real estate has become excess to USFK requirements.

   f. **Task 1135** Release of 15.72 acres of land, constituting a portion of Camp Mercer Installation held under Acq. No. ASCOM-378, and located in Kimpo-gun, Kyonggi-do. This request for release includes a total of 17 USFK-constructed buildings and facilities located on the Installation. This real estate has become excess to USFK requirements.

These minutes are considered as official documents pertaining to both
Governments and will not be released without mutual agreement.

Tasks 1130-1136

    g. **Task 1136** Release of 45.757 acres of land, constituting a portion
of ASP #46 Installation held under Acq. No. SAC-715, and located in Seoul
City. This request for release includes a total of 84 USFK-constructed
buildings and facilities, and a total of 10 Korean-constructed buildings and
facilities. This request for release is contigent upon the provision by the
Republic of Korea Ministry of National Defense, without cost to the US Government, of the following activities: (1) Construction of approximately 460 linear
feet of barbed wire security fencing at a specified location; (2) Construction of
approximately 1,585 linear feet of barbed wire security fencing with one
vehicle gate, at another location; (3) The relocation of Bldg. No. T-181 to the
USFK-retained communication area; and (4) The installation of water and
electric meters. The locations involved in activities (1) through (3) above
are indicated on a map in possession of the Republic of Korea Ministry of
National Defense and the USFK Engineer.

The Ministry of National Defense and the USFK Engineer will prepare the
necessary documents. It is recommended that the Joint Committee, SOFA,
approve these seven requests.

4. Security Classification: Unclassified.

_____
Brigadier General PAK Woo Bum
Chairman, ROK Component
Facilities and Areas Subcommittee

_____
Brigadier General Philip T. Boerger
Chairman, US Component
Facilities and Areas Subcommittee

APPROVED BY THE JOINT COMMITTEE ON
24 FEBRUARY 1972 AT SEVENTY-FIRST MEETING

_____
KIM DONG-WHIE
Republic of Korea
Representative

_____
ROBERT N. SMITH
Lieutenant General
United States Air Force
United States Representative

287

20

71st JC (Incl 10)
24 Feb 72

공   란

공 란

공 란

공   란

공 란

공 란

공   란

공 란

공　　　란

공　　　란

공　　란

공 란

These minutes are considered as official documents pertaining to both
Governments and will not be released without mutual agreement.

JOINT COMMITTEE
UNDER
THE REPUBLIC OF KOREA AND THE UNITED STATES
STATUS OF FORCES AGREEMENT

5 FEB 1972

MEMORANDUM FOR: THE JOINT COMMITTEE

SUBJECT: Designation of US Invited Contractor under Article XV,
Status of Forces Agreement

1. References:

   a. Paragraph 2, Article XV, Status of Forces Agreement.

   b. US Chairman, Commerce Subcommittee letter, dated 6 Oct
1971, subject as above (Incl 1).

   c. ROK Chairman, Commerce Subcommittee letter, dated 1 Nov
1971, subject as above (Incl 2).

2. The United States, after consultation with the ROK Commerce
Subcommittee and having duly considered its views, has designated
International Electronics Corporation as a US invited contractor for
execution of contract GS-00S-07831 for repair and maintenance of
non-tactical radio equipment.

3. Pertinent data concerning US or third country national employees
will be provided to the Joint Secretariat by established reporting
procedures.

2 Incl
as

ROBERT N. SMITH
Lieutenant General, USAF
United States Representative
Joint Committee

33

71st JC (Incl 12)
24 Feb 72

REPUBLIC OF KOREA - UNITED STATES
COMMERCE SUBCOMMITTEE

6 October 1971

SUBJECT: Designation of US Invited Contractor Under Article XV,
Status of Forces Agreement

ROK Chairman, Commerce Subcommittee

1. Reference paragraph 2, Article XV of the Status of Forces Agreement.

2. The Government of the Republic of Korea is informed through this written consultative process that the United States Forces, Korea, proposes to extend invited contractor status to the International Electronics Corporation for repair and maintenance of non-tactical radio equipment.

3. The following data are provided:

   a. Company Name: International Electronics Corporation

   b. Local Address: APO 96301

   c. Identification of US Citizen Employees: To be reported monthly.

   d. Number of US and ROK Employees: It is estimated that four (4) US and fourteen (14) Korean personnel will be employed under this contract.

   e. Reasons for Designation of an Invited Contractor:

   (1) Security requirements of the US Air Force. The contractor will be involved in the operation and maintenance of radio nets which directly affect the mission capabilities of the US Air Force. The increasing Air Force mission in Korea frequently requires revision of one or more nets and the contractor's assistance is required in system layout and planning, equipment selection and technical operation which may be classified and contain information not releasable to foreign nationals.

   (2) Unavailability of materials or services required by US standards:

   (a) Fully qualified, trained and experienced supervisors and technical personnel are essential to insure that all equipment is installed, tested and placed into operation to meet all specifications. The management of US equipment and supplies placed in the hands of the contractor requires that the contractor be responsible for and responsive to USAF policies and requirements.

34   71st JC (Incl 1 to Incl 12)
                                      24 Feb 72

These minutes are considered as official documents pertaining to both Governments and will not be released without mutual agreement.

6 October 1971

SUBJECT: Designation of US Invited Contractor Under Article XV, Status of Forces Agreement

(b) The contractor is required to comply with various Air Force manuals, regulations and other applicable publications which are technical in nature. All equipment is US design and manufactured and must be maintained to standards which can best be met by using US supervisory personnel.

(c) It is the policy of the manufacturer to provide price lists, operating and repair manuals and associated data only to their authorized representatives to warrant all equipment. This warranty is void if the equipment is serviced by other than an authorized representative.

(d) Replacement parts are available only from the manufacture's representative.

f. Location of Contract: US Air Forces bases in Korea

g. Type of Contract: Fixed Price requirements contract for maintenance and repair of non-tactical radio equipment.

h. Length of Contract: One year with option to extend for periods of one year.

i. USFK Sponsor: US Air Force, Korea

RICHARD T. CANN
Colonel, US Army
United States Chairman
Commerce Subcommittee

35

71st JC (Incl 1 to Incl 12)
24 Feb 72

MINISTRY OF COMMERCE AND INDUSTRY
REPUBLIC OF KOREA
SEOUL, KOREA

1 November 1971

Subject : Designation of US Invited Contractor under Article XV,
Status of Foreces Agreement

US Chairman, Commerce Subcommittee

1. Reference:

    a. Paragraph 2, Article XV, Status of Forces Agreement

    b. US Commerce Subcommittee Memorandum of Consultation, dated 6 October 1971 subject as above, pertaining to contract for repair and maintenance of non-tactical reoio equipment, US Air Force, Korea.

2. The US memorandum, reference 1b above, has been reviewed and the government of the Republic of Korea understands the requirement for an invited contractor in this instance.

Chung An Kil
Chairman
Commerce Subcommittee, ROK

36

71st JC (Incl 2 to Incl 12)
24 Feb 72

These minutes are considered as official documents pertaining to both
Governments and will not be released without mutual agreement.
JOINT COMMITTEE
UNDER
THE REPUBLIC OF KOREA AND THE UNITED STATES
STATUS OF FORCES AGREEMENT

5 FEB 1972

MEMORANDUM FOR: The Joint Committee

SUBJECT: Designation of US Invited Contractor Under Article XV,
Status of Forces Agreement

1. References:

    a. Paragraph 2, Article XV, Status of Forces Agreement.

    b. US Chairman, Commerce Subcommittee letter, dated 20 Oct
1971, subject as above (Incl 1).

    c. ROK Chairman, Commerce Subcommittee letter, dated 1 Nov
1971, subject as above (Incl 2).

2. The United States, after consultation with the ROK Commerce
Subcommittee and having duly considered its views, has designated
Air America, Incorporated as a US invited contractor for execution
of contract DOT-FA72PC-907 for maintenance of FAA T-39 aircraft,
Korea.

3. Pertinent data concerning US or third country national employees
will be provided to the Joint Secretariat by established reporting
procedures.

2 Incl
as

ROBERT N. SMITH
Lieutenant General, USAF
United States Representative
Joint Committee

37

71st JC (Incl 13)
24 Feb 72

REPUBLIC OF KOREA - UNITED STATES
COMMERCE SUBCOMMITTEE

20 October 1971

SUBJECT: Designation of US Invited Contractor Under Article XV, Status of Forces Agreement

ROK Chairman, Commerce Subcommittee

1. Reference paragraph 2, Article XV of the Status of Forces Agreement.

2. The Government of the Republic of Korea is informed through this written consultative process that the United States Forces, Korea proposes to extend invited contractor status to Air America, Inc. for maintenance of T-39 aircraft.

3. The following data are provided:

   a. Company Name: Air America

   b. Local Address: Osan Air Base, Korea

   c. Identification of US Citizen Employees: To be provided by periodic reports.

   d. Number of US and ROK Employees: One US and nine Koreans.

   e. Reasons for Designation of an Invited Contractor:

   (1) Local unavailability of material and services required by US standards. Contract specifies that the contractor must possess required technical skills and supplies for maintenance and repair services of the T-39 aircraft in accordance with FAA regulations. Mechanics are trained by FAA in accordance with FAA regulations.

   (2) Limitations of US Law. All maintenance services must comply with the Federal Aviation Regulations of the US Government.

   f. Location of Contract: Air Force bases, Korea

   g. Type of Contract: T-39 aircraft maintenance

38

71st JC (Incl 1 to Incl 13)
24 Feb 72

305   INCL 1

These minutes are considered as official documents pertaining to both Governments and will not be released without mutual agreement.

20 October 1971

SUBJECT: Designation of US Invited Contractor Under Article XV, Status of Forces Agreement

h. **Length of Contract:** One year with option to extend for additional periods of one year.

i. **USFK Sponsor:** US Air Forces Korea

RICHARD T. CANN
Colonel, US Army
United States Chairman
Commerce Subcommittee

39

71st JC (Incl 1 to Incl 13)
24 Feb 72

These minutes are considered as official documents pertaining to both Governments and will not be released without mutual agreement.

MINISTRY OF COMMERCE AND INDUSTRY
REPUBLIC OF KOREA
SEOUL, KOREA

1 November 1971

Subject : Designation of US Invited Contractor under Article XV,
Status of Forces Agreement

US Chairman, Commerce Subcommittee

1. Reference:

a. Paragraph 2, Article XV, Status of Forces Agreement

b. US Commerce Subcommittee Memorandum of Consultation,
dated 20 October 1971 subject as above, pertaining to contract
for maintenance of T-39 aircraft, Korea.

2. The US memorandum, reference 1b above, has been reviewed and
the government of the Republic of Korea understands the requirement
for an invited contractor in this instance.

Chung Min Kil
Chairman
Commerce Subcommittee, ROK

These minutes are considered as official documents pertaining to both Governments and will not be released without mutual agreement.

JOINT COMMITTEE
UNDER
THE REPUBLIC OF KOREA AND THE UNITED STATES
STATUS OF FORCES AGREEMENT

5 FEB 1972

MEMORANDUM FOR: The Joint Committee

SUBJECT: Designation of US Invited Contractor Under Article XV, Status of Forces Agreement

1. References:

   a. Paragraph 2, Article XV, Status of Forces Agreement.

   b. US Chairman, Commerce Subcommittee letter, dated 22 Oct 1971, subject as above (Incl 1).

   c. ROK Chairman, Commerce Subcommittee letter, dated 1 Nov 1971, subject as above (Incl 2).

2. The United States, after consultation with the ROK Commerce Subcommittee and having duly considered its views, has designated Southern Air Transport, Incorporated as a US invited contractor for execution of contract F11626-71-C-0042 for international air transportation services for the Military Airlift Command in Korea.

3. Pertinent data concerning US or third country national employees will be provided to the Joint Secretariat by established reporting procedures.

ROBERT N. SMITH
Lieutenant General, USAF
United States Representative
Joint Committee

2 Incl
as

41

71st JC (Incl 14)
24 Feb 72

These minutes are considered as official documents pertaining to both Governments an███ill not be released without mu███l agreement.

REPUBLIC OF KOREA - UNITED STATES
COMMERCE SUBCOMMITTEE

21 October 1971

SUBJECT: Designation of US Invited Contractor Under Article XV, Status of Forces Agreement

ROK Chairman, Commerce Subcommittee

1. Reference paragraph 2, Article XV of the Status of Forces Agreement.

2. The Government of the Republic of Korea is informed through this written consultative process that the United States Forces, Korea proposes to extend invited contractor status to the Southern Air Transport, Inc., for international air transportation services for the Military Airlift Command, United States Air Force.

3. The following data are provided:

    a. Company Name: Southern Air Transport, Inc.

    b. Local Address: Osan Air Base, Korea

    c. Identification of US Citizen Employees: To be provided by periodic reports.

    d. Number of US and ROK Employees: One US, twenty-three Koreans and one third-country national will be employed under this contract.

    e. Reasons for Designation of an Invited Contractor:

    (1) Security considerations. The contractor is required to transport classified cargo, registered mail and other regular mail for which only US registered carriers are authorized to transport.

    (2) Local unavailability of material and services required by US standards. Contract specifies that the contractor will provide B-727 aircraft with guaranteed allowable cabin load of 16.5 ton cargo or 105 passengers and properly trained manpower for this type aircraft.

    (3) Limitations of US Law. All equipment and operations must comply with the Federal Aviation Regulations of the US Government.

42

71st JC (Incl 1 to Incl 14)
24 Feb 72

These minutes are considered as official documents pertaining to both Governments and will not be released without mutual agreement.

21 October 1971

SUBJECT: Designation of US Invited Contractor Under Article XV, Status of Forces Agreement

    f. <u>Location of Contract</u>: Air Force bases, Korea

    g. <u>Type of Contract</u>: Contract for air transportation services for US military and other authorized personnel and cargo.

    h. <u>Length of Contract</u>: One year with option to extend three months.

    i. <u>USFK Sponsor</u>: US Air Forces Korea.

RICHARD T. CANN
Colonel, US Army
United States Chairman
Commerce Subcommittee

43

71st JC (Incl 1 to Incl 14)
24 Feb 72

MINISTRY OF COMMERCE AND INDUSTRY
REPUBLIC OF KOREA
SEOUL, KOREA

1 November 1971

Subject: Designation of US Invited Contractor under Article XV, Status of Forces Agreement

US Chairman, Commerce Subcommittee

1. Reference:

a. Paragraph 2, Article XV, Status of Forces Agreement

b. US Commerce Subcommittee Memorandum of Consultation, dated 21 October 1971 subject as above, pertaining to contract for international air transportation services for the Military Airlift Command, United States Air Force, Korea

2. The US memorandum, reference 1b above, has been reviewed and the government of the Republic of Korea understands the requirement for an invited contractor in this instance.

Chung Min Kil
Chairman
Commerce Subcommittee, ROK

44   71st JC (Incl 2 to Incl 14)
                      24 Feb 72

JNCL 2

These minutes are considered as official documents pertaining to both Governments and will not be released without mutual agreement.

JOINT COMMITTEE
UNDER
THE REPUBLIC OF KOREA AND THE UNITED STATES
STATUS OF FORCES AGREEMENT

24 February 1972

MEMORANDUM FOR: The Joint Committee

SUBJECT: Designation of US Invited Contractor Under Article XV, Stauts of Forces Agreement

1. References:

    a. Paragraph 2, Article XV, Status of Forces Agreement.

    b. US Chairman, Commerce Subcommittee letter, dated 19 Oct 71, subject as above (Incl 1).

    c. ROK Chairman, Commerce Subcommittee letter, dated 1 Nov 71, subject as above (Incl 2).

2. The United States, after consultation with the ROK Commerce Subcommittee and having duly considered its views, has designated Minnesota (3M) Services Supply Limited as a US invited contractor for execution of contract DAJB03-72-C-3034 for service and supply of 3M office copying machines, US Army installations.

3. Pertinent data concerning US or third country national employees will be provided to the Joint Secretariat by established reporting procedures.

2 Incl
as

ROBERT N. SMITH
for Lieutenant General, USAF
United States Representative
Joint Committee

45   71st JC (Incl 15)
24 Feb 72

These minutes are considered as official documents pertaining to both Governments an⬤will not be released without m⬤al agreement.

REPUBLIC OF KOREA - UNITED STATES
COMMERCE SUBCOMMITTEE

19 October 1971

SUBJECT: Designation of US Invited Contractor Under Article XV, Status of Forces Agreement

ROK Chairman, Commerce Subcommittee

1. Reference paragraph 2, Article XV of the Status of Forces Agreement.

2. The Government of the Republic of Korea is informed through this written consultative process that the United States Forces, Korea, proposes to extend invited contractor status to the Minnesota (3M) Services Supply Limited for contract for service and supply of 3M office copying machines, US Army installations.

3. The following data are provided:

a. Company Name: Minnesota (3M) Services Supply Limited.

b. Local Address: APO 96301.

c. Identification of US Citizen Employees: To be provided after award.

d. Number of US and ROK Employees: It is estimated that 2 US and 7 Koreans will be employed.

e. Reasons for Designation of an Invited Contractor:

(1) Limitation of US Procurement Law. Under Title 10 United States Code 2202 promulgated by the Armed Services Procurement Regulations (ASPR), procurement of supplies outside the US is subject to certain restrictions because of the Balance of Payments Program. Reference is made to paragraph 6-805, Part 8, Section VI of the Armed Services Procurement Regulations. This particular law places certain limitations on the procurement of supplies outside the US, but certain exceptions are provided in some cases so that local indigenous sources may be used. The interpretation in this particular case, of supplies for office equipment, is that no direct exception is provided and that procurement must be made from US firms.

46   71st JC (Incl 1 to Incl 15)
                      24 Feb 72

These minutes are considered as official documents pertaining to both Governments and ▇▇▇ not be released without mutu▇▇ agreement.

19 October 1971

SUBJECT: Designation of US Invited Contractor Under Article XV, Status of Forces Agreement

(2) Unavailability of materials and services by US standards. The office machines and equipment are of US design and manufacture. It is highly essential that the maintenance service and parts and supply sources function in accordance with US standards of high reliability of operation, minimum number of equipment failures and minimum down time for lack of service, parts and supplies. By US standards the contractors are expected to provide satisfactory performance to ordering activities with minimal administrative aid. In this case, US standards of service are best assured if the contract is US managed and supervised.

     f. <u>Location of Contract</u>: US Army installations, Korea.

     g. <u>Type of Contract</u>: Fixed Price Contract for Maintenance and Repair of 3M office copying machines.

     h. <u>Length of Contract</u>: Initially for 7 months, with option to extend for 12 months.

     i. <u>USFK Sponsor</u>: US Army Korea Procurement Agency.

RICHARD T. CANN
Colonel, US Army
United States Chairman
Commerce Subcommittee

47

71st JC (Incl 1 to Incl 15)
24 Feb 72

34

These minutes are considered as official documents pertaining to both Governments and ██ill not be released without mu███l agreement.

MINISTRY OF COMMERCE AND INDUSTRY
REPUBLIC OF KOREA
SEOUL, KOREA

1 November 1971

Subject: Designation of US Invited Contractor under Article XV, Status of Forces Agreement

US Chairman, Commerce Subcommittee

1. Reference:

    a. Paragraph 2, Article XV, Status of Forces Agreement

    b. US Commerce Subcommittee Memorandum of Consultation, dated 19 October 1971 subject as above, pertaining to contract for service and supply of 3M office copying machines, US Army installations.

2. The US memorandum, reference 1b above, has been reviewed and the government of the Republic of Korea understands the requirement for an invited contractor in this instance.

Chung Min Kil
Chairman
Commerce Subcommittee, ROK

These minutes are considered as official documents pertaining to both Governments and will not be released without mutual agreement.

JOINT COMMITTEE
UNDER
THE REPUBLIC OF KOREA AND THE UNITED STATES
STATUS OF FORCES AGREEMENT

5 FEB 1972

MEMORANDUM FOR: The Joint Committee

SUBJECT: Designation of US Invited Contractor Under Article XV, Status of Forces Agreement

1. References:

    a. Paragraph 2, Article XV, Status of Forces Agreement.

    b. US Chairman, Commerce Subcommittee letter, dated 29 July 1971, subject as above (Incl 1).

    c. ROK Chairman, Commerce Subcommittee letter, dated 11 August 1971, subject as above (Incl 2).

2. The United States, after consultation with the ROK Commerce Subcommittee and having duly considered its views, has designated Universal American Ent. Inc., the US member firm of the ROK - US joint venture, as a US invited contractor for execution of contract DAJB03-72-C-6049 for facilities engineering (Pyongtaek and Sihung-ni).

3. Pertinent data concerning US or third country national employees will be provided to the Joint Secretariat by established reporting procedures.

2 Incl
as

ROBERT N. SMITH
Lieutenant General, USAF
United States Representative
Joint Committee

49

71st JC (Incl 16)
24 Feb 72

REPUBLIC OF KOREA - UNITED STATES
COMMERCE SUBCOMMITTEE

29 July 1971

SUBJECT: Designation of US Invited Contractor Under
           Article XV, Status of Forces Agreement

ROK Chairman, Commerce Subcommittee

1. Reference: Paragraph 2, Article XV, of the Status of Forces Agreement.

2. The Government of the Republic of Korea is informed through this written consultative process that the United States Forces, Korea, proposes to extend invited contractor status to the US member of the successful negotiated bidder among qualified joint venture firms for the forthcoming Facilities Engineering contract for the Pyongtaek/Sihungni Area, Korea.

3. The following data are provided:

    a. <u>Company Name:</u> Names of the US firms to be considered are inclosed.

    b. <u>Local Address:</u> To be submitted upon designation.

    c. <u>Identification of US Citizen Employees</u>: To be submitted upon designation.

    d. <u>Number of US and ROK Employees:</u> It is estimated that 14 US and 466 Korean personnel will be employed.

    e. <u>Reasons for Designation of a Joint Venture Contractor:</u> Open competitive bidding is not practical because:

    (1) Security considerations for handling the classified portions of the project require US personnel.

    (2) Special management and technical skills are required.

    (3) Management experience in this type of operation is required.

50   **71st JC (Incl 1 to Incl 16)**
                      24 Feb 72

These minutes are considered as official documents pertaining to both Governments and will not be released without mutual agreement.

SUBJECT: Designation of US Invited Contractor   29 July 1971
          Under Article XV, Status of Forces Agreement

     f. Location of Contract: Pyongtaek/Sihungni Area, Korea.

     g. Type of Contract: A Cost-Plus-Fixed Fee contract
for the management, operation, maintenance and repair of
real property facilities.

     h. Length of Contract: 1 January 1972 through 30 June
1972. The contract will have a 30 day transition period
at the end of the contract.

     i. Sponsoring Component Commander: Commanding General,
Eighth United States Army.

                              RICHARD T. CANN
                              Colonel, US Army
                              United States Chairman
                              Commerce Subcommittee

                           51   71st JC (Incl 1 to Incl 16)
                                           24 Feb 72

MINISTRY OF COMMERCE AND INDUSTRY
REPUBLIC OF KOREA
SEOUL, KOREA

11 August 1971

Subject: Designation of US Invited Contractor under Article XV, Status of Forces Agreement

US Chairman, Commerce Subcommittee

1. Reference:

a. Paragraph 2, Article XV, Status of Forces Agreement

b. US Commerce Subcommittee Memorandum of Consultation, dated 29 July 1971, subject as above, pertaining to contract for Facilities Engineering contract for the Pyongtaek/Sihungni Area, Korea.

2. The US memorandum reference 1b above, has been reviewed and the Government of the Republic of Korea understands the requirement for an invited contractor status to the US member firm of the ROK-US joint venture contract in this instance.

Chung Min Kil
Chairman
Commerce Subcommittee, ROK

52   71st JC (Incl 2 to Incl 16)
            24 Feb 72

Incl 2

These minutes are considered as official documents pertaining to both Governments and will not be released without mutual agreement.

**JOINT COMMITTEE
UNDER
THE REPUBLIC OF KOREA AND THE UNITED STATES
STATUS OF FORCES AGREEMENT**

24 February 1972

MEMORANDUM FOR: The Joint Committee

SUBJECT: Withdrawal of US Invited Contractor Status Under Article XV, SOFA

1. Reference: Paragraph 2(a), Article XV, Status of Forces Agreement.

2. Morrison-Knudsen International Company, Incorporated has completed all contracts with the United States which require work in the Republic of Korea and in accordance with the above reference, their designation as an invited contractor is withdrawn.

FM Romanick Capt USN

for ROBERT N. SMITH
Lieutenant General, USAF
United States Representative
Joint Committee

_320

53

71st JC (Incl 17)
24 Feb 72

These minutes are considered as official documents pertaining to both Governments and will not be released without mutual agreement.

ROK-US Joint Committee Press Release
Fifth Anniversary of Entry into Force of SOFA
9 February 1972

The fifth anniversary of the entry into force of the ROK-US Status of Forces Agreement (SOFA) is being observed on 9 February 1972. The ROK-US SOFA is a comprehensive agreement containing 31 articles covering almost all facets of the relations between the ROK and US Governments relating to the presence of US military forces in Korea. The SOFA provides that this agreement will remain in force while the 1954 ROK-US Defense Treaty remains in force unless terminated earlier by agreement between the two Governments.

The successful implementation of the SOFA during its first five years has been the work of the ROK-US Joint Committee which was established in accordance with SOFA provisions to implement this Agreement and to deal with all problems except those concerning telecommunications. This Government-to-Government body, which includes a ROK Representative who is the Director of the Bureau of European and American Affairs and a US Representative who is the Chief of Staff, United States Forces, Korea, has held seventy formal meetings and innumerable other conferences in the last five years, and has taken up hundreds of topics relating to the implementation of the ROK-US SOFA. The current ROK Representative, Mr. KIM Dong-Whie, Director of the European and American Bureau of the Foreign Ministry, is

54

71st JC (Incl 18)
24 Feb 72

These minutes are considered as official documents pertaining to both Governments and will not be released without mutual agreement.

assisted on the Joint Committee by eight senior Bureau directors from six major Ministries as well as by a SOFA Secretariat which is headed by the Chief of the North America Second Section of the MOFA, Mr. KIM Young Sup. The US Representative who, for the past 34 months, has been Lieutenant General Robert N. Smith, Chief of Staff, USFK, is supported on the US component of the Joint Committee, by represent- atives of all the major components of USFK as well as by the USFK Staff Judge Advocate, an Embassy SOFA Political Advisor, and a US SOFA Secretariat which is headed by the senior American civilian offi- cer in USFK, Mr. Robert A. Kinney.

Since the JC Committee deals with all problems relating to the presence of US forces in the ROK, it has organized 12 joint ROK-US Subcommittees for the purpose of giving advice and making recommend- ations to the Joint Committee. During the first five years of operations, the Joint Committee has assigned a total of 1212 tasks to these Subcom- mittees. The Subcommittees have submitted mutually agreed recom- mendations on 1176 of these tasks, which, in turn, have been approved by the ROK-US Joint Committee. Many of the 36 tasks outstanding at this time were recently assigned to the respective Subcommittees for deliberation and recommendation. The SOFA provides that in the event the Joint Committee cannot resolve a problem, the problem shall be referred to the respective Governments. Thus far, in its

55

71st JC (Incl 18)
24 Feb 72

first five years of operations, the Joint Committee has not referred any problems to higher levels of their Governments for it has either resolved them on a mutually satisfactory basis, or is still working on them.

One of the busiest of the twelve Joint Committee Subcommittees is its Facilities and Areas Subcommittee, which deals with the acquisition and re'ease of facilities and areas required by the United States military forces — the ROK. During the first five years of the SOFA, the Joint Committee has assigned 1139 tasks to this Subcommittee, and the Subcommittee, in turn, has submitted 1113 recommendations which have been accepted by the Joint Committee. Only 26 tasks are outstanding in this Subcommittee as of the end of the first five years of the SOFA, ten of which were assigned within the past two weeks.

The SOFA provides that the ROK Government may assume criminal jurisdiction over USFK personnel under certain circumstances, in accordance with the provisions of the SOFA Criminal Jurisdiction Article (XXII). From 1967 through 30 January 1972, the ROK Government had assumed jurisdiction over US personnel in 191 cases with 157 convictions and three acquittals thus far. Of the 157 personnel convicted, 114 were fined, 36 had confinement suspended, and seven were sent to the ROK prison at Suwon. At present, only one US citizen who is in Korea under the SOFA is serving his term in a ROK

prison. Many of the cases involving US personnel in Korea, over which the US military authorities have jurisdiction in accordance with SOFA provisions, have been tried by US military courts martial. The ROK Government, however, assumes jurisdiction over cases "of particular importance" to the Republic of Korea.

The SOFA Labor Article (XVII) has exerted a positive influence in developing stable and effective labor relations between the USFK and its more than 27,000 Korean direct-hire and US invited contractor employees. Provisions of Article XVII relating to mediation of disputes has provided an effective instrument for resolution of disputes between the Foreign Organizations Employees Union (FOEU) and the USFK. USFK wage levels for its Korean employees are established on the basis of periodic wage surveys in the ROK. The enlightened labor relations policies of the USFK, coupled with close cooperation of the FOEU and the ROK Government have resulted in continuing improvement in the generally favorable labor relations between the Korean nationals working for USFK and the US command in Korea. In the first five years of the SOFA, all labor disputes have been settled in accordance with provisions of the SOFA.

The SOFA has assigned the responsibility for the settlement of most claims involving USFK personnel to the ROK Government, and through 31 January 1972, a total of 3664 claims have been processed

These minutes are considered as official documents pertaining to both Governments ar ⬤ will not be released without m ⬤ al agreement.

under Article XXIII of the SOFA. Of these claims, a total of 2268 have been paid on the agreed basis of 75 percent by the United States and 25 percent by the Republic of Korea. A total of 149 claims out of the 3664 submitted have been disallowed.

In its operation, the Joint Committee has met the changing situations confronting it and it has provided that in urgent situations, exigent action can be taken by the US and ROK Representatives without formally convening a Joint Committee meeting. A recent illustration of the dynamic operation of the Joint Committee is its establishment of an Ad Hoc Subcommittee on Civil-Military Relations in September 1971 in order to deal more effectively with problems in civil-military relations in the Korean communities adjacent to US military installations. This Subcommittee has made information gathering field trips to almost all the major US bases and adjacent Korean communities in Korea, and thus far has submitted a series of 19 recommendations, all of which were approved by the Joint Committee, to improve relations between US military personnel and the Korean people. The US-ROK Ad Hoc Subcommittee has supported the current program of the ROK Government to improve the conditions in these camp communities through the ROK inter-ministerial "Base Community Clean-Up Committee."

The Ad Hoc Subcommittee on Civil-Military Relations has seven panels which work on specific areas of civil-military relations, including local community and governmental relations, ROK police-US military police cooperation and coordination, health and sanitation, narcotics and drug control, larceny and black marketing, race rela- tions and equality of treatment, and people-to-people projects. It is anticipated that the camp communities will be better and more comfort- able for all concerned as a result of these activities.

Other Joint Committee subcommittees have been organized to func- tion in various areas of SOFA responsibility, including Criminal Juris- diction, Civil Jurisdiction, Finance, Commerce, Transportation, Entry and Exit, and Labor, respectively. Only the Joint Committee, however, can make decisions; the Subcommittees only give advice and make rec- commendations.

During its first five years of operation, the ROK-US Joint Commit- tee has demonstrated that the ROK-US SOFA is a living and vital agree- ment which has exerted a positive influence in the promotion of con- tinued ROK-US friendship and strengthening our mutual defense against Communist aggression.

-59

71st JC (Incl 18)
24 Feb 72

These minutes are considered as official documents pertaining to both Governments and will not be released without mutual agreement.

**JOINT COMMITTEE
UNDER
THE REPUBLIC OF KOREA AND THE UNITED STATES
STATUS OF FORCES AGREEMENT**

24 February 1972

MEMORANDUM FOR: Chairmen, Finance (Personnel Affairs)
Subcommittee

SUBJECT: Declaration and Certification on Imports Consigned to
Persons Subject to the ROK-US SOFA

1. Reference: Recommendation of the Finance (Personnel Affairs) Subcommittee on the subject of determination of procedures relating specifically to the forms and methods of presentation of the appropriate certification to be made on various USFK imports, approved by the ROK-US Joint Committee on 11 April 1967, and contained as Inclosure 5 to the official minutes of the fifth meeting of the ROK-US Joint Committee on 11 April 1967.

2. The declaration and certification process as described in reference has to date been applied not only to imports by the agencies specified in paragraph 2 of SOFA Article IX, but also to imports consigned to individuals who are subject to the ROK-US SOFA.

3. It is requested that mutual consultation be undertaken to determine whether any revision is required in current procedures in effect for the declaration and certification of imports consigned by name to persons who are subject to the ROK-US SOFA. If it is determined that such revision is required, it is further requested that a recommendation be transmitted to the Joint Committee on this subject.

KIM DONG-WHIE
Republic of Korea
Representative

ROBERT N. SMITH
Lieutenant General
United States Air Force
United States Representative

60

71st JC (Incl 19)
24 Feb 72

These minutes are considered as official documents pertaining to both Governments and will not be released without mutual agreement.

JOINT ROK-US PRESS RELEASE
SEVENTY-FIRST ROK-US JOINT COMMITTEE MEETING
24 FEBRUARY 1972

The ROK-US Joint Committee received the sixth report and seven additional recommendations of its Ad Hoc Subcommittee on Civil-Military Relations at its seventy-first meeting held in the US SOFA Conference Room on 24 February. The Joint Committee has thus far approved 26 recommendations of the Ad Hoc Subcommittee and its seven panels, which are designed to improve relations between American servicemen and the Korean people.

The Joint Committee also approved nine recommendations of its Facilities and Areas Subcommittee and assigned ten new tasks to that Subcommittee.

The US Representative, LTG Robert N. Smith, presided at this Joint Committee meeting and designated five US invited contractors, in accordance with Joint Committee procedures. The next meeting of the Committee is scheduled to be held on 23 March in the ROK Capitol Building with the ROK Representative, Mr. KIM Dong-Whie, presiding.

71st JC (Incl 20)
24 Feb 72

61

대한민국 외무부
공보관실
전화 74-3576

보 도 자 료

이 기사는 제공처인 외무부를
밝히고 보도할수 있음

외무보도   호

년   월   일   시   분 발표

한.미 합동위원회 제 71차 회의
공 동 발 표 문

72. 2. 24.

  2월 24일 주한미군 SOFA   회의실에서 개최된 한.미 합동위원회는 군.민관계 임시분과위원회의 제 6차 보고서와 7개의 추가건의를 접수 하였다.

  합동위원회는 지금까지 주한미군과 한국 국민간의 관계개선을 위하여 설치된 임시분과위원회 및 그 산하 7개의 조사반이 제시한 26개의 건의를 채택하였다.

  또한 합동위원회는 시설구역 분과위원회가 제시한 9개의 건의를 채택하고 10개의 새로운 과제를 동 분과위원회에 위촉 하였다.

  미국측 대표인 Robert N. Smith   중장이 금차 회의를 주재 하였으며, 5명의 초청계약자를 합동위원회 운영절차에 따라 지정하였다.

  차기 회의는 합동위 한국측 대표의 사회로 중앙청에서 3월 23일 개최될 예정이다.

327

3. 제72차, 1972. 3.28

330

기 안 용 지

분류기호 문서번호	미이 723 -	(전화번호 　　　　)	전결규정 조항 **국장**　전결사항	
처리기간				
시행일자			国	장
보존년한				

| 보조기관 | 과　장 | 彻 | | | | 협 | | |

| 기안책임자 | 김성심 | 북미2과 (72. 3. 13 | | |

경유			발	
수신	수신처 참조			
참조			신	

| 제　목 | 한.미 합동위원회 회의개최 통지. |

오는 1972년 3월 23일 (목요일) 15:30 시에 외무부

회의실에서 한.미 합동위원회 제 72차회의가 개최될 예정이오니 각 위원

께서는 회의에 필히 참석하여 주시기 바라며, 의제 및 회의자료는 추후

통보 위계입니다.　끝.

수신처 : 법무부장관 (법무실장, 검찰국장, 출입국관리국장),

　　　　국방부장관 (기획국장, 시설국장),　재무부장관 (관세국장),

　　　　상공부장관 (상역국장),　교통부장관 (종합수송담당관),

　　　　노동청장 (노정국장).

공통서식1-2(갑)
1967. 4. 4. 승인

190mm × 268mm (1급인쇄용지70g/㎡)
조달청 (3.31)

AGENDA ITEM I   1. US Presentation

(1. FOR YOUR INFORMATION: The ROK Representative will
convene the meeting and will invite the US Representative to present
sixteen new tasks for assignment to the Facilities and Areas Subcommittee.)

2. Before presenting Agenda Item I, the United States Representative
would like to note that Colonel Carl G. Schneider, Vice Commander of the
314th Air Division/Air Forces Korea, who is now in the USA, will be
leaving the Joint Committee. Colonel Schneider has been an extremely
able and effective member of the Joint Committee and its Ad Hoc Subcommittee on Civil-Military Relations. However, as you may know, Colonel
Schneider has been nominated for promotion to Brigadier General and has
been selected to become the Assistant Chief of Staff, J3, United States
Forces, Korea, upon the departure of Major General Colladay in late
April. Therefore, although we will miss him on the Joint Committee,
on behalf of the US component, I wish to congratulate him on his promotion and new assignment, and I am looking forward to working directly
with him in this new capacity.

3. I should also like to introduce at this time Colonel Schneider's
replacement, Colonel K. D. Dunaway, to the other members of the Joint
Committee. Colonel Dunaway was formerly the Director of Operations
of the 314th Air Division/Air Forces Korea. On behalf of the US component
I wish to welcome Colonel Dunaway to the Joint Committee.

AGENDA ITEM I continued

(4. FOR YOUR INFORMATION: The ROK Representative will congratulate Colonel Schneider on his promotion and will welcome Colonel Dunaway to the Joint Committee. He will then ask the US Representative to present the new tasks to the Facilities and Areas Subcommittee.)

5. The United States Representative would like to present sixteen new tasks for assignment to the Facilities and Areas Subcommittee. These consist of two requests for the acquisition of real estate on a permanent use basis, five requests for the acquisition of Temporary Use Permits, six requests for the extension of existing Temporary Use Permits, and three requests for the release of real estate. All details concerning these sixteen new tasks are contained in memoranda which have been distributed to both sides.

6. It is proposed that these sixteen new tasks be assigned to the Facilities and Areas Subcommittee.

(7. FOR YOUR INFORMATION: The ROK SOFA Secretary has indicated that the ROK Representative will concur in this proposal.)

2

AGENDA ITEM I   2. ROK Presentation

(1. FOR YOUR INFORMATION: The ROK Representative will proceed to present the remaining five new tasks for assignment to the Facilities and Areas Subcommittee. These five new tasks all involve requests for release of relatively small parcels of real estate.)

2. The United States Representative is happy to concur in the assignment of the five specified new tasks to the Facilities and Areas Subcommittee.

(1. FOR YOUR INFORMATION: The Ad Hoc Subcommittee on Civil-Military Relations, at its seventh meeting on 18 February 1972, approved among other actions a recommendation submitted by its Panel on Larceny and Black Marketing. This recommendation subsequently was approved by the Joint Committee at its seventy-first meeting on 24 February 1972. The recommendation provides "That US military authorities, in consultation with ROK Government authorities, develop a list of additional items to be added to the PX and Commissary controlled item ration system, and that the procedures for monitoring the outflow of items beyond the reasonable needs of an individual be strengthened.")

(2. FOR YOUR INFORMATION: With regard to the implementation of this recommendation, it was mutually agreed in discussions between the US and ROK Secretariat personnel that the most appropriate method for implementation would be through the assignment of a task requesting implementation to the Finance (Personnel Affairs) Subcommittee, since the subject matter of the recommendation falls within the area of responsibility of that Subcommittee. Accordingly, the ROK Representative will propose a task assignment in this matter.)

(3. FOR YOUR INFORMATION: During Panel discussions on this subject, the ROK side informally indicated that their concern focused primarily upon the volume of liquor, beer, and cigarettes flowing into the ROK from US bases.)

AGENDA ITEM II continued

4. The United States Representative is pleased to concur in the assignment of the specified task to the Finance (Personnel Affairs) Subcommittee.

AGENDA ITEM III

(1. FOR YOUR INFORMATION: The ROK Representative will invite
the US Representative to present four recommendations received from the
Facilities and Areas Subcommittee, all of them involving releases of
parcels of real estate. Since the ROK Representative has no Facilities'
and Areas recommendations to present at this meeting, upon conclusion
of the US Representative's presentation of this agenda item, he will
propose turning to Agenda Item IV.)

2. The United States Representative would like to present four
recommendations received from the Facilities and Areas Subcommittee.
All of these four recommendations involve the release of land and facilities
at four separate locations throughout Korea. Details concerning these
recommendations will be found in memoranda which have been distributed to both sides.

3. It is proposed that the Joint Committee approve these four
recommendations of the Facilities and Areas Subcommittee.

(4. FOR YOUR INFORMATION: The ROK SOFA Secretary has
indicated that the ROK Representative will concur in this proposal.)

(1. FOR YOUR INFORMATION: The ROK Representative will

propose the Joint Committee approval of the Seventh Report of the

Ad Hoc Subcommittee on Civil-Military Relations along with the four

recommendations included therein. One of these recommendations

from the Panel on Local Community and Governmental Relations con--

cerns measures to be taken by the owners or managers of the estab-

lishments frequented by US servicemen to maintain control and order

The last three recommendations relate to the situation in the Camp

Humphreys-Anjong-ni area. The first of these recommendations

requests that the situation in the Camp Humphreys-Anjongni area

be called to the attention of the ROK "Base Community-Clean-Up

Committee, " stressing the importance of the opportunity for the ROK

Government to assist the local Korean authorities in taking the

necessary steps to eliminate the presently unsatisfactory conditions

in Anjong-ni. The second recommendation calls upon the USFK

and its component commands, especially the command at Camp

Humphreys, to encourage and assist the ROK authorities to deal

promptly and effectively in renovation of Anjong-ni. The third

recommendation concerns the four back-alley clubs which are

currently off limits and proposes a course of action which would

result in local Korean authorities in consultation with local US military

authorities to develop plans and programs to widen alleys adjacent

AGENDA ITEM IV continued

to off-limit clubs into streets capable of handling two-way vehicular

traffic. The recommendation proposes lifting the off limits at a mutually

agreed time when the standards previously agreed upon for the re-opening

of the clubs in Anjong-ni are achieved. The four off-limits clubs must

be accessible to emergency vehicles prior to the re-opening but programs

to develop streets capable of handling two-way vehicular traffic may con-

tinue after the return of the clubs to on limits. Should the plans and pro-

grams fail to be implemented within the period agreed upon between the

Korean and US authorities, those back-alley clubs may be put off limits

again at the discretion of the US military authorities.)

2. The United States Representative is happy to concur in the

Republic of Korea Representative's proposal to accept the Seventh Report

of the Ad Hoc Subcommittee and to approve the four recommendations

therein. I would particularly like to note the recommendations regarding

the Camp Humphreys-Anjong-ni area and to commend the Ad Hoc Sub-

committee for its comprehensive work on this subject with the objective

of improving civil-military relations in the area. With the increasing

importance of Camp Humphreys, the Ad Hoc Subcommittee's proposal

to stress the opportunities for the Republic of Korea's interministerial

"Base Community Clean-Up Committee" to assist local Korean authorit.es

in the area should materially facilitate improvement of the situation at

Anjong-ni. The Ad Hoc Subcommittee proposal to restore the four off-

limits clubs to on-limits status is a mutually agreeable plan to resolve this

2

AGENDA ITEM IV continued

situation. This proposal provides that the local Korean authorities and businessmen, in consultation with US military authorities, will develop mutually agreed plans and programs for widening the alleys adjacent to the off-limits clubs into streets accessible to vehicular traffic. Such a development in Anjong-ni should promote public safety, facilitate the maintenance of law and order, and provide a better environment for effective Korean-American civil-military relations.

3

공　　　　란

공   란

공 란

공 란

공 란

공 란

공   란

공   란

AGENDA ITEM V

ROK Presentation

(1. FOR YOUR INFORMATION: The ROK Representative will present a memorandum from the Utilities Subcommittee, dated 17 March 1972, concerning a change in the rates for water service supplied by the City of Taejon to all users in that area, including USFK. He will propose acceptance of this memorandum by the Joint Committee and will probably note that details concerning the rate change are contained in the memorandum which has already been distributed to both sides.)

(2. FOR YOUR INFORMATION: The US side has carefully reviewed the new water rate table, and has determined that the change in water rates applicable to USFK is no less favorable than rates accorded any other comparable user under the new rate table, as required by paragraph 2 of Article VI of the SOFA. Hence, there is no obstacle to acceptance by USFK of the new water rates.)

(3. FOR YOUR INFORMATION: With the closure of Stonestown Installation in Taejon, USFK no longer has any units in that area using Taejon City water supplies. Therefore, all that is involved from a financial viewpoint is the retroactive payment of the new rate from 27 September 1971, the date the US side was notified of the rate change, through February 1972, involving a sum of approximately $1700.)

4. The United States Representative is happy to concur in accepting the Utility Subcommittee's memorandum as evidence of

349

SOFA 한.미국 합동위원회 회의록, 제70-72차. 1972 355

AGENDA ITEM VI continued

completion of the consultations required by Article VI of the SOFA

pertaining to the increase in rates for water service supplied by the

City of Taejon, effective 27 September 1971.

350

AGENDA ITEM VII   US Presentation

(1. FOR YOUR INFORMATION: The ROK Representative will

request the US Representative to present this agenda item.)

2. The United States Representative wishes to note for the record

that the United States Status of Forces Agreement Secretariat has

furnished the following information to the Republic of Korea Status of

Forces Agreement Secretariat in accordance with the provisions of

the Status of Forces Agreement and Joint Committee decisions.

a. Five copies of reports on the United States armed forces dis-

position of cases for the month of January 1972.

b. One copy of pertinent information on cargo consigned to United

States armed forces non-appropriated fund organizations in the Republic

of Korea for the month of February 1972.

c. Twenty copies of the report of United States armed forces

personnel, the civilian component, invited contractors, and the depend-

ents of each, entering or departing the Republic of Korea during the

month of February 1972.

d. Twenty copies of the USFK monthly update of the listing of all

United States invited contractor employees and dependents as of 29 February

1972.

(3. FOR YOUR INFORMATION: The ROK SOFA Secretary has

indicated that the ROK Representative will acknowledge receipt of

these documents.)

(1. FOR YOUR INFORMATION: In accordance with the procedure for designating the date of the next Joint Committee meeting, the ROK Representative will ask the US Representative if he would like to propose the date, time, and place for the next meeting.)

2. The United States Representative would like to propose that the seventy-third meeting of the Joint Committee be held in the United States Status of Forces Agreement Conference Room on Thursday, 27 April 1972, at 1530 hours.

(3. FOR YOUR INFORMATION: The ROK SOFA Secretary has indicated that the ROK Representative will concur in the proposed date, time, and place for the seventy-third Joint Committee meeting.)

AGENDA ITEM ~~IX~~ VIII   ROK PRESENTATION

(1. FOR YOUR INFORMATION: The ROK Representative will propose approval of the joint press release as drafted by the two SOFA Secretaries and as distributed in advance.)

2. The United States Representative is happy to approve the joint press release for the seventy-second Joint Committee meeting as distributed in advance.

353

(1. FOR YOUR INFORMATION: The ROK Representative will ask the US Representative if he has any further items to present at this meeting.)

2. I have no further items to present at this meeting, Mr. Kim.

(3. FOR YOUR INFORMATION: The ROK Representative will state that since there is no other business to come before the Joint Committee, he declares the seventy-second meeting of the Joint Committee adjourned.)

ADDED AGENDA ITEM   US Presentation

1. The United States Representative would like to propose the assignment of an exigent task to the Transportation Subcommittee, relating to
distinctive license plates for privately-owned vehicles of United States
Forces Korea personnel and United States invited contractors. I am
sorry that we have not handled this proposed task along with other Agenda
items, but this question came to my attention only today, and it appears
to be of such importance that it deserves the urgent attention of the
United States-Republic of Korea Joint Committee.

2. The United States-Republic of Korea Joint Committee approved
a recommendation of the Transportation Subcommittee on 30 December
1971 specifying that privately-owned vehicles of United States Forces
Korea personnel and United States invited contractors be reregistered
and given new license plates of a mutually agreed distinctive design.
This reregistration of the privately-owned vehicles of United States
Forces Korea personnel and United States invited contractors was accomplished in February and March 1972. One of the primary objectives of
our two Governments, I believe, in this reregistration and issuing of
new United States Forces Korea licenses plates of a distinctive design
was to insure the ready identification of the vehicles of United States
Forces Korea in Korea under the SOFA, and to prevent any unauthorized
use by or transfer to unauthorized personnel, thereby defeating the

355

purpose of the Joint Committee and possibly depriving the Ministry of Finance of customs duties.

3. It has come to our attention that the objectives of the Joint Committee in instituting this reregistration and issuing of new licenses may be being subverted by the issuance of the distinctive blue 2-series plates of the United States Forces Korea and invited contractor vehicles to other personnel not ~ it'ed to the licensing and registration of vehicles under United States-Republic of Korea Status of Forces Agreement. It is for this reason that I propose an exigent task to the Transportation Subcommittee to enable them to expeditiously review this problem and to propose procedures designed to insure that the mutually agreed distinctive blue 2-series license plates be issued only for vehicles of United States Forces Korea personnel and United States invited contractors. With the assignment of this task, it is hoped that the Transportation Subcommittee can review all aspects of this problem and arrive at mutually agreed procedures to insure that the provisions of the SOFA and the intent of the Joint Committee-approved procedures are upheld.

2

356

MINUTES OF THE SEVENTY-SECOND MEETING

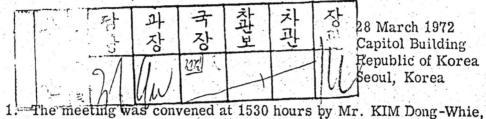

28 March 1972
Capitol Building
Republic of Korea
Seoul, Korea

1. The meeting was convened at 1530 hours by Mr. KIM Dong-Whie,

the ROK Representative, who presided at the meeting. A copy of the

agenda is attached as Inclosure 1.

2. The following were in attendance:

ROK	US
Mr. KIM Dong-Whie	LTG Robert N. Smith, USAF
Mr. KIM Chong Kyung	Captain Frank M. Romanick, USN
Mr. LEE Chong Won	COL David P. Heekin, USA
MG CHO Jae Joon	COL K. D. Dunaway, USAF
BG PAK Woo Bum	COL Bruce T. Coggins, USA
Mr. JUNG Ik Won	Mr. Richard W. Finch, US Embassy
Mr. KIM Young Sup	Mr. Robert A. Kinney, USFK
Mr. KIM Kee Joe	MAJ Dick J. Petersen, USAF
Mr. CHUNG Tai Ik	MR. Francis K. Cook, USFK
Mr. KWON Chan	

3. The US Representative, LTG Robert N. Smith, noted that Colonel

Carl G. Schneider, Vice Commander of the 314th Air Division/Air Forces

Korea, who is now in the USA, will be leaving the Joint Committee. He

stated that Colonel Schneider has been an extremely able and effective

member of the Joint Committee and its Ad Hoc Subcommittee on Civil-

Military Relations. However, Colonel Schneider has been nominated for

promotion to Brigadier General and has been selected to become the

Assistant Chief of Staff, J3, USFK, upon the departure of Major General

Colladay in late April. Therefore, the US Representative commented

that, although Colonel Schneider will be missed on the Joint Committee,

on behalf of the US component, he wished to congratulate him on his

357

promotion and new assignment, and stated that he was looking forward to working directly with him in this new capacity.

4. The US Representative also presented Colonel Schneider's replacement, Colonel K. D. Dunaway, to the other members of the Joint Committee. He stated that Colonel Dunaway was formerly the Director of Operations of the 314th Air Division/Air Forces Korea. On behalf of the US component, LTG Smith welcomed Colonel Dunaway to the Joint Committee.

5. The ROK Representative stated he would like to extend heartfelt congratulations to Colonel Schneider on his pending promotion to Brigadier General. He stated that Colonel Schneider will be missed as an able and dedicated member of the Joint Committee. He said he highly valued all the efforts and contributions Colonel Schneider has made in the activi= ties of the SOFA Joint Committee and of the Ad Hoc Subcommittee on Civil-Military Relations. The ROK Representative said he believed that Colonel Schneider / would be successful in his new assignment and would continue to contribute toward common defense interests of both countries in Korea.

6. On behalf of the Korean component, the ROK Representative extended a warm welcome to Colonel K. D. Dunaway to the Joint Committee. He stated that he was looking forward to working together with Colonel Dunaway in the Joint Committee.

2

7. The US Representative presented sixteen new tasks for assignment to the Facilities and Areas Subcommittee. These consisted of two requests for the acquisition of real estate on a permanent use basis (Inclosures 2 and 3), five requests for the acquisition of Temporary Use Permits (Inclosures 4-6), six requests for the extension of existing Temporary Use Permits (Inclosures 7-10), and three requests for the release of real estate (Inclosures 11 and 12). He stated that details concerning these sixteen new tasks are contained in memoranda which had been distributed to both sides. He proposed that these sixteen tasks be assigned to the Facilities and Areas Subcommittee and the ROK Representative concurred.

8. The ROK Representative presented five new tasks of Facilities and Areas Subcommittee (Inclosures 13-17). He said all of these five tasks involved requests for release of parcels of real estate. The ROK Representative proposed assignment of these five new tasks to the Facilities and Areas Subcommittee, and the US Representative concurred.

9. The ROK Representative stated that the Ad Hoc Subcommittee on Civil-Military Relations, at its seventh meeting on 18 February 1972, approved a recommendation submitted by its panel on Larceny and Black Marketing. The recommendation subsequently was approved by the Joint Committee at its seventy-first meeting on 24 February 1972. This recommendation provided "That US military authorities in consultation

3

with ROK Government authorities, develop a list of additional items to be added to the PX and commissary controlled item ration system, and that the procedures for monitoring the outflow of items beyond the reasonable needs of an individual be strengthened." With regard to the implementation of this recommendation, the ROK Representative proposed the assignment of a task on this subject to the Finance (Personnel Affairs) Subcommittee. The US Representative concurred.

10. The US Representative presented four recommendations received from the Facilities and Areas Subcommittee (Inclosure 19). He stated that all of these four recommendations involved the release of land and facilities at four separate locations throughout Korea. He proposed that the Joint Committee approve these four recommendations of the Facilities and Areas Subcommittee. The ROK Representative concurred.

11. The ROK Representative stated that he was pleased to note that the Ad Hoc Subcommittee on Civil-Military Relations, after making its second fact-finding trip to the Anjong-ni-Camp Humphreys area, has presented recommendations which have been worked out/mutually on a agreeable basis with a view to resolving the problems existing in that area. The ROK Representative proposed that this Seventh Report, together with its four recommendations, be approved and recorded in the minutes of this Joint Committee meeting. These four recommenda-

4

360

tions include three on the Camp Humphreys-Anjong-ni area and one
from the Panel on Local Community and Governmental Relations.

12. The US Representative stated that he was happy to concur in the
ROK Representative's proposal to accept the Seventh Report of the Ad
Hoc Subcommittee and to approve the four recommendations therein.
He stated that he would particularly like to note the recommendations regarding the Camp Humphreys-Anjong-ni area and to commend the Ad Hoc
Subcommittee for its comprehensive work toward improving civil-
military relations in the area. He said that, with the increasing importance of Camp Humphreys, the Ad Hoc Subcommittee's proposal to stress
the opportunities for the ROK interministerial "Base Community Clean-
Up Committee" to assist local Korean authorities in the area should
materially faciliate improvement of the situation at Anjong-ni. He
stated that the Ad Hoc Subcommittee's proposal to restore the four off-
limits clubs to on-limits status provides that the local Korean authorities
and businessmen, in consultation with US military authorities, develop
mutually agreed plans and programs for widening the alleys adjacent to
the off-limits clubs into streets accessible to vehicular traffic. He stated
that such a development in Anjong-ni should promote public safety, facilitate the maintenance of law and order, and provide a better environment
for effective Korean-American civil-military relations.

5

36l

13. The ROK Representative proposed that the Joint Committee accept the Utility Subcommittee's memorandum dated 17 March 1972 (Inclosure 20) as evidence of the completion of the consultations required by Article VI of the SOFA pertaining to the increase in rates for water service supplied by the City of Taejon, effective 27 September 1971.

14. The US Representative stated that he was happy to concur in accepting the Utility Subcommittee's memorandum as evidence of completion of the consultations required by Article VI of the SOFA pertaining to the increase in rates for water service supplied by the City of Taejon, effective 27 September 1971.

15. The US Representative noted for the record that the US SOFA Secretariat had furnished the following information to the ROK SOFA Secretariat in accordance with the provisions of the SOFA and Joint Committee decisions.

a. Five copies of reports on the US armed forces disposition of cases for the month of January 1972.

b. One copy of pertinent information on cargo consigned to US armed forces non-appropriated fund organizations in the ROK for the month of February 1972.

c. Twenty copies of the report of US armed forces personnel, the civilian component, invited contractors, and the dependents of each, entering or departing the ROK during the month of February 1972.

6

16. The ROK Representative acknowledged the receipt of the reports as enumerated by the US Representative.

17. The US Representative proposed that the seventy-third meeting of the Joint Committee be held in the US SOFA Conference Room on Thursday, 27 April 1972, at 1530 hours. The ROK Representative concurred.

18. The ROK Representative proposed that the Joint Committee
(Inclosure 21)
adopt the joint press release/as prepared and distributed in advance by both secretaries of the Joint Committee. The US Representative concurred.

19. The meeting was adjourned at 1630 hours.

21 Incl

KIM DONG-WHIE
Republic of Korea
Representative

ROBERT N. SMITH
Lieutenant General
United Stats Air Force
United States Representative

7

AGENDA FOR THE SEVENTY-SECOND MEETING
OF THE ROK-US JOINT COMMITTEE
1530 HOURS, 28 MARCH 1972, ROK CAPITOL BUILDING

I.   Assignment of Tasks to Facilities and Areas Subcommittee.

     1.   Sixteen Tasks - US Presentation.

     2.   Five Tasks - ROK Presentation.

II.   Assignment of Task to Finance (Personnel Affairs) Subcommittee - ROK Presentation.

III.   Recommendation of Facilities and Areas Subcommittee - US Presentation.

IV.   Consideration of Seventh Report and Recommendations of Ad Hoc Subcommittee on Civil-Military Relations - ROK and US Presentations.

V.   Memorandum from Utilities Subcommittee - ROK Presentation.

VI.   Memoranda Presented to the ROK Government by the US in the Implementation of the SOFA - US Presentation.

VII.   Proposed Time of Next Meeting - 1630 Hours, Thursday, 27 April 1972, in the US SOFA Conference Room.

VIII.   Agreement on Joint Press Release.

IX.   Adjourn.

364

**JOINT COMMITTEE
UNDER
THE REPUBLIC OF KOREA AND THE UNITED STATES
STATUS OF FORCES AGREEMENT**

23 March 1972

MEMORANDUM FOR: Chairmen, Facilities and Areas Subcommittee

SUBJECT: Request for Acquisition of Real Estate

1. SOFA provides in Article II, paragraph 2, that the Governments of the Republic of Korea and the United States may agree that facilities and areas or portions thereof, shall be returned to the Republic of Korea or that additional facilities and areas may be provided.

2. Pursuant to paragraph 1 above, it is requested that a recommendation be presented to the Joint Committee concerning a request for the acquisition, on a permanent exclusive use basis, of one Korean-constructed building composed of wood and masonry containing approximately 3,339 square feet of building space. This building was constructed on USFK land acquired on an exclusive use basis, and is located within the Kunsan Air Base held under Acquisition No. PAC-KUNSAN-233. The building is presently vacant.

KIM DONG-WHIE
Republic of Korea
Representative

ROBERT N. SMITH
Lieutenant General
United States Air Force
United States Representative

23 March 1972

MEMORANDUM FOR: Chairmen, Facilities and Areas Subcommittee

SUBJECT: Request for Acquisition of Real Estate

1. SOFA provides in Article II, paragraph 2, that the Governments of the Republic of Korea and the United States may agree that facilities and areas or portions thereof, shall be returned to the Republic of Korea or that additional facilities and areas may be provided.

2. Pursuant to paragraph 1 above, it is requested that a recommendation be presented to the Joint Committee concerning a request for the acquisition, on a permanent use basis, of a total of 1.736 acres of land in three non-contiguous areas, located in Pochon-gun, Kyonggi-do. This real estate is require to upgrade Pochon R217 Airfield.

KIM DONG-WHIE	ROBERT N. SMITH
Republic of Korea	Lieutenant General
Representative	United States Air Force
	United States Representative

23 March 1972

MEMORANDUM FOR: Chairmen, Facilities and Areas Subcommittee

SUBJECT: Request for Acquisition of Temporary Use Permit

1. SOFA provides in Article II, paragraph 2, that the Governments of the Republic of Korea and the United States may agree that facilities and areas or portions thereof, shall be returned to the Republic of Korea or that additional facilities and areas may be provided.

2. Pursuant to paragraph 1 above, it is requested that a recommendation be presented to the Joint Committee concerning a request for the acquisition of a Temporary Use Permit, involving 31.00 acres of river bed land, located in Chilgok-gun, Kyongsangbuk-do, for a period of twelve months following the date of any approval by the US-ROK Joint Committee of a recommendation on this subject. This real estate is required to provide a source of gravel and sand materials for construction projects.

KIM DONG-WHIE
Republic of Korea
Representative

ROBERT N. SMITH
Lieutenant General
United States Air Force
United States Representative

**JOINT COMMITTEE
UNDER
THE REPUBLIC OF KOREA AND THE UNITED STATES
STATUS OF FORCES AGREEMENT**

23 March 1972

MEMORANDUM FOR: Chairmen, Facilities and Areas Subcommittee

SUBJECT: Requests for Acquisition of Temporary Use Permits

1. SOFA provides, in Article II, paragraph 2, that the Governments of the Republic of Korea and the United States may agree that facilities and areas or portions thereof shall be returned to the Republic of Korea or that additional facilities and areas may be provided.

2. Pursuant to paragraph 1 above, it is requested that recommendations be presented to the Joint Committee concerning requests for the following actions:

    a. Acquisition of a Temporary Use Permit, involving approximately 30.40 acres forming a tributary stream bed located in Pochon-gun, Kyonggi-do, for a period of twelve months following the date of any approval of a recommendation on this subject by the US-ROK Joint Committee. This real estate is required to provide a source of gravel rock materials required in the upgrading construction program for the Pochon R-217 Airfield.

    b. Acquisition of a Temporary Use Permit, involving 42.551 acres of land located in Kwangsang-gun, Chollanam-do, for a period of four months following the date of any approval of a recommendation on this subject by the US-ROK Joint Committee. This real estate is required for topographic survey and soil exploration to select a site for a hazardous cargo pad at Kwangju Air Base.

KIM DONG-WHIE
Republic of Korea
Representative

ROBERT N. SMITH
Lieutenant General
United States Air Force
United States Representative

23 March 1972

MEMORANDUM FOR: Chairmen, Facilities and Areas Subcommittee

SUBJECT: Requests for Acquisition of Temporary Use Permits

1. SOFA provides in Article II, paragraph 2, that the Governments of the Republic of Korea and the United States may agree that facilities and areas or portions thereof, shall be returned to the Republic of Korea or that additional facilities and areas may be provided.

2. Pursuant to paragraph 1 above, it is requested that recommendations be presented to the Joint Committee concerning requests for the following actions:

a. Acquisition of a Temporary Use Permit for the establishment of one navigational aid site in Wando-gun, Chollanam-do, to be known as Wan-do, for the period 1 May 1972 through 31 December 1972. This site will be used for the conduct of joint surveys by the US Naval Oceanographic Office and the ROK Hydrographic Office. The precise location of this site is indicated on a map in the possession of the Republic of Korea Ministry of National Defense and the Real Estate Division of the Engineer, USFK.

b. Acquisition of a Temporary Use Permit for the establishment of one navigational aid site in Wando-gun, Chollanam-do, to be known as Saengil-to, for the period 1 May 1972 through 31 December 1972. This site will be used for the conduct of joint surveys by the US Naval Oceanographic Office and the ROK Hydrographic Office. The precise location of this site is indicated on a map in the possession of the Republic of Korea Ministry of National Defense and the Real Estate Division of the Engineer, USFK.

KIM DONG-WHIE
Republic of Korea
Representative

ROBERT N. SMITH
Lieutenant General
United States Air Force
United States Representative

23 March 1972

MEMORANDUM FOR: Chairmen, Facilities and Areas Subcommittee

SUBJECT: Requests for Extension of Temporary Use Permits

1. SOFA provides in Article II, paragraph 2, that the Governments of the Republic of Korea and the United States may agree that facilities and areas or portions thereof shall be returned to the Republic of Korea or that additional facilities and areas may be provided.

2. Pursuant to paragraph 1 above, it is requested that recommendations be presented to the Joint Committee concerning requests for the following actions:

a. Extension of Temporary Use Permit K-H-T-16 from 1 May 1972 through 31 December 1972. A general description of real estate currently held under this Temporary Use Permit is as follows:

Name of Navigational Aid Site	Location
(1) Oeraro-do	Kohung-gun, Chollanam-do
(2) Kultong	Buk Cheju-gun, Cheju-do
(3) Pyoson-ni	Namcheju-gun, Cheju-do
(4) Mosulpo	Namcheju-gun, Cheju-do
(5) Changbong-do, P	Puchon-gun, Kyonggi-do
(6) Changbong-do, A	Puchon-gun, Kyonggi-do
(7) Chawol-to, P	Sosan-gun, Chungchongnam-do
(8) Chawol-to, A	Sosan-gun, Chungchongnam-do

b. Extension of Temporary Use Permit K-H-T-21, involving one navigational aid site named Kogum-do, located in Kohung-gun, Chollanam-do, from 1 May 1972 through 31 December 1972.

c. Extension of Temporary Use Permit K-H-T-23 from 15 September 1972 through 31 December 1972. A general description of real estate currently held under this Temporary Use Permit is as follows:

Name of Navigational Aid Site	Location
(1) Yongsang-ni	Bukcheju-gun, Cheju-do
(2) Pogil-to	Wando-gun, Chollanam-do
(3) Imja-do	Muan-gun, Chollanam-do
(4) Chin-do	Chindo-gun, Chollanam-do
(5) Taehuksan-do	Muan-gun, Chollanam-do

3. This real estate is required for the continued conduct of joint surveys by the US Naval Oceanographic Office and the ROK Hydrographic Office. The specific locations of sites involved are indicated on maps in the possession of the Republic of Korea Ministry of National Defense and the Real Estate Division of the Engineer, USFK.

KIM DONG-WHIE
Republic of Korea
Representative

ROBERT N. SMITH
Lieutenant General
United States Air Force
United States Representative

23 March 1972

MEMORANDUM FOR: Chairmen, Facilities and Areas Subcommittee

SUBJECT: Request for Extension of Temporary Use Permit

1. SOFA provides in Article II, paragraph 2, that the Governments of the Republic of Korea and the United States may agree that facilities and areas or portions thereof shall be returned to the Republic of Korea or that additional facilities and areas may be provided.

2. Pursuant to paragraph 1 above, it is requested that a recommendation be presented to the Joint Committee concerning a request for the extension of Temporary Use Permit K-E-T-105, involving approximately 100 acres of land located in Yangyang-gun, Kangwon-do, for the period 1 April 1972 through 31 March 1973. This real estate is required for continued topographic survey and exploratory drilling at R-407 Airfield.

KIM DONG-WHIE
Republic of Korea
Representative

ROBERT N. SMITH
Lieutenant General
United States Air Force
United States Representative

372

23 March 1972

MEMORANDUM FOR: Chairmen, Facilities and Areas Subcommittee

SUBJECT: Request for Extension of Temporary Use Permit

1. SOFA provides in Article II, paragraph 2, that the Governments of the Republic of Korea and the United States may agree that facilities and areas or portions thereof, shall be returned to the Republic of Korea or that additional facilities and areas may be provided.

2. Pursuant to paragraph 1 above, it is requested that a recommendation be presented to the Joint Committee concerning a request for the extension of Temporary Use Permit SAC-T-17, involving 190.35 acres of land in two non-contiguous areas, and located in Pyongtaek-gun, Kyonggi-do. Extension is requested for the period 1 April 1972 through 31 March 1973. This land has been used for training exercises since 1962, and there is a continuing need for its use for that purpose.

KIM DONG-WHIE
Republic of Korea
Representative

ROBERT N. SMITH
Lieutenant General
United States Air Force
United States Representative

23 March 1972

MEMORANDUM FOR: Chairmen, Facilities and Areas Subcommittee

SUBJECT: Request for Extension of Temporary Use Permit.

1. SOFA provides in Article II, paragraph 2, that the Governments of the Republic of Korea and the United States may agree that facilities and areas or portions thereof shall be returned to the Republic of Korea or that additional facilities and areas may be provided.

2. Pursuant to paragraph 1 above, it is requested that a recommendation be presented to the Joint Committee concerning a request for the extension of Temporary Use Permit K-E-T-106, involving approximately 193.00 acres of land located in Chechon-gun, Chungchongbuk-do, from 1 April 1972 through 31 March 1973. This real estate is required for continued use for the purpose of topographic survey and exploratory drilling at R-605 Airfield.

KIM DONG-WHIE
Republic of Korea
Representative

ROBERT N. SMITH
Lieutenant General
United States Air Force
United States Representative

23 March 1972

MEMORANDUM FOR: Chairmen, Facilities and Areas Subcommittee

SUBJECT: Requests for Release of Real Estate

1. SOFA provides in Article II, paragraph 2, that the Governments of the Republic of Korea and the United States may agree that facilities and areas or portions thereof, shall be returned to the Republic of Korea or that additional facilities and areas may be provided.

2. Pursuant to paragraph 1 above, it is requested that recommendations be presented to the Joint Committee concerning requests for the following actions:

   a. Release of 84.446 acres of land, constituting a portion of Seattle Installation currently held under Acquisition No. AAC-395, and located in Inchon City, Kyonggi-do. This request for release includes a total of 16 Korean-constructed buildings and facilities and a total of 77 USFK-constructed buildings and facilities located on the Installation. This real estate has become excess to USFK requirements.

   b. Release of 0.07 acre of land, containing one Korean-constructed building, constituting Taegu RTO Facility held under Acquisition No. PAC-166, and located in Taegu City, Kyongsangbuk-do. This real estate has become excess to USFK requirements.

KIM DONG-WHIE
Republic of Korea
Representative

ROBERT N. SMITH
Lieutenant General
United States Air Force
United States Representative

23 March 1972

MEMORANDUM FOR: Chairmen, Facilities and Areas Subcommittee

SUBJECT: Request for Release of Real Estate

1. SOFA provides in Article II, paragraph 2, that the Governments of the Republic of Korea and the United States may agree that facilities and areas or portions thereof, shall be returned to the Republic of Korea or that additional facilities and areas may be provided.

2. Pursuant to paragraph 1 above, it is requested that a recommendation be presented to the Joint Committee concerning a request for the release of a USFK-constructed communications facility, comprising 156,322 linear feet of aerial and underground communications cable line, located within Pochon-gun, Kyonggi-do. There is no land involved in this request for release. This facility has become excess to USFK requirements.

KIM DONG-WHIE
Republic of Korea
Representative

ROBERT N. SMITH
Lieutenant General
United States Air Force
United States Representative

23 March 1972

MEMORANDUM FOR: Chairmen, Facilities and Areas Subcommittee

SUBJECT: Request for Partial Release of Real Estate

1. SOFA provides in Article II, paragraph 2, that the Governments of the Republic of Korea and the United States may agree that facilities and areas or portions thereof, shall be returned to the Republic of Korea or that additional facilities and areas may be provided.

2. Pursuant to paragraph 1 above, it is requested that a recommendation be presented to the Joint Committee concerning a request for the release of approximately 108 square feet of real estate, constituting a portion of the area under acquisition by the USA Far East District Engineer, and located in Bangsandong, Choongu-ku, Seoul City.

KIM DONG-WHIE   ROBERT N. SMITH
Republic of Korea   Lieutenant General
Representative   United States Air Force
                                       United States Representative

23 March 1972

MEMORANDUM FOR: Chairmen, Facilities and Areas Subcommittee

SUBJECT: Request for the Release of Real Estate

1. SOFA provides in Article II, paragraph 2, that the Governments of the Republic of Korea and the United States may agree that facilities and areas or portions thereof, shall be returned to the Republic of Korea or that additional facilities and areas may be provided.

2. Pursuant to paragraph 1 above, it is requested that a recommendation be presented to the Joint Committee concerning a request for the release of approximately 3.87 acres of land, constituting a portion of Seattle Installation currently held under Acquisition No. AAC-395, and located in Inchon City, Kyonggi-do.

KIM DONG-WHIE
Republic of Korea
Representative

ROBERT N. SMITH
Lieutenant General
United States Air Force
United States Representative

23 March 1972

MEMORANDUM FOR: Chairmen, Facilities and Areas Subcommittee

SUBJECT: Request for the Release of Real Estate

1. SOFA provides in Article II, paragraph 2, that the Governments of the Republic of Korea and the United States may agree that facilities and areas or portions thereof, shall be returned to the Republic of Korea or that additional facilities may be provided.

2. Pursuant to paragraph 1 above, it is requested that a recommendation be presented to the Joint Committee concerning a request for the release of a portion of the real estate currently held under Acquisition No. SAC-677, which is used by USFK as a dairy plant and which is located in Yongdungpo-dong, Yongdungpo-ku, Seoul City.

KIM DONG-WHIE
Republic of Korea
Representative

ROBERT N. SMITH
Lieutenant General
United States Air Force
United States Representative

23 March 1972

MEMORANDUM FOR: Chairmen, Facilities and Areas Subcommittee

SUBJECT: Request for Partial Release of Real Estate

1. SOFA provides in Article II, paragraph 2, that the Governments of the Republic of Korea and the United States may agree that facilities and areas or portions thereof shall be returned to the Republic of Korea or that additional facilities and areas may be provided.

2. Pursuant to paragraph 1 above, it is requested that a recommendation be presented to the Joint Committee concerning a request for release of 1.00 acre of land which is a portion of the area held under Acquisition No. CAV-130 and located at Camp Edwards, Youngtae-ri, Walryong-myun, Paju-gun, Kyonggi-do. This real estate is required for the military use by the ROK Army.

KIM DONG-WHIE
Republic of Korea
Representative

ROBERT N. SMITH
Lieutenant General
United States Air Force
United States Representative

380

28 March 1972

MEMORANDUM FOR: Chairmen, Facilities and Areas Subcommittee

SUBJECT: Request for Release of Real Estate

1. SOFA provides in Article II, paragraph 2, that the Governments of the Republic of Korea and the United States may agree that facilities and areas or portions thereof shall be returned to the Republic of Korea or that additional facilities and areas may be provided.

2. Pursuant to paragraph 1 above, it is requested that a recommendation be presented to the Joint Committee concerning a request for the release of 0.6 acre of land, constituting Fire Station No. 10 currently held under Acquisition No. SAC-95, and located in Hengdang-dong, Songdong-ku, Seoul City.

KIM DONG-WHIE
Republic of Korea
Representative

ROBERT N. SMITH
Lieutenant General
United States Air Force
United States Representative

381

23 March 1972

MEMORANDUM FOR: Chairmen, Finance (Personnel Affairs)
Subcommittee

SUBJECT: Request for Implementation of Recommendation of the
Panel on Larceny and Black Marketing

1.   The Ad Hoc Subcommittee on Civil-Military Relations, at its
seventh meeting on 18 February 1972, among other actions approved
a recommendation submitted by its Panel on Larceny and Black Marketing. This recommendation subsequently was approved by the US-
ROK Joint Committee at its seventy-first meeting on 24 February 1972.

2.   The text of the aforementioned recommendation is as follows:

"That US military authorities, in consultation with ROK Government authorities, develop a list of additional items to be added to the
PX and Commissary controlled item ration system, and that the procedures for monitoring the outflow of items beyond the reasonable
needs of an individual be strengthened."

3.   Since the subject matter of paragraph 2 falls within the area of
responsibility of the Finance (Personnel Affairs) Subcommittee, mutual
consultation is requested toward the end of formulating a recommendation in this matter for transmittal to the Joint Committee.

KIM DONG-WHIE
Republic of Korea
Representative

ROBERT N. SMITH
Lieutenant General
United States Air Force
United States Representative

REPUBLIC OF KOREA - UNITED STATES
FACILITIES AND AREAS SUBCOMMITTEE

16 March 1972

MEMORANDUM FOR: THE JOINT COMMITTEE

1. Subcommittee Members:

United States	Republic of Korea
BG Philip T. Boerger, Chairman	BG PAK Woo Bum, Chairman
COL Leonard Edelstein, Alt. Chairman	Mr. MIN Won Sik, Secty
COL Eugene T. Blanton, USAF	Mr. KANG Hong Suk, Asst Secty
MAJ William S. Littlefield, J4, USFK	LTC SHIN Sang Pil
MAJ Allen D. Adams, USAFCS, K	Mr. KIM Young Sup
CPT James H. Smith, USAF	Mr. SONG Jae Kun
Mr. Francis K. Cook, J5, USFK	Mr. CHOE Byong Hoon
Mr. S. F. O'Hop, ENJ-RE, Secty	Mr. SOUNG Baek Jon
Mr. E. H. Brummett, ENJ-RE,	Mr. DO Tae Ku
Alt. Secty	Mr. SUH Chin Hwan
	Mr. LEE Soung Woo
	Mr. PARK Dahl Young
	Mr. BAE Jeung Sun

2. Subject of Recommendation: Requests of Release of Real Estate, Joint
Committee memorandum, dated 24 February 1972.

3. Recommendation: Tasks 1146-1149 The following requests for release
of real estate have been accepted by the Ministry of National Defense:

    a. Task 1146 Release of 11.467 acres of land, constituting a portion of
Kanghwa-do Installation, currently held under Acq. Nos. Inchon-268, ASCOM-
379, and K-E-401, and located in Kanghwa-gun, Kyonggi-do. This request for
release includes a total of 56 USFK-constructed buildings and facilities located
on that Installation. This real estate has become excess to USFK requirements.

b. **Task 1147** Release of 37.89 acres of land, constituting the A-102 Airfield which is a portion of Market Installation held under Acq. No. AAC-396, and located in Inchon City, Kyonggi-do. This request for release includes two Korean-constructed buildings and a total of 68 USFK-constructed buildings and facilities. This real estate has become excess to USFK requirements.

c. **Task 1148** Release of one Korean-constructed building (No. S-230), constituting a portion of the acquisition held under Acq. No. PAC-Taegu-113, and located on Camp Henry Installation, Taegu City, Kyongsangbuk-do. This building has deteriorated beyond economical repair and maintenance.

d. **Task 1149** Release of 13.36 acres of land, constituting Stonestown Installation, currently held under Acq. No. SAC-PAC-135, and located in Taejon City, Chungchongnam-do. This request for release includes a total of 20 Korean-constructed buildings and facilities and a total of 70 USFK-constructed buildings and facilities which are located on the Installation. This real estate has become excess to USFK requirements.

The Ministry of National Defense and the USFK Engineer will prepare the necessary documents. It is recommended that the Joint Committee, SOFA, approve this recommendation.

4. Security Classification: Unclassified

Brigadier General PAK Woo Bum
Chairman, ROK Component
Facilities and Areas Subcommittee

Brigadier General Philip T. Boerger
Chairman, US Component
Facilities and Areas Subcommittee

384

2

공   란

공   란

REPUBLIC OF KOREA-UNITED STATES
UTILITIES SUBCOMMITTEE

17 March 1972

MEMORANDUM TO: The Joint Committee

SUBJECT: Consultation on Rate/Tariff Changes

1. Subcommittee Members:

ROK	US
Mr. SUH Suck Joon, Chairman	COL Richard T. Cann, Chairman
Mr. PARK Woon Suh, Secretary	COL Norman W. Hammes, Alt Chairman
Mr. KIM Woon Cho, Member	LTC Charles J. Turner, Secretary
Mr. NOH Chin Shik, Member	CDR John P. Smith, Member
Mr. CHUNG Chae Jin, Member	Mr. William E. Woodford, Member
Mr. KIM Jong Ho, Member	MAJ Robert E. Frazier, Member
Mr. SONG Hae Joon, Member	Mr. Samuel Pollock, Member
Mr. PAIK Joong Sup, Member	Mr. Don Leland, Member
Mr. SHIN Kyong Shick, Member	MAJ Jewell D. Raymond, Member
Mr. KIM Sung Shil, Member	Mr. Francis K. Cook, Member

2. **Subject of Recommendation:** Agreed Minute 1 to Article VI, ROK-US SOFA, provides that any changes determined by the authorities of the Republic of Korea in priorities, conditions, and rates or tariffs, applicable to the United States armed forces shall be the subject of consultation in the Joint Committee prior to their effective date.

3. The Republic of Korea has initiated consultation concerning a change in rates or tariffs for the cost of water purchased from the City of Taejon, effective 27 September 1971, under contract DABJO3-69-C-0275 (Inclosure 1).

4. The United States component of the Utilities Subcommittee has received the ROK request for consultation and has determined that the requested change in rates or tariffs is no less favorable than those accorded any other comparable user (see inclosure 2).

5. It is recommended that the two inclosures referenced in paragraphs 3 and 4 be accepted by the Joint Committee as evidence of consultation contemplated by Article VI of the Status of Forces Agreement.

2 Incl

RICHARD T. CANN, COL, USA
United States Chairman
Utilities Subcommittee

SUH SUCK JOON
Republic of Korea Chairman
Utilities Subcommittee

REPUBLIC OF KOREA-UNITED STATES

UTILITIES SUBCOMMITTEE

27 September, 1971

SUBJECT :   Change in Water Supply Rate Schedule applicable to the
US Armed Forces under Article VI of the Status of Forces
Agreement.

TO :   US Chairman, Utilities Subcommittee

1.   Reference : Paragraph 2 and Agreed Minute 1 of Article VI of
the Status of Force Agreement.

2.   The Government of the United States is informed through this
written consultative process that the Republic of Korea proposes to change the following rate/tariff at locations below:

Rate/Tariff   Location

Water Supply   The city of Taejon

3.   The following date are provide:

a.   Effective date.

Although the rate change are effective from 1 May, 1970
in Taejon, the new rate will be applied to the US Forces'
use in accordance with the agreement set forth in the
letter dated 15 November, 1969.

b.   Rate schedule of proposed change.

Refer to item " d ".

c.   Rate schedule showing rates that are charged all classes
of users. (attached)

Inclosure 1

d. Calculation of old and new rate

description	old rate (won)	new rate (won)
Basic rate for the first 30m^3	300	700
Excess charge per m^3	15	40

e. Reason for revision of rate base.
    To cover the rising prime cost.

4. The Government of ROK advises the Government of the United States that priorities, conditions, and rates or tariffs being changed are no less favorable than those accorded any other user. The view of the Government of the United States is solicited as soon as possible. You may be assured that your views will be greatly appreciated.

Suck Joon Suh
Suck Joon Suh
Chairman
ROK Utilities Subcommittee

(attached)

Water Rate Schedule of the city of Taejon

Description	Unit	Monthly basic rate		Charge above Minimun (per 1 m³)
		Q'ty(m³)	Rate(won)	
Special use	1 house 1 place	30	700	40
Commercial	"	20	450	40
Recreation	1 place	-	-	40
Bath house	1 house 1 place	200	4,000	25
Construction	1 place	-	-	35
Industrial use	1 house 1 place	20,000	200,000	15
Domestic	1 house	10	150	20
Public	1 house	5	60	20

REPUBLIC OF KOREA - UNITED STATES
UTILITIES SUBCOMMITTEE

15 March 1972

SUBJECT: Change in Water Supply Rate Schedule Applicable to the US Armed Forces under Article VI of the Status of Forces Agreement

TO: Republic of Korea Chairman, Utilities Subcommittee

1. References:

    a. Paragraph 2 and Agreed Minute 1 of Article VI of the Status of Forces Agreement.

    b. ROK component of the Utilities Subcommittee Memorandum of Consultation, dated 27 September 1971, subject as above, pertaining to the rate change in water supply for the City of Taejon.

2. The ROK memorandum, reference 1b above, has been reviewed and the United States component of the Utilities Subcommittee fully understands the requirement for change in the water supply rates in this instance and will join with the ROK component of the Utilities Subcommittee in presenting a memorandum on the rates to the Joint Committee.

RICHARD T. CANN
United States Chairman
Utilities Subcommittee

Inclosure 2

28 March 1972

MEMORANDUM FOR: Chairmen, Transportation Subcommittee

SUBJECT: Distinctive License Plates for Privately-Owned Vehicles
of USFK Personnel and Invited Contractors

1. The first sentence of paragraph 2 of the Agreed Procedures for
licensing and registration of privately-owned vehicles of United
States Forces, Korea personnel (Inclosure 1 to Inclosure 12 to the
minutes of the twenty-eighth meeting of the US-ROK Joint Committee) approved by the Joint Committee at its twenty-eighth meeting
on 3 July 1968 states:

"The Government of the Republic of Korea will produce
a requisite number of license plates and seals to a design
and specification of its choice."

2. The first sentence of paragraph 2 of the Agreed Procedures for
licensing and registration of privately-owned vehicles of United
States armed forces invited contractors in Korea (Inclosure 1 to Inclosure 17 to the minutes of the thirty-second meeting of the US-
ROK Joint Committee) approved by the Joint Commi_ tee at its thirty-
second meeting on 7 November 1968 is identical to the above.

3. Officials of the Republic of Korea indicated informally late in
1971 that they desired all privately-owned vehicles of US Forces,
Korea personnel and invited contractors be re-registered with new
license plates of a distinctive design. The United States Forces,
Korea desired to re-register the privately-owned vehicles of its
personnel and United States armed forces invited contractors with
a distinctive and readily identifiable license plate. A task was assigned to the Transportation Subcommittee on 6 December 1971 to
insure that the new license plate issued be of a design and specification which is mutually agreeable. This recommendation of the Transportation Subcommittee to resolve this task was approved by the
Joint Committee on 30 December 1971 and the privately-owned vehicles of USFK personnel and US invited contractors were re-registered
and given the agreed distinctive plates in February and March 1972.

393

The Joint Committee agreed that these distinctive license plates will be issued on an annual basis and that revalidation of vehicle registration will be accomplished concurrently.

4. The Transportation Subcommittee is assigned another task to review the problem of the issuance of these new distinctive license plates and to propose procedures designed to insure that the mutually agreed distinctive plates be issued only for vehicles of USFK personnel and US invited contractors.

KIM DONG-WHIE
Republic of Korea
Representative

ROBERT N. SMITH
Lieutenant General
United States Air Force
United States Representative

JOINT ROK-US PRESS RELEASE
SEVENTY-SECOND ROK-US JOINT COMMITTEE MEETING
28 MARCH 1972

The ROK-US SOFA Joint Committee received the seventh report of its Ad Hoc Subcommittee on Civil-Military Relations and approved four recommendations submitted to it by this Subcommittee at its seventy-second meeting held in the ROK Capitol Building on 28 March 1972. These recommendations include one from the Panel on Local Community and Governmental Relations and three relating to ROK and US proposals to improve civil-military relations in the Camp Humphreys-Anjong-ni area.

The ROK-US Joint Committee also approved four recommendations of the Facilities and Areas Subcommittee and assigned twenty-one new tasks to that Subcommittee. The Finance (Personnel Affairs) Subcommittee was also assigned a new task and a memorandum from the Utilities Subcommittee was approved.

The ROK Representative, Mr. KIM Dong-Whie, presided at this meeting. The next meeting of the SOFA Joint Committee is scheduled for 27 April 1972 in the US SOFA Conference Room.

기 안 용 지

분류기호 문서번호	미이 720 -	(전 화 번 호 　　)	국장 　 전 결 사 항
처 리 기 간			
시 행 일 자			
보 존 년 한			북 　 장
보 조 기 관	과 장		협
기 안 책 임 자	김성심	북미 2과 (72.	
경 유			
수 신	수신처 참조		1972. 4. 20 외무부 / 1972. 4 20
참 조			
제 목	한.미 합동위원회 회의록 송부		

1. 한미 군대지위협정에 따른 한.미 합동위원회 제 72차 회의가
72. 3. 28. 개최되었는 바, 동회의 회의록을 별첨 송부하오니 합동위
결의사항중 귀부 소관사항을 시행하시고 그 결과를 당부에 통보하여
주시기 바랍니다.

2. 본 회의록은 한.미 양측의 합의에 의하여서만 공개할수 있는
문서이오니, 유념하시기 바랍니다.

	정서

첨부 : 합동위원회 제 72차 회의록. 끝.

	관인

수신처 : 경제기획원장관 (물가정책관), 내무부장관 (치안국장, 지방국장),
법무부장관 (법무 실장, 검찰국장, 출입국관리국장), 재무부장관
(세제국장, 관세국장), 상공부장관 (상역국장), 국방부장관
(기획국장, 시설국장), 교통부장관 (종합수송담당관), 난비정. 397
노동청장 (노정국장), 주미, 주일, 주비, 주중 대사. 2047

396

Governments and will not be released without mutual agreement.

**JOINT COMMITTEE
UNDER
THE REPUBLIC OF KOREA AND THE UNITED STATES
STATUS OF FORCES AGREEMENT**

MINUTES OF THE SEVENTY-SECOND MEETING

28 March 1972
Capitol Building
Republic of Korea
Seoul, Korea

1. The meeting was convened at 1530 hours by Mr. KIM Dong-Whie, the ROK Representative, who presided at the meeting. A copy of the agenda is attached as Inclosure 1.

2. The following were in attendance:

ROK	US
Mr. KIM Dong-Whie	LTG Robert N. Smith, USAF
Mr. KIM Chong Kyung	Captain Frank M. Romanick, USN
Mr. LEE Chong Won	COL David P. Heekin, USA
MG CHO Jae Joon	COL K. D. Dunaway, USAF
BG PAK Woo Bum	COL Bruce T. Coggins, USA
Mr. JUNG Ik Won	Mr. Richard W. Finch, US Embassy
Mr. KIM Young Sup	Mr. Robert A. Kinney, USFK
Mr. KIM Kee Joe	MAJ Dick J. Petersen, USAF
Mr. CHUNG Tai Ik	Mr. Francis K. Cook, USFK
Mr. KWON Chan	

3. The US Representative, LTG Robert N. Smith, noted that Colonel Carl G. Schneider, Vice Commander of the 314th Air Division/Air Forces Korea, who is now in the USA, will be leaving the Joint Committee. He stated that Colonel Schneider has been an extremely able and effective member of the Joint Committee and its Ad Hoc Subcommittee on Civil-Military Relations. However, Colonel Schneider has been nominated for promotion to Brigadier General and has been selected to become the Assistant Chief of Staff, J3, USFK, upon the departure of Major General Colladay in late April. Therefore, the US Representative commented that, although Colonel Schneider will be missed on the Joint Committee, on behalf of the US component, he wished to congratulate him on his promotion and new assignment, and stated that he was looking forward to working directly with him in this new capacity.

72d JC
28 Mar 72

These minutes are considered as official documents pertaining to both Governments and will not be released without mutual agreement.

4. The US Representative also introduced Colonel Schneider's replacement, Colonel K. D. Dunaway, to the other members of the Joint Committee. He stated that Colonel Dunaway was formerly the Director of Operations of the 314th Air Division/Air Forces Korea. On behalf of the US component, LTG Smith welcomed Colonel Dunaway to the Joint Committee.

5. The ROK Representative stated he would like to extend heartfelt congratulations to Colonel Schneider on his pending promotion to Brigadier General. He stated that Colonel Schneider will be missed as an able and dedicated member of the Joint Committee. He said he highly valued all the efforts and contributions Colonel Schneider has made in the activities of the SOFA Joint Committee and of the Ad Hoc Subcommittee on Civil-Military Relations. The ROK Representative said he believed that Colonel Schneider would be successful in his new assignment and would continue to contribute toward common defense interests of both countries in Korea.

6. On behalf of the Korean component, the ROK Representative extended a warm welcome to Colonel K. D. Dunaway to the Joint Committee. He stated that he was looking forward to working together with Colonel Dunaway in the Joint Committee.

7. The US Representative presented sixteen new tasks for assignment to the Facilities and Areas Subcommittee. These consisted of two requests for the acquisition of real estate on a permanent use basis (Inclosures 2 and 3), five requests for the acquisition of Temporary Use Permits (Inclosures 4-6), six requests for the extension of existing Temporary Use Permits (Inclosures 7-10), and three requests for the release of real estate (Inclosures 11 and 12). He stated that details concerning these sixteen new tasks are contained in memoranda which had been distributed to both sides. He proposed that these sixteen tasks be assigned to the Facilities and Areas Subcommittee and the ROK Representative concurred.

8. The ROK Representative presented five new tasks of Facilities and Areas Subcommittee (Inclosures 13-17). He said all of these five tasks involved requests for release of parcels of real estate. The ROK Representative proposed assignment of these five new tasks to the Facilities and Areas Subcommittee, and the US Representative concurred.

2   72d JC
                               28 Mar 72

ese minutes are considered as official documents pertaining to both
Governments and will not be released without mutual agreement.

9. The ROK Representative stated that the Ad Hoc Subcommittee
on Civil-Military Relations, at its seventh meeting on 18 February 1972,
approved a recommendation submitted by its Panel on Larceny and Black
Marketing. The recommendation (Inclosure 18) subsequently was approved by the Joint Committee at its seventy-first meeting on 24 February
1972. This recommendation provided "That US military authorities in
consultation with ROK Government authorities, develop a list of additional
items to be added to the PX and commissary controlled item ration system,
and that the procedures for monitoring the outflow of items beyond the
reasonable needs of an individual be strengthened." With regard to the
implementation of this recommendation, the ROK Representative proposed the assignment of a task on this subject to the Finance (Personnel
Affairs) Subcommittee. The US Representative concurred.

10. The US Representative presented four recommendations received from the Facilities and Areas Subcommittee (Inclosure 19). He
stated that all of these four recommendations involved the release of
land and facilities at four separate locations throughout Korea. He proposed that the Joint Committee approve these four recommendations of
the Facilities and Areas Subcommittee. The ROK Representative concurred.

11. The ROK Representative stated that he was pleased to note
that the Ad Hoc Subcommittee on Civil-Military Relations, after making
its second fact-finding trip to the Anjong-ni-Camp Humphreys area, has
presented recommendations which have been worked out on a mutually
agreeable basis with a view to resolving the problems existing in that
area. The ROK Representative proposed that this Seventh Report, together with its four recommendations (Inclosure 20), be approved and
recorded in the minutes of this Joint Committee meeting. These four
recommendations include three on the Camp Humphreys-Anjong-ni
area and one from the Panel on Local Community and Governmental
Relations.

12. The US Representative stated that he was happy to concur in
the ROK Representative's proposal to accept the Seventh Report of the
Ad Hoc Subcommittee and to approve the four recommendations therein. He stated that he would particularly like to note the recommendations regarding the Camp Humphreys-Anjong-ni area and to commend
the Ad Hoc Subcommittee for its comprehensive work toward improving civil-military relations in the area. He said that, with the increasing importance of Camp Humphreys, the Ad Hoc Subcommittee's proposal

3   72d JC
                          28 Mar 72

These minutes are considered as official documents pertaining to both Governments and will not be released without mutual agreement.

to stress the opportunities for the ROK interministerial "Base Community Clean-Up Committee" to assist local Korean authorities in the area should materially facilitate improvement of the situation at Anjong-ni. He stated that the Ad Hoc Subcommittee's proposal to restore the four off-limits clubs to on-limits status provides that the local Korean authorities and businessmen, in consultation with US military authorities, develop mutually agreed plans and programs for widening the alleys adjacent to the off-limits clubs into streets accessible to vehicular traffic. He stated that such a development in Anjong-ni should promote public safety, facilitate the maintenance of law and order, and provide a better environment for effective Korean-American civil-military relations.

13. The ROK Representative proposed that the Joint Committee accept the Utility Subcommittee's memorandum dated 17 March 1972 (Inclosure 21) as evidence of the completion of the consultations required by Article VI of the SOFA pertaining to the increase in rates for water service supplied by the City of Taejon, effective 27 September 1971.

14. The US Representative stated that he was happy to concur in accepting the Utility Subcommittee's memorandum as evidence of completion of the consultations required by Article VI of the SOFA pertaining to the increase in rates for water service supplied by the City of Taejon, effective 27 September 1971.

15. The US Representative noted for the record that the US SOFA Secretariat had furnished the following information to the ROK SOFA Secretariat in accordance with the provisions of the SOFA and Joint Committee decisions.

a. Five copies of reports on the US armed forces disposition of cases for the month of January 1972.

b. One copy of pertinent information on cargo consigned to US armed forces non-appropriated fund organizations in the ROK for the month of February 1972.

c. Twenty copies of the report of US armed forces personnel, the civilian component, invited contractors, and the dependents of each, entering or departing the ROK during the month of February 1972.

4   72d JC
                                          28 Mar 72

These minutes are considered as official documents pertaining to both Governments and will not be released without mutual agreement.

16. The ROK Representative acknowledged the receipt of the reports as enumerated by the US Representative.

17. The US Representative proposed that the seventy-third meeting of the Joint Committee be held in the US SOFA Conference Room on Thursday, 27 April 1972, at 1530 hours. The ROK Representative concurred.

18. The ROK Representative proposed that the Joint Committee adopt the joint press release (Inclosure 22) as prepared and distributed in advance by both secretaries of the Joint Committee. The US Representative concurred.

19. The meeting was adjourned at 1630 hours.

22 Incl

_____
KIM DONG-WHIE
Republic of Korea
Representative

7M Romanich Cptasn
for
_____
ROBERT N. SMITH
Lieutenant General
United States Air Force
United States Representative

5   72d JC
28 Mar 72

AGENDA FOR THE SEVENTY-SECOND MEETING
OF THE ROK-US JOINT COMMITTEE
1530 HOURS, 28 MARCH 1972, ROK CAPITOL BUILDING

I.   Assignment of Tasks to Facilities and Areas Subcommittee.

    1. Sixteen Tasks - US Presentation.

    2. Five Tasks - ROK Presentation.

II.   Assignment of Task to Finance (Personnel Affairs) Subcommittee - ROK Presentation.

III.   Recommendation of Facilities and Areas Subcommittee - US Presentation.

IV.   Consideration of Seventh Report and Recommendations of Ad Hoc Subcommittee on Civil-Military Relations - ROK and US Presentations.

V.   Memorandum from Utilities Subcommittee - ROK Presentation.

VI.   Memoranda Presented to the ROK Government by the US in the Implementation of the SOFA - US Presentation.

VII.   Proposed Time of Next Meeting - 1630 Hours, Thursday, 27 April 1972, in the US SOFA Conference Room.

VIII. Agreement on Joint Press Release.

IX.   Adjourn.

6

72d JC (Incl 1)
28 Mar 72

These minutes are considered as official documents pertaining to both Governments and will not be released without mutual agreement.

.28 March 1972

MEMORANDUM FOR: Chairmen, Facilities and Areas Subcommittee

SUBJECT: Request for Acquisition of Real Estate

1. SOFA provides in Article II, paragraph 2, that the Governments of the Republic of Korea and the United States may agree that facilities and areas or portions thereof, shall be returned to the Republic of Korea or that additional facilities and areas may be provided.

2. Pursuant to paragraph 1 above, it is requested that a recommendation be presented to the Joint Committee concerning a request for the acquisition, on a permanent exclusive use basis, of one Korean-constructed building composed of wood and masonry containing approximately 3, 339 square feet of building space. This building was constructed on USFK land acquired on an exclusive use basis, and is located within the Kunsan Air Base held under Acquisition No. PAC-KUNSAN-233. The building is presently vacant.

KIM DONG-WHIE
Republic of Korea
Representative

ROBERT N. SMITH
Lieutenant General
United States Air Force
United States Representative

7

72d JC (Incl 2)

28 Mar 72

These minutes are considered as official documents pertaining to both Governments and will not be released without mutual agreement.

**JOINT COMMITTEE
UNDER
THE REPUBLIC OF KOREA AND THE UNITED STATES
STATUS OF FORCES AGREEMENT**

28 March 1972

MEMORANDUM FOR: Chairmen, Facilities and Areas Subcommittee

SUBJECT: Request for Acquisition of Real Estate

1. SOFA provides in Article II, paragraph 2, that the Governments of the Republic of Korea and the United States may agree that facilities and areas or portions thereof, shall be returned to the Republic of Korea or that additional facilities and areas may be provided.

2. Pursuant to paragraph 1 above, it is requested that a recommendation be presented to the Joint Committee concerning a request for the acquisition, on a permanent use basis, of a total of 1.736 acres of land in three non-contiguous areas, located in Pochon-gun, Kyonggi-do. This real estate is require to upgrade Pochon R217 Airfield.

KIM DONG-WHIE
Republic of Korea
Representative

for ROBERT N. SMITH
Lieutenant General
United States Air Force
United States Representative

8

72d JC (Incl 3)
28 Mar 72

These minutes are considered as official documents pertaining to both Governments and will not be released without mutual agreement.

**JOINT COMMITTEE
UNDER
THE REPUBLIC OF KOREA AND THE UNITED STATES
STATUS OF FORCES AGREEMENT**

28 March 1972

MEMORANDUM FOR: Chairmen, Facilities and Areas Subcommittee

SUBJECT: Request for Acquisition of Temporary Use Permit

1. SOFA provides in Article II, paragraph 2, that the Governments of the Republic of Korea and the United States may agree that facilities and areas or portions thereof, shall be returned to the Republic of Korea or that additional facilities and areas may be provided.

2. Pursuant to paragraph 1 above, it is requested that a recommendation be presented to the Joint Committee concerning a request for the acquisition of a Temporary Use Permit, involving 31.00 acres of river bed land, located in Chilgok-gun, Kyongsangbuk-do, for a period of twelve months following the date of any approval by the US-ROK Joint Committee of a recommendation on this subject. This real estate is required to provide a source of gravel and sand materials for construction projects.

KIM DONG-WHIE
Republic of Korea
Representative

for ROBERT N. SMITH
Lieutenant General
United States Air Force
United States Representative

9

72d JC (Incl 4)
28 Mar 72

These minutes are considered as official documents pertaining to both Governments and will not be released without mutual agreement.

**JOINT COMMITTEE
UNDER
THE REPUBLIC OF KOREA AND THE UNITED STATES
STATUS OF FORCES AGREEMENT**

28 March 1972

MEMORANDUM FOR: Chairmen, Facilities and Areas Subcommittee

SUBJECT: Requests for Acquisition of Temporary Use Permits

1. SOFA provides, in Article II, paragraph 2, that the Governments of the Republic of Korea and the United States may agree that facilities and areas or portions thereof shall be returned to the Republic of Korea or that additional facilities and areas may be provided.

2. Pursuant to paragraph 1 above, it is requested that recommendations be presented to the Joint Committee concerning requests for the following actions:

a. Acquisition of a Temporary Use Permit, involving approximately 30.40 acres forming a tributary stream bed located in Pochon-gun, Kyonggi-do, for a period of twelve months following the date of any approval of a recommendation on this subject by the US-ROK Joint Committee. This real estate is required to provide a source of gravel rock materials required in the upgrading construction program for the Pochon R-217 Airfield.

b. Acquisition of a Temporary Use Permit, involving 42.551 acres of land located in Kwangsang-gun, Chollanam-do, for a period of four months following the date of any approval of a recommendation on this subject by the US-ROK Joint Committee. This real estate is required for topographic survey and soil exploration to select a site for a hazardous cargo pad at Kwangju Air Base.

KIM DONG-WHIE
Republic of Korea
Representative

ROBERT N. SMITH
Lieutenant General
United States Air Force
United States Representative

10

72d JC (Incl 5)
28 Mar 72

These minutes are considered as official documents pertaining to both
Governments ● will not be released without ● ual agreement.

**JOINT COMMITTEE
UNDER
THE REPUBLIC OF KOREA AND THE UNITED STATES
STATUS OF FORCES AGREEMENT**

28 March 1972

MEMORANDUM FOR: Chairmen, Facilities and Areas Subcommittee

SUBJECT: Requests for Acquisition of Temporary Use Permits

1. SOFA provides in Article II, paragraph 2, that the Governments
of the Republic of Korea and the United States may agree that facilities and areas or portions thereof, shall be returned to the Republic
of Korea or that additional facilities and areas may be provided.

2. Pursuant to paragraph 1 above, it is requested that recommendations be presented to the Joint Committee concerning requests for
the following actions:

a. Acquisition of a Temporary Use Permit for the establishment
of one navigational aid site in Wando-gun, Chollanam-do, to be known
as Wan-do, for the period 1 May 1972 through 31 December 1972. This
site will be used for the conduct of joint surveys by the US Naval
Oceanographic Office and the ROK Hydrographic Office. The precise
location of this site is indicated on a map in the possession of the Republic of Korea Ministry of National Defense and the Real Estate Division
of the Engineer, USFK.

b. Acquisition of a Temporary Use Permit for the establishment
of one navigational aid site in Wando-gun, Chollanam-do, to be known
as Saengil-to, for the period 1 May 1972 through 31 December 1972.
This site will be used for the conduct of joint surveys by the US Naval
Oceanographic Office and the ROK Hydrographic Office. The precise
location of this site is indicated on a map in the possession of the Republic of Korea Ministry of National Defense and the Real Estate Division of the Engineer, USFK.

KIM DONG-WHIE
Republic of Korea
Representative

ROBERT N. SMITH
Lieutenant General
United States Air Force
United States Representative

11

72d JC (Incl 6)
28 Mar 72

SOFA 한.미국 합동위원회 회의록, 제70-72차. 1972 413

Governments and will not be released without mutual agreement.

28 March 1972

MEMORANDUM FOR: Chairmen, Facilities and Areas Subcommittee

SUBJECT: Requests for Extension of Temporary Use Permits

1. SOFA provides in Article II, paragraph 2, that the Governments of the Republic of Korea and the United States may agree that facilities and areas or portions thereof shall be returned to the Republic of Korea or that additional facilities and areas may be provided.

2. Pursuant to paragraph 1 above, it is requested that recommendations be presented to the Joint Committee concerning requests for the following actions:

a. Extension of Temporary Use Permit K-H-T-16 from 1 May 1972 through 31 December 1972. A general description of real estate currently held under this Temporary Use Permit is as follows:

Name of Navigational Aid Site	Location
(1) Oeraro-do	Kohung-gun, Chollanam-do
(2) Kultong	Buk Cheju-gun, Cheju-do
(3) Pyoson-ni	Namcheju-gun, Cheju-do
(4) Mosulpo	Namcheju-gun, Cheju-do
(5) Changbong-do, P	Puchon-gun, Kyonggi-do
(6) Changbong-do, A	Puchon-gun, Kyonggi-do
(7) Chawol-to, P	Sosan-gun, Chungchongnam-do
(8) Chawol-to, A	Sosan-gun, Chungchongnam-do

12

72d JC (Incl 7)
28 Mar 72

These minutes are considered as official documents pertaining to both Governments and will not be released without mutual agreement.

b. Extension of Temporary Use Permit K-H-T-21, involving one navigational aid site named Kogum-do, located in Kohung-gun, Chollanam-do, from 1 May 1972 through 31 December 1972.

c. Extension of Temporary Use Permit K-H-T-23 from 15 September 1972 through 31 December 1972. A general description of real estate currently held under this Temporary Use Permit is as follows:

Name of Navigational Aid Site	Location
(1) Yongsang-ni	Bukcheju-gun, Cheju-do
(2) Pogil-to	Wando-gun, Chollanam-do
(3) Imja-do	Muan-gun, Chollanam-do
(4) Chin-do	Chindo-gun, Chollanam-do
(5) Taehuksan-do	Muan-gun, Chollanam-do

3. This real estate is required for the continued conduct of joint surveys by the US Naval Oceanographic Office and the ROK Hydrographic Office. The specific locations of sites involved are indicated on maps in the possession of the Republic of Korea Ministry of National Defense and the Real Estate Division of the Engineer, USFK.

KIM DONG-WHIE
Republic of Korea
Representative

ROBERT N. SMITH
Lieutenant General
United States Air Force
United States Representative

13

72d JC (Incl 7)
28 Mar 72

These minutes are considered as official documents pertaining to both Governments and will not be released without mutual agreement.

**JOINT COMMITTEE
UNDER
THE REPUBLIC OF KOREA AND THE UNITED STATES
STATUS OF FORCES AGREEMENT**

28 March 1972

MEMORANDUM FOR: Chairmen, Facilities and Areas Subcommittee

SUBJECT: Request for Extension of Temporary Use Permit

1. SOFA provides in Article II, paragraph 2, that the Governments of the Republic of Korea and the United States may agree that facilities and areas or portions thereof shall be returned to the Republic of Korea or that additional facilities and areas may be provided.

2. Pursuant to paragraph 1 above, it is requested that a recommendation be presented to the Joint Committee concerning a request for the extension of Temporary Use Permit K-E-T-105, involving approximately 100 acres of land located in Yangyang-gun, Kangwon-do, for the period 1 April 1972 through 31 March 1973. This real estate is required for continued topographic survey and exploratory drilling at R-407 Airfield.

KIM DONG-WHIE
Republic of Korea
Representative

for ROBERT N. SMITH
Lieutenant General
United States Air Force
United States Representative

14

72d JC (Incl 8)
28 Mar 72

410

ıese mınu.es are consı.ere. as o.ficial .ocuments pertaining to both Governments and will not be released without mutual agreement.

**JOINT COMMITTEE
UNDER
THE REPUBLIC OF KOREA AND THE UNITED STATES
STATUS OF FORCES AGREEMENT**

28 March 1972

MEMORANDUM FOR: Chairmen, Facilities and Areas Subcommittee

SUBJECT: Request for Extension of Temporary Use Permit

1. SOFA provides in Article II, paragraph 2, that the Governments of the Republic of Korea and the United States may agree that facilities and areas or portions thereof, shall be returned to the Republic of Korea or that additional facilities and areas may be provided.

2. Pursuant to paragraph 1 above, it is requested that a recommendation be presented to the Joint Committee concerning a request for the extension of Temporary Use Permit SAC-T-17, involving 190.35 acres of land in two non-contiguous areas, and located in Pyongtaek-gun, Kyonggi-do. Extension is requested for the period 1 April 1972 through 31 March 1973. This land has been used for training exercises since 1962, and there is a continuing need for its use for that purpose.

KIM DONG-WHIE
Republic of Korea
Representative

for ROBERT N. SMITH
Lieutenant General
United States Air Force
United States Representative

15   72d JC (Incl 9)
                  28 Mar 72

These minutes are considered as official documents pertaining to both Governments and will not be released without mutual agreement.

**JOINT COMMITTEE
UNDER
THE REPUBLIC OF KOREA AND THE UNITED STATES
STATUS OF FORCES AGREEMENT**

28 March 1972

MEMORANDUM FOR: Chairmen, Facilities and Areas Subcommittee

SUBJECT: Request for Extension of Temporary Use Permit.

1. SOFA provides in Article II, paragraph 2, that the Governments of the Republic of Korea and the United States may agree that facilities and areas or portions thereof shall be returned to the Republic of Korea or that additional facilities and areas may be provided.

2. Pursuant to paragraph 1 above, it is requested that a recommendation be presented to the Joint Committee concerning a request for the extension of Temporary Use Permit K-E-T-106, involving approximately 193.00 acres of land located in Chechon-gun, Chungchongbuk-do, from 1 April 1972 through 31 March 1973. This real estate is required for continued use for the purpose of topographic survey and exploratory drilling at R-605 Airfield.

KIM DONG-WHIE
Republic of Korea
Representative

ROBERT N. SMITH
Lieutenant General
United States Air Force
United States Representative

16

72d JC (Incl 10)
28 Mar 72

These minutes are considered as official documents pertaining to both
Governments ● d will not be released without ● tual agreement.

28 March 1972

MEMORANDUM FOR: Chairmen, Facilities and Areas Subcommittee

SUBJECT: Requests for Release of Real Estate

1. SOFA provides in Article II, paragraph 2, that the Governments of
the Republic of Korea and the United States may agree that facilities
and areas or portions thereof, shall be returned to the Republic of
Korea or that additional facilities and areas may be provided.

2. Pursuant to paragraph 1 above, it is requested that recommendations be presented to the Joint Committee concerning requests for the
following actions:

    a. Release of 84.446 acres of land, constituting a portion of Se-
attle Installation currently held under Acquisition No. AAC-395, and
located in Inchon City, Kyonggi-do. This request for release includes
a total of 16 Korean-constructed buildings and facilities and a total of
77 USFK-constructed buildings and facilities located on the Installation.
This real estate has become excess to USFK requirements.

    b. Release of 0.07 acre of land, containing one Korean-constructed
building, constituting Taegu RTO Facility held under Acquisition No. PAC-
166, and located in Taegu City, Kyongsangbuk-do. This real estate has
become excess to USFK requirements.

KIM DONG-WHIE
Republic of Korea
Representative

ROBERT N. SMITH
Lieutenant General
United States Air Force
United States Representative

17

72d JC (Incl 11)
28 Mar 72

These minutes are considered as official documents pertaining to both Governments and will not be released without mutual agreement.

**JOINT COMMITTEE
UNDER
THE REPUBLIC OF KOREA AND THE UNITED STATES
STATUS OF FORCES AGREEMENT**

28 March 1972

MEMORANDUM FOR: Chairmen, Facilities and Areas Subcommittee

SUBJECT: Request for Release of Real Estate

1. SOFA provides in Article II, paragraph 2, that the Governments of the Republic of Korea and the United States may agree that facilities and areas or portions thereof, shall be returned to the Republic of Korea or that additional facilities and areas may be provided.

2. Pursuant to paragraph 1 above, it is requested that a recommendation be presented to the Joint Committee concerning a request for the release of a USFK-constructed communications facility, comprising 156,322 linear feet of aerial and underground communications cable line, located within Pochon-gun, Kyonggi-do. There is no land involved in this request for release. This facility has become excess to USFK requirements.

KIM DONG-WHIE
Republic of Korea
Representative

ROBERT N. SMITH
Lieutenant General
United States Air Force
United States Representative

18

72d JC (Incl 12)
28 Mar 72

These minutes are considered as official documents pertaining to both Governments and will not be released without mutual agreement.

28 March 1972

MEMORANDUM FOR: Chairmen, Facilities and Areas Subcommittee

SUBJECT: Request for Partial Release of Real Estate

1. SOFA provides in Article II, paragraph 2, that the Governments of the Republic of Korea and the United States may agree that facilities and areas or portions thereof, shall be returned to the Republic of Korea or that additional facilities and areas may be provided.

2. Pursuant to paragraph 1 above, it is requested that a recommendation be presented to the Joint Committee concerning a request for the release of approximately 108 square feet of real estate, constituting a portion of the area under acquisition by the USA Far East District Engineer, and located in Bangsandong, Choongu-ku, Seoul City.

KIM DONG-WHIE
Republic of Korea
Representative

for

ROBERT N. SMITH
Lieutenant General
United States Air Force
United States Representative

19

72d JC (Incl 13)
28 Mar 72

These minutes are considered as official ducuments pertaining to both Governments and will not be released without mutual agreement.

JOINT COMMITTEE
UNDER
THE REPUBLIC OF KOREA AND THE UNITED STATES
STATUS OF FORCES AGREEMENT

28 March 1972

MEMORANDUM FOR: Chairmen, Facilities and Areas Subcommittee

SUBJECT: Request for the Release of Real Estate

1. SOFA provides in Article II, paragraph 2, that the Governments of the Republic of Korea and the United States may agree that facilities and areas or portions thereof, shall be returned to the Republic of Korea or that additional facilities and areas may be provided.

2. Pursuant to paragraph 1 above, it is requested that a recommendation be presented to the Joint Committee concerning a request for the release of approximately 3.87 acres of land, constituting a portion of Seattle Installation currently held under Acquisition No. AAC-395, and located in Inchon City, Kyonggi-do.

KIM DONG-WHIE
Republic of Korea
Representative

ROBERT N. SMITH
Lieutenant General
United States Air Force
United States Representative

20

72d JC (Incl 14)
28 Mar 72

These minutes are considered as official documents pertaining to both Governments and will not be released without mutual agreement.

JOINT COMMITTEE
UNDER
THE REPUBLIC OF KOREA AND THE UNITED STATES
STATUS OF FORCES AGREEMENT

28 March 1972

MEMORANDUM FOR: Chairmen, Facilities and Areas Subcommittee

SUBJECT: Request for the Release of Real Estate

1. SOFA provides in Article II, paragraph 2, that the Governments of the Republic of Korea and the United States may agree that facilities and areas or portions thereof, shall be returned to the Republic of Korea or that additional facilities may be provided.

2. Pursuant to paragraph 1 above, it is requested that a recommendation be presented to the Joint Committee concerning a request for the release of a portion of the real estate currently held under Acquisition No. SAC-677, which is used by USFK as a dairy plant and which is located in Yongdungpo-dong, Yongdungpo-ku, Seoul City.

KIM DONG-WHIE
Republic of Korea
Representative

ROBERT N. SMITH
Lieutenant General
United States Air Force
United States Representative

21

72d JC (Incl 15)
28 Mar 72

417

These minutes are considered as official minutes pertaining to both
Governments and will not be released without mutual agreement.

**JOINT COMMITTEE
UNDER
THE REPUBLIC OF KOREA AND THE UNITED STATES
STATUS OF FORCES AGREEMENT**

28 March 1972

MEMORANDUM FOR: Chairmen, Facilities and Areas Subcommittee

SUBJECT: Request for Partial Release of Real Estate

1. SOFA provides in Article II, paragraph 2, that the Governments of
the Republic of Korea and the United States may agree that facilities
and areas or portions thereof shall be returned to the Republic of
Korea or that additional facilities and areas may be provided.

2. Pursuant to paragraph 1 above, it is requested that a recommendation be presented to the Joint Committee concerning a request for release of 1.00 acre of land which is a portion of the area held under
Acquisition No. CAV-130 and located at Camp Edwards, Youngtae-ri,
Walryong-myun, Paju-gun, Kyonggi-do. This real estate is required
for the military use by the ROK Army.

_____
KIM DONG-WHIE
Republic of Korea
Representative

_____
for ROBERT N. SMITH
Lieutenant General
United States Air Force
United States Representative

22

72d JC (Incl 16)
28 Mar 72

These minutes are considered as official documents pertaining to both Governments and will not be released without mutual agreement.

JOINT COMMITTEE
UNDER
THE REPUBLIC OF KOREA AND THE UNITED STATES
STATUS OF FORCES AGREEMENT

28 March 1972

MEMORANDUM FOR: Chairmen, Facilities and Areas Subcommittee

SUBJECT: Request for Release of Real Estate

1. SOFA provides in Article II, paragraph 2, that the Governments of the Republic of Korea and the United States may agree that facilities and areas or portions thereof shall be returned to the Republic of Korea or that additional facilities and areas may be provided.

2. Pursuant to paragraph 1 above, it is requested that a recommendation be presented to the Joint Committee concerning a request for the release of 0.6 acre of land, constituting Fire Station No. 10 currently held under Acquisition No. SAC-95, and located in Hengdang-dong, Songdong-ku, Seoul City.

KIM DONG-WHIE
Republic of Korea
Representative

ROBERT N. SMITH
Lieutenant General
United States Air Force
United States Representative

23

72d JC (Incl 17)
28 Mar 72

These minutes are considered as official documents pertaining to both Governments and will not be released without mutual agreement.

**JOINT COMMITTEE
UNDER
THE REPUBLIC OF KOREA AND THE UNITED STATES
STATUS OF FORCES AGREEMENT**

28 March 1972

MEMORANDUM FOR: Chairmen, Finance (Personnel Affairs) Subcommittee

SUBJECT: Request for Implementation of Recommendation of the Panel on Larceny and Black Marketing

1. The Ad Hoc Subcommittee on Civil-Military Relations, at its seventh meeting on 18 February 1972, among other actions approved a recommendation submitted by its Panel on Larceny and Black Marketing. This recommendation subsequently was approved by the US-ROK Joint Committee at its seventy-first meeting on 24 February 1972.

2. The text of the aforementioned recommendation is as follows:

"That US military authorities, in consultation with ROK Government authorities, develop a list of additional items to be added to the PX and Commissary controlled item ration system, and that the procedures for monitoring the outflow of items beyond the reasonable needs of an individual be strengthened."

3. Since the subject matter of paragraph 2 falls within the area of responsibility of the Finance (Personnel Affairs) Subcommittee, mutual consultation is requested toward the end of formulating a recommendation in this matter for transmittal to the Joint Committee.

KIM DONG-WHIE
Republic of Korea
Representative

ROBERT N. SMITH
Lieutenant General
United States Air Force
United States Representative

420

24

72d JC (Incl 18)
28 Mar 72

These minutes are considered as official documents pertaining to both
Governments ar⬛ will not be released without m⬛al agreement.

REPUBLIC OF KOREA - UNITED STATES
FACILITIES AND AREAS SUBCOMMITTEE

16 March 1972

MEMORANDUM FOR: THE JOINT COMMITTEE

1. Subcommittee Members:

United States	Republic of Korea
BG Philip T. Boerger, Chairman	BG PAK Woo Bum, Chairman
COL Leonard Edelstein, Alt. Chairman	Mr. MIN Won Sik, Secty
COL Eugene T. Blanton, USAF	Mr. KANG Hong Suk, Asst Secty
MAJ William S. Littlefield, J4, USFK	LTC SHIN Sang Pil
MAJ Allen D. Adams, USAFCS, K	Mr. KIM Young Sup
CPT James H. Smith, USAF	Mr. SONG Jae Kun
Mr. Francis K. Cook, J5, USFK	Mr. CHOE Byong Hoon
Mr. S. F. O'Hop, ENJ-RE, Secty	Mr. SOUNG Baek Jon
Mr. E. H. Brummett, ENJ-RE,	Mr. DO Tae Ku
Alt. Secty	Mr. SUH Chin Hwan
	Mr. LEE Soung Woo
	Mr. PARK Dahl Young
	Mr. BAE Jeung Sun

2. Subject of Recommendation: Requests of Release of Real Estate, Joint
Committee memorandum, dated 24 February 1972.

3. Recommendation: Tasks 1146-1149 The following requests for release
of real estate have been accepted by the Ministry of National Defense:

a. Task 1146 Release of 11.467 acres of land, constituting a portion of
Kanghwa-do Installation, currently held under Acq. Nos. Inchon-268, ASCOM-
379, and K-E-401, and located in Kanghwa-gun, Kyonggi-do. This request for
release includes a total of 56 USFK-constructed buildings and facilities located
on that Installation. This real estate has become excess to USFK requirements.

These minutes are considered as official documents pertaining to both Governments and will not be released without mutual agreement.

Tasks 1146-1149

b. **Task 1147** Release of 37.89 acres of land, constituting the A-102 Airfield which is a portion of Market Installation held under Acq. No. AAC-396, and located in Inchon City, Kyonggi-do. This request for release includes two Korean-constructed buildings and a total of 68 USFK-constructed buildings and facilities. This real estate has become excess to USFK requirements.

c. **Task 1148** Release of one Korean-constructed building (No. S-230), constituting a portion of the acquisition held under Acq. No. PAC-Taegu-113, and located on Camp Henry Installation, Taegu City, Kyongsangbuk-do. This building has deteriorated beyond economical repair and maintenance.

d. **Task 1149** Release of 13.36 acres of land, constituting Stonestown Installation, currently held under Acq. No. SAC-PAC-135, and located in Taejon City, Chungchongnam-do. This request for release includes a total of 20 Korean-constructed buildings and facilities and a total of 70 USFK-constructed buildings and facilities which are located on the Installation. This real estate has become excess to USFK requirements.

The Ministry of National Defense and the USFK Engineer will prepare the necessary documents. It is recommended that the Joint Committee, SOFA, approve this recommendation.

4. Security Classification: Unclassified

_____   _____
Brigadier General PAK Woo Bum   Brigadier General Philip T. Boerger
Chairman, ROK Component   Chairman, US Component
Facilities and Areas Subcommittee   Facilities and Areas Subcommittee

APPROVED BY THE JOINT COMMITTEE ON
28 MARCH 1972 AT SEVENTY-SECOND MEETING

_____   _____
KIM DONG-WHIE   ROBERT N. SMITH
Republic of Korea   Lieutenant General
Representative   United States Air Force
                                    United States Representative

                                    72d JC (Incl 19)
                    26   28 Mar 72

공   란

공   란

공 란

공 란

공   란

공   란

공   란

These minutes are considered as official documents pertaining to both Governments and will not be released without mutual agreement.

REPUBLIC OF KOREA-UNITED STATES
UTILITIES SUBCOMMITTEE

17 March 1972

MEMORANDUM TO: The Joint Committee

SUBJECT: Consultation on Rate/Tariff Changes

1. Sub ommittee Members:

ROK	US
Mr. SUH Suck Joon, Chairman	COL Richard T. Cann, Chairman
Mr. PARK Woon Suh, Secretary	COL Norman W. Hammes, Alt Chairman
Mr. KIM Woon Cho, Member	LTC Charles J. Turner, Secretary
Mr. NOH Chin Shik, Member	CDR John P. Smith, Member
Mr. CHUNG Chae Jin, Member	Mr. William E. Woodford, Member
Mr. KIM Jong Ho, Member	MAJ Robert E. Frazier, Member
Mr. SONG Hae Joon, Member	Mr. Samuel Pollock, Member
Mr. PAIK Joong Sup, Member	Mr. Don Leland, Member
Mr. SHIN Kyong Shick, Member	MAJ Jewell D. Raymond, Member
Mr. KIM Sung Shil, Member	Mr. Francis K. Cook, Member

2. <u>Subject of Recommendation:</u> Agreed Minute 1 to Article VI, ROK-US SOFA, provides that any changes determined by the authorities of the Republic of Korea in priorities, conditions, and rates or tariffs, applicable to the United States armed forces shall be the subject of consultation in the Joint Committee prior to their effective date.

3. The Republic of Korea has initiated consultation concerning a change in rates or tariffs for the cost of water purchased from the City of Taejon, effective 27 September 1971, under contract DABJO3-69-C-0275 (Inclosure 1).

4. The United States component of the Utilities Subcommittee has received the ROK request for consultation and has determined that the requested change in rates or tariffs is no less favorable than those accorded any other comparable user (see inclosure 2).

34

72d JC (Incl 21)

28 Mar 72

These minutes are considered as official documents pertaining to both Governments and will not be released without mutual agreement.

5. It is recommended that the two inclosures referenced in paragraphs 3 and 4 be accepted by the Joint Committee as evidence of consultation contemplated by Article VI of the Status of Forces Agreement.

2 Incl

SUH SUCK JOON
Republic of Korea Chairman
Utilities Subcommittee

RICHARD T. CANN, COL, USA
United States Chairman
Utilities Subcommittee

APPROVED BY THE JOINT COMMITTEE ON
28 MARCH 1972 AT SEVENTY-SECOND MEETING

KIM DONG-WHIE
Republic of Korea
Representative

ROBERT N. SMITH
Lieutenant General
United States Air Force
United States Representative

35

72d JC (Incl 21)
28 Mar 72

REPUBLIC OF KOREA-UNITED STATES

UTILITIES SUBCOMMITTEE

27 September, 1971

SUBJECT :   Change in Water Supply Rate Schedule applicable to the US Armed Forces under Article VI of the Status of Forces Agreement.

TO :   US Chairman, Utilities Subcommittee

1.   Reference : Paragraph 2 and Agreed Minute 1 of Article VI of the Status of Force Agreement.

2.   The Government of the United States is informed through this written consultative procese that the Republic of Korea proposes to change the following rate/tariff at locations below:

Rate/Tariff	Location
Water Supply	The city of Taejon

3.   The following date are provide:

a.   Effective date.

Although the rate change are effective from 1 May, 1970 in Taejon, the new rate will be applied to the US Forces' use in accordance with the agreement set forth in the letter dated 15 November, 1969.

b.   Rate schedule of proposed change.
Refer to item " d ".

c.   Rate schedule showing rates that are charged all classes of users. (attached)

72d JC (Incl 21)

432   Inclosure 1   36   28 Mar 72

These minutes are considered as official documents pertaining to both Governments and will not be released without mutual agreement.

d. Calculation of old and new rate

description	old rate (won)	new rate (won)
Basic rate for the first $30m^3$	300	700
Excess charge per m^3	15	40

e. Reason for revision of rate base.

To cover the rising prime cost.

4. The Government of ROK advises the Government of the United States that priorities, conditions, and rates or tariffs being changed are no less favorable than those accorded any other user. The view of the Government of the United States is solicited as soon as possible. You may be assured that your views will be greatly appreciated.

Suck Joon Suh
Chairman
ROK Utilities Subcommittee

72d JC (Incl 21)
28 Mar 71

37

These minutes are considered as official documents pertaining to both Governments and will not be released without mutual agreement.

(attached)

<u>Water Rate Schedule of the city of Taejon</u>

Description	Unit	Monthly basic rate		Charge above Minimun (per 1 m^3)
		Q'ty(m^3)	Rate(won)	
Special use	1 house 1 place	30	700	40
Commercial	"	20	450	40
Recreation	1 place	–	–	40
Bath house	1 house 1 place	200	4,000	25
Construction	1 place	–	–	35
Industrial use	1 house 1 place	20,000	200,000	15
Domestic	1 house	10	150	20
Public	1 house	5	60	20

38

72d JC (Incl 21)
28 Mar 72

These minutes are considered as official documents pertaining to both Governments a[n]d will not be released without m[utu]al agreement.

REPUBLIC OF KOREA - UNITED STATES
UTILITIES SUBCOMMITTEE

15 March 1972

SUBJECT: Change in Water Supply Rate Schedule Applicable to the US Armed Forces under Article VI of the Status of Forces Agreement

TO: Republic of Korea Chairman, Utilities Subcommittee

1. References:

   a. Paragraph 2 and Agreed Minute 1 of Article VI of the Status of Forces Agreement.

   b. ROK component of the Utilities Subcommittee Memorandum of Consultation, dated 27 September 1971, subject as above, pertaining to the rate change in water supply for the City of Taejon.

2. The ROK memorandum, reference 1b above, has been reviewed and the United States component of the Utilities Subcommittee fully understands the requirement for change in the water supply rates in this instance and will join with the ROK component of the Utilities Subcommittee in presenting a memorandum on the rates to the Joint Committee.

RICHARD T. CANN
United States Chairman
Utilities Subcommittee

72d JC (Incl 21)
28 Mar 72

435

39

Inclosure 2

JOINT ROK-US PRESS RELEASE
SEVENTY-SECOND ROK-US JOINT COMMITTEE MEETING
28 MARCH 1972

The ROK-US SOFA Joint Committee received the seventh report of its Ad Hoc Subcommittee on Civil-Military Relations and approved four recommendations submitted to it by this Subcommittee at its seventy-second meeting held in the ROK Capitol Building on 28 March 1972. These recommendations include one from the Panel on Local Community and Governmental Relations and three relating to ROK and US proposals to improve civil-military relations in the Camp Humphreys-Anjong-ni area.

The ROK-US Joint Committee also approved four recommendations of the Facilities and Areas Subcommittee and assigned twenty-one new tasks to that Subcommittee. The Finance (Personnel Affairs) Subcommittee was also assigned a new task and a memorandum from the Utilities Subcommittee was approved.

The ROK Representative, Mr. KIM Dong-Whie, presided at this meeting. The next meeting of the SOFA Joint Committee is scheduled for 27 April 1972 in the US SOFA Conference Room.

72d JC (Incl 22)
28 Mar 72

436

40

대한민국 외무부
공보관실
전화 74-3576

보 도 자 료

이 기사는 제공처인 외무부를
밝히고 보도할수 있음

외무보도   호

년 월 일 시 분 발표

한.미 합동위원회 제72차회의
공 동 발 표 문
72. 3. 28.

한.미 합동위원회 제72차 회의가 72. 3. 28. 한국 중앙청 회의실에서 개최되었다.

본 합동위원회는 군민관계 임시분과위원회의 제7차 보고서를 접수하고 동 임시분과위원회가 제출한 4개의 건의를 승인하였다. 이들 건의의 하나는 지방행정 관계 조사반이 제출하고 다른 세개의 건의는 안정리지역 캠프 험프리 기지내의 군민관계를 개선하기 위한 한국과 미국의 제안에 관한 것입니다.

본 합동위원회는 시설구역분과위원회의 4개의 건의를 승인하고 동 분과위원회에 21개의 신규 과제를 부여하였다.

또한 재무분과위원회에 1개의 신규 과제를 부여하고 공공용역 분과위원회가 제출한 각서를 승인하였다.

한국 대표 김동휘 구미국장이 본 회의를 사회하였으며, 차기회의는 1972. 4. 27. 미국 SOFA 회의실에서 개최될 예정이다.

437

외교문서 비밀해제: 주한미군지위협정(SOFA) 26
주한미군지위협정(SOFA) 한·미 합동위원회 3

초판인쇄 2024년 03월 15일
초판발행 2024년 03월 15일

지은이 한국학술정보(주)
펴낸이 채종준
펴낸곳 한국학술정보(주)
주 소 경기도 파주시 회동길 230(문발동)
전 화 031-908-3181(대표)
팩 스 031-908-3189
홈페이지 http://ebook.kstudy.com
E-mail 출판사업부 publish@kstudy.com
등 록 제일산-115호(2000. 6. 19)

ISBN 979-11-7217-037-0 94340
       979-11-7217-011-0 94340 (set)